To Andrew and Elena

Wireless Java:
Developing with J2ME,
Second Edition

JONATHAN KNUDSEN

Apress™

Wireless Java: Developing with J2ME, Second Edition
Copyright ©2003 by Jonathan Knudsen

ISBN (pbk): 1-59059-077-5
Printed and bound in the United States of America 12345678910

Trademarked names may appear in this book. Rather than use a trademark symbol with every occurrence of a trademarked name, we use the names only in an editorial fashion and to the benefit of the trademark owner, with no intention of infringement of the trademark.

Technical Reviewer: Michael Yuan
Editorial Directors: Dan Appleman, Gary Cornell, Simon Hayes, Martin Streicher, Karen Watterson, John Zukowski
Managing and Production Editor: Grace Wong
Copy Editor: Rebecca Rider
Proofreader: Gregory Teague
Compositor: Diana Van Winkle, Van Winkle Design Group
Indexer: Valerie Perry
Artist and Cover Designer: Kurt Krames
Manufacturing Manager: Tom Debolski

Distributed to the book trade in the United States by Springer-Verlag New York, Inc., 175 Fifth Avenue, New York, NY, 10010 and outside the United States by Springer-Verlag GmbH & Co. KG, Tiergartenstr. 17, 69112 Heidelberg, Germany

In the United States, phone 1-800-SPRINGER, email orders@springer-ny.com, or visit http://www.springer-ny.com.
Outside the United States, fax +49 6221 345229, email orders@springer.de, or visit http://www.springer.de.
For information on translations, please contact Apress directly at 2560 Ninth Street, Suite 219, Berkeley, CA 94710. Phone 510-549-5930, fax: 510-549-5939, email info@apress.com, or visit http://www.apress.com.

The information in this book is distributed on an "as is" basis, without warranty. Although every precaution has been taken in the preparation of this work, neither the author nor Apress shall have any liability to any person or entity with respect to any loss or damage caused or alleged to be caused directly or indirectly by the information contained in this work.

The source code for this book is available to readers at http://www.apress.com in the Downloads section.

Contents at a Glance

Contents

Acknowledgments

THANKS TO ALL the folks at Apress for helping get this book done. Thanks to Gary Cornell for talking me into this book in the first place. Grace Wong was my project manager, a job I could never have. She was very nice about all of my delays and a pleasure to work with. My copy editor, Rebecca Rider, put up with my formatting idiosyncrasies and tightened the book up a lot. Thanks to Michael Yuan for an excellent technical review.

My family now has permission to slap me upside the head if I ever consider taking on a project like this again. Thanks to everyone—Kristen, Daphne, Luke, Andy, and Elena—for putting up with me.

About the Author

JONATHAN KNUDSEN IS the author of several other Java books, including *Learning Java, Java 2D Graphics*, and *Java Cryptography*. He is also the author of *The Unofficial Guide to LEGO MINDSTORMS Robots*, but, sadly, was unable to parlay that success into a full-time career. Jonathan has written numerous articles about Java and a few about LEGO robots as well. He is the father of four children and enjoys bicycling and playing the piano. For more information, see http://jonathanknudsen.com/.

Preface

THIS BOOK DESCRIBES how to program mobile telephones, pagers, and other small devices using Java technology. It is about the Mobile Information Device Profile (MIDP), which is part of Java 2 Platform, Micro Edition (J2ME). It is concise and complete, describing all of MIDP, as well as moving into several advanced topics like XML and cryptography.

This second edition covers MIDP 2.0, which includes many exciting enhancements. Three entirely new chapters have been added, and the rest of the book has been meticulously updated.

Who Are You?

You're probably reading this book because you're excited about building wireless applications with Java. This book is aimed at people who already have experience programming in Java. At a minimum, you should understand the Java programming language and the fundamentals of object-oriented programming. Some chapters delve into subjects that in themselves could occupy entire books. These chapters include suggested reading if you want to get up to speed on a particular subject.

If you are unfamiliar with Java, I suggest you read an introductory book or take a course. *Learning Java, Second Edition* (O'Reilly 2002) is a good introduction to Java for programmers who are already experienced in another language such as C or C++.

The Structure of This Book

This book is organized into fifteen chapters and one appendix. There are basically three sections. The first two chapters are introductory material. Chapters 3 through 12 provide complete coverage of the MIDP APIs. Chapters 13 through 15 cover advanced topics. The complete breakdown of chapters is listed here:

- Chapter 1, "Introduction," provides context and motivation for the rest of the book. J2ME is explained in detail, gradually zooming in to MIDP.

- Chapter 2, "Building MIDlets," is intended to be a teaser. It includes an example application that allows you to look up the definitions of words over the Internet using any MIDP device. Along the way you'll learn a lot about developing applications for the MIDP platform.

- Chapter 3, "All About MIDlets," goes into detail about the life cycle and packaging of MIDP applications. It includes new material on the MIDP 2.0 security architecture.

- Chapter 4, "Almost the Same Old Stuff," describes the pieces of the MIDP API that will be familiar to Java programmers.

- Chapter 5, "Creating a User Interface," is the first of a handful of chapters devoted to MIDP's user-interface packages. It provides an overview of MIDP's user-interface package and goes into detail about the simple visual components.

- Chapter 6, "Lists and Forms," picks up where Chapter 5 left off, describing MIDP's advanced user-interface components.

- Chapter 7, "Custom Items," shows how to create your own form items in MIDP 2.0.

- Chapter 8, "Persistent Storage," describes MIDP's mechanism for storing data.

- Chapter 9, "Connecting to the World," contains all the juicy details about how MIDP applications can send and receive data over the Internet.

- Chapter 10, "Programming a Custom User Interface," describes the low level API that can be used for specialized application user interfaces.

- Chapter 11, "The Game API," describes MIDP 2.0's new features for creating games, including sprites and tiled layers.

- Chapter 12, "Sound and Music," is all about MIDP 2.0's new multimedia capabilities. You'll learn how to produce simple tones as well as play sampled audio data.

- Chapter 13, "Performance Tuning," describes techniques for coping with the limited resources that are available on small devices.

- Chapter 14, "Parsing XML," examines the spectrum of small XML parsers that are currently available. It describes how to port parsers to MIDP and briefly discusses the usage involved with each parser.

- Chapter 15, "Protecting Network Data," discusses how to protect valuable data on the insecure Internet. It includes two sample applications that demonstrate cryptographic techniques for protecting data.

- Finally, an Appendix contains a complete API reference for the classes and interfaces that make up MIDP. The method signatures for the public API of each class and interface are listed for handy quick reference. In this second edition, the API reference is flagged to make it easy to see which methods are new in MIDP 2.0.

CHAPTER 1

Introduction

JAVA™ 2 PLATFORM, Micro Edition (J2ME) is the second revolution in Java's short history. When Java was introduced in 1995, it looked like the future of computing was in *applets*, small programs that could be downloaded and run on demand. A slow Internet forced applets out of the mainstream. Java, as a platform, did not really take off until the advent of *servlets*, Java programs that run on a server (essentially a replacement for CGI). Java further expanded into the server side of things, eventually picking up the moniker of Java 2 Platform, Enterprise Edition (J2EE). This was the first revolution, the blitz of server-side Java.

The second revolution is the explosion of small-device Java, and it's happening now. The market for small devices is expanding rapidly, and Java is important for two reasons. First, developers can write code and have it run on dozens of small platforms, without change. Second, Java has important safety features for downloadable code.

Understanding J2ME

J2ME isn't a specific piece of software or specification. All it means is Java for small devices. Small devices range in size from pagers, mobile phones, and personal digital assistants (PDAs), all the way up to things like set-top boxes that are just shy of being desktop PCs.

J2ME is divided into *configurations*, *profiles*, and *optional APIs*, which provide specific information about APIs and different families of devices. A configuration is designed for a specific kind of device based on memory constraints and processor power. It specifies a Java Virtual Machine (JVM) that can be easily ported to devices supporting the configuration. It also specifies some subset of the Java 2 Platform, Standard Edition (J2SE) APIs that will be used on the platform, as well as additional APIs that may be necessary.

Profiles are more specific than configurations. A profile is based on a configuration and adds APIs for user interface, persistent storage, and whatever else is necessary to develop running applications.

Optional APIs define specific additional functionality that may be included in a particular configuration. The whole caboodle—configuration, profile, and optional APIs—that is implemented on a device is called a *stack*. For example, a possible future device stack might be CLDC/MIDP + Mobile Media API. See the section later on platform standardization for information on JSR 185, which will define standard J2ME stacks.

Currently, there are a handful of configurations and profiles, as illustrated in Figure 1-1.

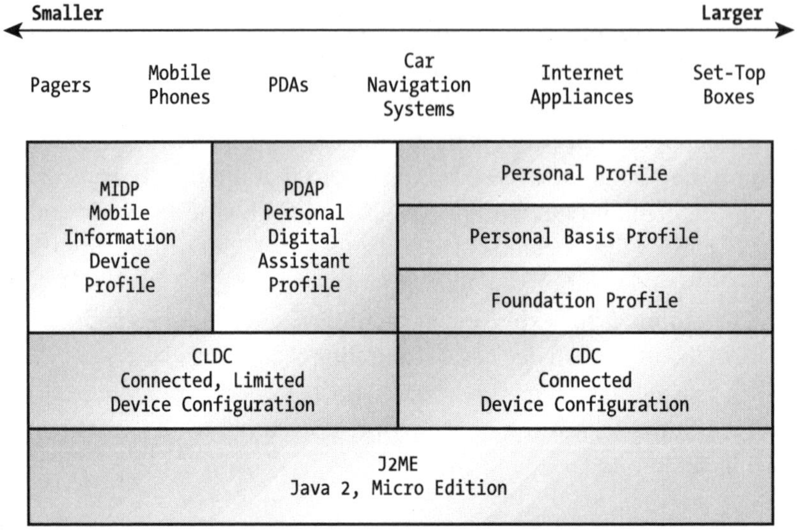

Figure 1-1. The J2ME universe

The Java Community Process

The Java Community Process (JCP) is designed to ensure that Java technology is developed according to community consensus. The process is described here:

http://jcp.org/introduction/overview/

Configurations and profiles first appear in the world as Java Specification Requests (JSRs). You can see a list of current JSRs here:

http://jcp.org/jsr/all/

To give you a flavor of what's happening in the J2ME world, Table 1-1 shows some of the configurations, profiles, and optional APIs that are available and under development. This is not a comprehensive list; for more information, check out the JCP web site at http://jcp.org/.

Table 1-1. J2ME Configurations, Profiles, and Optional APIs

CONFIGURATIONS

JSR	NAME	URL
30	Connected, Limited Device Configuration (CLDC) 1.0	http://jcp.org/jsr/detail/30.jsp
139	Connected, Limited Device Configuration (CLDC) 1.1	http://jcp.org/jsr/detail/139.jsp
36	Connected Device Configuration	http://jcp.org/jsr/detail/36.jsp

PROFILES

JSR	NAME	URL
37	Mobile Information Device Profile 1.0	http://jcp.org/jsr/detail/37.jsp
118	Mobile Information Device Profile 2.0	http://jcp.org/jsr/detail/118.jsp
75	PDA Profile 1.0	http://jcp.org/jsr/detail/75.jsp
46	Foundation Profile	http://jcp.org/jsr/detail/46.jsp
129	Personal Basis Profile	http://jcp.org/jsr/detail/129.jsp
62	Personal Profile	http://jcp.org/jsr/detail/62.jsp

OPTIONAL APIS

JSR	NAME	URL
66	RMI Optional Package	http://jcp.org/jsr/detail/66.jsp
82	Java APIs for Bluetooth	http://jcp.org/jsr/detail/82.jsp
120	Wireless Messaging API	http://jcp.org/jsr/detail/120.jsp
135	Mobile Media API	http://jcp.org/jsr/detail/135.jsp
179	Location API for J2ME	http://jcp.org/jsr/detail/179.jsp

Configurations

A configuration specifies a JVM and some set of core APIs for a specific family of devices. Currently there are two: the Connected Device Configuration (CDC) and the Connected, Limited Device Configuration (CLDC).

Connected Device Configuration

A *connected device* has, at a minimum, 512KB of read-only memory (ROM), 256KB of random access memory (RAM), and some kind of network connection. The CDC is designed for devices like television set-top boxes, car navigation systems, and high end PDAs. The CDC specifies that a full JVM (as defined in the Java Virtual Machine Specification, 2nd edition) must be supported.

The configurations and profiles of J2ME are generally described in terms of their memory capacity. Usually a minimum amount of ROM and RAM is specified. For small devices, it makes sense to think in terms of volatile and non-volatile memory. The *non-volatile memory* is capable of keeping its contents intact as the device is turned on and off. ROM is one type, but non-volatile memory could also be flash memory or battery-backed RAM. *Volatile memory* is essentially workspace and does not maintain its contents when the device is turned off.

The CDC is being developed under the Java Community Process. For more information on the CDC, see `http://java.sun.com/products/cdc/`. A Linux reference implementation is available.

The CDC is the basis of the Personal Profile stack. The Personal Profile is the next generation of PersonalJava, a Java application environment that is similar to JDK 1.1.8.

Connected, Limited Device Configuration

CLDC is the configuration that interests us, because it encompasses mobile phones, pagers, PDAs, and other devices of similar size. CLDC is aimed at smaller devices than the CDC. The name is a little misleading; really, the CLDC is designed for a small device with a limited network connection—"Limited Connection Device Configuration" might have been more accurate.

The CLDC is designed for devices with 160KB to 512KB of memory available for the Java platform. If you've ever watched J2SE gobble up tens of megabytes of memory on your desktop computer, you'll appreciate the challenge of J2ME. The "limited connection" simply refers to a network connection that is intermittent and probably not very fast. (Most mobile telephones, for example, typically achieve data rates of 9.6Kbps.) Between the small screen size, limited memory, and slow network connection, applications designed in the CLDC space should be very sparing with the use of the network connection.

The CLDC is based around a small JVM called the KVM. Its name comes from the fact that it is a JVM whose size is measured in kilobytes rather than megabytes. While the CLDC is a specifications document, the KVM refers to a specific piece of software.[1] Because of its small size, the KVM can't do everything a JVM does in the J2SE world.

- Native methods cannot be added at runtime. All native functionality is built into the KVM.

- The KVM only includes a subset of the standard bytecode verifier. This means that the task of verifying classes is split between the CLDC device and some external mechanism. This has serious security implications, as we'll discuss later.

You can find more information at the CLDC home page, `http://java.sun.com/products/cldc/`. Most deployed devices implement CLDC 1.0, but CLDC 1.1 is almost complete as this is written. CLDC 1.1 includes enhancements to CLDC 1.0, including support for floating-point data types.

Platform Standardization

Given the profusion of configurations, profiles, and especially optional APIs, how do you know what APIs are likely to be available on typical devices? Sun's answer to this question is JSR 185 (`http://jcp.org/jsr/detail/185.jsp`), impressively titled *Java Technology for the Wireless Industry*. This specification aims to standardize software stacks to bring coherence to the J2ME world.

In the next generation of J2ME, a concept called Building Blocks is supposed to replace configurations and profiles. A *Building Block* is just some subset of a J2SE API. For example, one Building Block might be created from a subset of the J2SE `java.io` package. Conceptually, a Building Block represents a smaller chunk of information than a configuration. Profiles, then, will be built on top of a set of Building Blocks rather than a configuration.

The definition of Building Blocks is a JSR, which is briefly described here: `http://jcp.org/jsr/detail/68.jsp`. Progress on JSR 68 has been extremely slow since its creation in June 2000. I suggest keeping your eyes on JSR 185 instead.

---

1. The KVM was originally part of the Spotless system, a Sun research project. See `http://www.sun.com/research/spotless/`.

Profiles

A profile is layered on top of a configuration (and someday, perhaps, on Building Blocks), adding the APIs and specifications necessary to develop applications for a specific family of devices.

Current Profiles

Several different profiles are being developed under the Java Community Process. Table 1-1 (shown earlier) provides a bird's-eye view.

The Foundation Profile is a specification for devices that can support a rich networked J2ME environment. It does not support a user interface; other profiles can be layered on top of the Foundation Profile to add user interface support and other functionality.

Layered on top of the Foundation Profile are the Personal Basis Profile and the Personal Profile. The combination of CDC + Foundation Profile + Personal Basis Profile + Personal Profile is designed as the next generation of the PersonalJava application runtime environment (see http://java.sun.com/products/personaljava/). As such, the Personal Profile has the specific goal of backward compatibility with previous versions of PersonalJava.

The PDA Profile (PDAP), which is built on CLDC, is designed for palmtop devices with a minimum of 512KB combined ROM and RAM (and a maximum of 16MB). It sits midway between the Mobile Information Device Profile (MIDP) and the Personal Profile. It includes an application model based on MIDlets but uses a subset of the J2SE Abstract Windowing Toolkit (AWT) for graphic user interface. Although the PDAP specification is nearly finished, to my knowledge no hardware manufacturer has announced that it will be implementing PDAP. The J2ME world currently is covered by MIDP on the small end and Personal Profile on the higher end.

Mobile Information Device Profile

The focus of this book is the Mobile Information Device Profile (MIDP). According to the specification, a Mobile Information Device has the following characteristics:

- 128KB of non-volatile memory for the MIDP implementation

- 32KB of volatile memory for the runtime heap

- 8KB of non-volatile memory for persistent data

- A screen of at least 96 × 54 pixels

- Some capacity for input, either by keypad, keyboard, or touch screen

- Two-way network connection, possibly intermittent

Try to imagine a device that might be a MIDP device: mobile telephones and advanced pagers are right in the groove, but entry-level PDAs could also fit this description.

More information about MIDP, including a link to the official specification document, is at http://java.sun.com/products/midp/.

This book covers both MIDP 1.0 and MIDP 2.0. MIDP 2.0 features numerous enhancements, including support for multimedia, a new game user interface API, support for HTTPS connection, and other features. It is fully backward compatible with MIDP 1.0. I will indicate features that are specific to MIDP 2.0 throughout the rest of the book.

Anatomy of MIDP Applications

The APIs available to a MIDP application come from packages in both CLDC and MIDP, as shown in Figure 1-2. Packages marked with a + are new in CLDC 1.1 and MIDP 2.0.

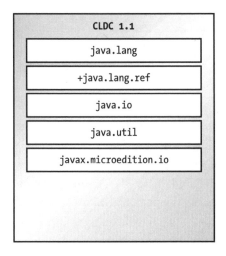
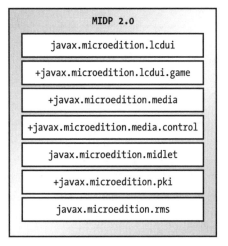

Figure 1-2. MIDP packages

CLDC defines a core of APIs, mostly taken from the J2SE world. These include fundamental language classes in `java.lang`, stream classes from `java.io`, and simple collections from `java.util`. CLDC also specifies a generalized network API in `javax.microedition.io`.

 NOTE *According to the MIDP 2.0 specification, MIDP 2.0 will most likely be paired with CLDC 1.1, although it is certainly possible for MIDP 2.0 to be implemented atop CLDC 1.0. The first implementations of MIDP 2.0 will be paired with CLDC 1.0, as the MIDP 2.0 specification is further along in the Java Community Process than the CLDC 1.1 specification.*

Optionally, device vendors may also supply Java APIs to access device-specific features. MIDP devices, then, will typically be able to run several different flavors of applications. Figure 1-3 shows a map of the possibilities.

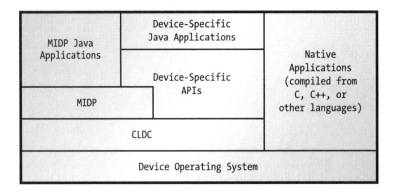

Figure 1-3. MIDP software components

Each device implements some kind of operating system (OS). Native applications run directly on this layer and represent the world as it is today—many different kinds of devices, each with its own OS and native applications.

Layered on top of the device OS is the CLDC (including the KVM) and the MIDP APIs. MIDP applications use only the CLDC and MIDP APIs. Device-specific Java applications may also use Java APIs supplied by the device vendor.

Advantages of MIDP

Given the spectrum of configurations and profiles, why is this book about MIDP? First, MIDP comes at a critical time, a time when MIDP devices, like mobile phones, are an exploding market. Simultaneously, MIDP devices are achieving the kind of processing power, memory consumption, and Internet connectivity that makes them an attractive platform for distributed applications. MIDP 1.0 is already deployed on millions of handsets all over the world, and MIDP 2.0 holds much promise for the future.

Second, of course, MIDP is the first J2ME profile that is ready for prime time. If you read into the next chapter, you can write MIDP applications today.

Portability

The advantage of using Java over using other tools for small device application development is portability. You could write device applications with C or C++, but the result would be specific to a single platform. An application written using the MIDP APIs will be directly portable to any MIDP device.

If you've been following Java's development for any time, this should sound familiar. It's the same "Write Once, Run Anywhere" (WORA) mantra that Sun's been repeating since 1995. Unfortunately, WORA is a bit of a four-letter word for developers who struggled with cross-platform issues in JDK 1.0 and JDK 1.1 (particularly the browser implementations). While Java's cross-platform capabilities in Java 2 are generally successful, WORA still has the taint of an unfulfilled promise.

Does MIDP deliver painless cross-platform functionality? Yes. There will always be platform-specific bugs in MIDP implementations, but I believe MIDP works as advertised because it is so much smaller than desktop Java. Less code means fewer bugs when porting to multiple platforms. Most of the cross-platform incompatibilities of JDK 1.0 and JDK 1.1 were caused by the nightmare of trying to fit disparate windowing systems into the AWT's peer-based component architecture. MIDP has nothing approaching the complexity of AWT, which means there's an excellent possibility that MIDP applications will seamlessly run on multiple platforms right out of the starting gate. Furthermore, while the JDK 1.0 test suite only included a few dozen tests, the MIDP compatibility test suite includes several thousand tests.

Security

A second compelling reason for using Java for small device development is security. Java is well known for its ability to safely run downloaded code like applets. This is a perfect fit—it's easy to imagine nifty applications dynamically downloading to your mobile phone.

But it's not quite such a rosy picture. For one thing, the KVM used in the CLDC only implements a partial bytecode verifier, which means that part of the important task of bytecode verification is performed off the MIDP device.

Second, the CLDC does not allow for application-defined classloaders. This means that any kind of dynamic application delivery is dependent on device-specific mechanisms. As you'll see, application deployment is not specifically defined in the CLDC or MIDP.

MIDP applications do offer one important security promise: they can never escape from the confines of the KVM. This means that, barring bugs, a MIDP application will never be able to write to device memory that doesn't belong to the KVM. A MIDP application will never mess up another application on the same device or the device OS itself.[2] This is the killer feature of MIDP. It allows manufacturers and carriers to open up application development to the world, more or less free from certification and verification programs, without the fear that rogue coders will write applications that crash phones.

In MIDP 2.0, MIDlet suites can be cryptographically signed, then verified on the device, which gives users some security about executing downloaded code. A new permissions architecture also allows the user to deny untrusted code access to certain API features. For example, if you install a suspicious-looking MIDlet suite on your phone, you can prevent it from making network connections.

---

2.   A MIDP application could conceivably launch a denial-of-service attack, (i.e., sucking up all the processor's time or bringing the device OS to a standstill). It's widely acknowledged that there's not much defense against denial-of-service attacks. Applications and applets in J2SE suffer from the same vulnerability.

MIDP Vendors

Several large players have thrown their weight behind MIDP. A quick browse of the JSR page for MIDP exposes the most important companies.

Two Asian companies led the charge to provide network services for Java-enabled mobile phones. In Korea, LG TeleCom deployed a service called ez-i in mid-2000. Later that same year, NTT DoCoMo deployed their wildly popular i-mode. The APIs developed for LG TeleCom (KittyHawk) and NTT DoCoMo (i-Appli) are similar to MIDP but were completed before the MIDP 1.0 specification.

In the United States, Motorola was the first manufacturer to produce a MIDP telephone. The i50sx and i85s were released on April 2, 2001, with service provided by Nextel. Motorola has since expanded its offerings with a handful of new devices.

Nokia has also made serious commitments to MIDP, and the expert group that created the MIDP specification includes an impressive list of manufacturers—Ericsson, Hitachi, Nokia, Sony, Symbian, and many more. You can go read the industry predictions if you wish—a gazillion MIDP phones sold in the next three years, and so on. It's a safe bet that your MIDP application will have a large market. For a comprehensive listing of MIDP devices, visit `http://wireless.java.sun.com/device/`.

Fragmentation

Platform fragmentation is a serious concern in the MIDP community. Many devices that implement MIDP 1.0 also include device-specific APIs. These APIs access device-specific features or provide functionality that wasn't addressed in MIDP 1.0's least-common-denominator specification. Current software vendors, particularly game developers, sometimes create and distribute multiple versions of an application, each tailored to a specific platform. Obviously this is a concern: part of the point of using MIDP in the first place is the ability to write one set of code and deploy it on multiple platforms.

I won't pretend to know how this particular drama is going to play out. I believe that MIDP 2.0 addresses many, possibly all, of the shortcomings of MIDP 1.0. Its timing is good, so the adoption and deployment of MIDP 2.0 devices may provide a standard, unified platform for wireless development.

Another fragmentation issue is the confusion surrounding the assembly of configurations, profiles, and optional APIs into a software stack. As a developer, you want to understand exactly what set of APIs will be available or are likely to be available, but there seem to be so many choices and so many possibilities. JSR 185 (`http://jcp.org/jsr/detail/185.jsp`) aims to bring clarity to this issue.

Summary

J2ME is the Java platform for small devices, a broad field that covers pretty much everything smaller than a breadbox. Because J2ME spans such a diverse selection of hardware, it is divided into configurations, profiles, and optional APIs. A configuration specifies a subset of J2SE functionality and the behavior of the JVM, while profiles are generally more specific to a family of devices with similar characteristics. Optional APIs offer added functionality in a flexible package. The Mobile Information Device Profile, which is the focus of this book, includes APIs for devices like mobile phones and two-way pagers.

CHAPTER 2

Building MIDlets

MIDP APPLICATIONS ARE piquantly called MIDlets, a continuation of the naming theme begun by *applets* and *servlets*. Writing MIDlets is relatively easy for a moderately experienced Java programmer. After all, the programming language is still Java. Furthermore, many of the fundamental APIs from java.lang and java.io are basically the same in the MIDP as they are in J2SE. Learning the new APIs (in the javax.microedition hierarchy) is not terribly difficult, as you'll see in the remainder of this book.

The actual development process, however, is a little more complicated for MIDlets than it is for J2SE applications. Beyond a basic compile-and-run cycle, MIDlets require some additional tweaking and packaging. The complete build cycle looks like this:

Edit Source Code > Compile > Preverify > Package > Test or Deploy

To show how things work, and to give you a taste of MIDlet development, this chapter is dedicated to building and running a simple MIDlet. In later chapters, we'll delve into the details of the MIDP APIs. In this chapter, you'll get a feel for the big picture of MIDlet development.

Tooling Up

MIDlets are developed on regular desktop computers, although the MIDlet itself is designed to run on a small device. To develop MIDlets, you'll need some kind of development kit, either from Sun or another vendor. Remember, MIDP is only a specification; vendors are free to develop their own implementations.

The world is full of MIDlet development tools if you know where to look. Furthermore, many of these tools are freely available.

The bare bones set of tools is Sun's MIDP reference implementation. This includes the preverify tool (more on this later), a MIDP device emulator, source code, and documentation. You can download the MIDP reference implementation by following the links from http://java.sun.com/products/midp/. However, I don't recommend using the reference implementation unless you really enjoy being in the middle of the gritty details of building and packaging MIDlets. (You should also investigate the reference implementation if you are interested in porting the MIDP runtime to a new device or platform.)

A much better tool for beginners is Sun's J2ME Wireless Toolkit, available from `http://java.sun.com/products/j2mewtoolkit/`. The J2ME Wireless Toolkit (or J2MEWTK, as it's affectionately known) includes a GUI tool that automates some of the tedious details of building and packaging MIDlets, providing a simple path from source code to running MIDlets. At the same time, the J2ME Wireless Toolkit is a relatively lightweight solution, almost a miniature IDE, not something that will choke your machine.

Larger IDEs are available in abundance, from device manufacturers, wireless carriers, and IDE vendors, including the following:

- Borland JBuilder MobileSet:
  `http://www.borland.com/jbuilder/mobileset/`

- IBM WebSphere Studio Device Developer:
  `http://www-3.ibm.com/software/pervasive/products/wsdd/`

- Metrowerks CodeWarrior Wireless Studio:
  `http://www.metrowerks.com/MW/Develop/Wireless/Wireless_Studio/default.htm`

- Research In Motion BlackBerry Java Development Environment:
  `http://www.blackberry.net/developers/na/java/start/download.shtml`

- Sun ONE Studio, Mobile Edition:
  `http://wwws.sun.com/software/sundev/jde/features/me-features.html`

- Zucotto Wireless WHITEboard SDK:
  `http://www.zucotto.com/products/wb/whiteboard.html`

You can use whatever development kit you wish. I suggest you start with the J2ME Wireless Toolkit, which is easy to use and authoritative. I'll be using the J2ME Wireless Toolkit throughout the rest of the book. Other development environments generally use the J2ME Wireless Toolkit as a plugin anyhow, so your experiences are likely to be similar no matter what tool you use. You'll notice details about the development environment most in this chapter, where I'll go into detail about the build tools and the emulators. For much of the remainder of this book, I'll be describing the MIDP APIs, so it won't really matter which development kit you use.

Creating Source Code

Writing Java source code is the same as it always was: use your favorite text editor to create a source file with a *.java* extension. The example we'll build and run is Jargoneer, a MIDlet that looks up words in the Jargon File. The Jargon File is a comprehensive lexicon of hacker slang (find out more by visiting http://www.tuxedo.org/~esr/jargon/).

When you enter a word into Jargoneer, it connects to a server to find the definition. Running this MIDlet will allow you to appear cool in the company of your hacker friends. When someone uses an unfamiliar word, like "cruft" or "grok," you can surreptitiously key the word into your mobile phone and see a definition in a few seconds.

Jargoneer's source code is provided in Listing 2-1. If you don't want to type it in, you can download all of the code examples in this book from the Downloads page at http://www.apress.com.

Listing 2-1. Jargoneer's *Source Code*

```java
import java.io.*;

import javax.microedition.io.*;
import javax.microedition.midlet.*;
import javax.microedition.lcdui.*;

public class Jargoneer extends MIDlet
    implements CommandListener, Runnable {
  private Display mDisplay;

  private Command mExitCommand, mFindCommand, mCancelCommand;

  private TextBox mSubmitBox;
  private Form mProgressForm;
  private StringItem mProgressString;

  public Jargoneer() {
    mExitCommand = new Command("Exit", Command.EXIT, 0);
    mFindCommand = new Command("Find", Command.SCREEN, 0);
    mCancelCommand = new Command("Cancel", Command.CANCEL, 0);

    mSubmitBox = new TextBox("Jargoneer", "", 32, 0);
    mSubmitBox.addCommand(mExitCommand);
    mSubmitBox.addCommand(mFindCommand);
    mSubmitBox.setCommandListener(this);
```

```
    mProgressForm = new Form("Lookup progress");
    mProgressString = new StringItem(null, null);
    mProgressForm.append(mProgressString);
  }

  public void startApp() {
    mDisplay = Display.getDisplay(this);

    mDisplay.setCurrent(mSubmitBox);
  }

  public void pauseApp() {}

  public void destroyApp(boolean unconditional) {}

  public void commandAction(Command c, Displayable s) {
    if (c == mExitCommand) {
      destroyApp(false);
      notifyDestroyed();
    }
    else if (c == mFindCommand) {
      // Show the progress form.
      mDisplay.setCurrent(mProgressForm);
      // Kick off the thread to do the query.
      Thread t = new Thread(this);
      t.start();
    }
  }

  public void run() {
    String word = mSubmitBox.getString();
    String definition;

    try { definition = lookUp(word); }
    catch (IOException ioe) {
      Alert report = new Alert(
          "Sorry",
          "Something went wrong and that " +
          "definition could not be retrieved.",
          null, null);
      report.setTimeout(Alert.FOREVER);
      mDisplay.setCurrent(report, mSubmitBox);
      return;
    }
```

```
    Alert results = new Alert("Definition", definition,
        null, null);
    results.setTimeout(Alert.FOREVER);
    mDisplay.setCurrent(results, mSubmitBox);
}

private String lookUp(String word) throws IOException {
    HttpConnection hc = null;
    InputStream in = null;
    String definition = null;

    try {
        String baseURL = "http://65.215.221.148:8080/wj2/jargoneer?word=";
        String url = baseURL + word;
        mProgressString.setText("Connecting...");
        hc = (HttpConnection)Connector.open(url);
        hc.setRequestProperty("Connection", "close");
        in = hc.openInputStream();

        mProgressString.setText("Reading...");
        int contentLength = (int)hc.getLength();
        if (contentLength == -1) contentLength = 255;
        byte[] raw = new byte[contentLength];
        int length = in.read(raw);

        // Clean up.
        in.close();
        hc.close();

        definition = new String(raw, 0, length);
    }
    finally {
        try {
            if (in != null) in.close();
            if (hc != null) hc.close();
        }
        catch (IOException ignored) {}
    }

    return definition;
}
```

Compiling a MIDlet

Writing MIDlets is an example of cross-compiling, where you compile code on one platform and run it on another. In this case, you'll be compiling a MIDlet using J2SE on your desktop computer. The MIDlet itself will run on a mobile phone, pager, or other mobile information device that supports MIDP.

The J2ME Wireless Toolkit takes care of the details as long as you put the source code in the right directory.

1. Start the toolkit, called KToolbar.

2. Choose **New Project...** from the toolbar to create a new project.

3. When the J2ME Wireless Toolkit asks you for the name of the project and the MIDlet class name, use "Jargoneer" for both.

4. Click **OK** twice to dismiss the project settings window.

Figure 2-1 shows the New Project dialog.

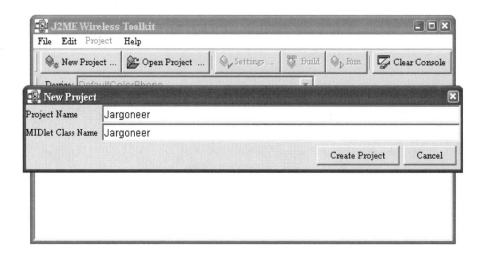

Figure 2-1. Creating a new project with the J2ME Wireless Toolkit

The J2ME Wireless Toolkit represents projects as subdirectories of its *apps* directory. The following diagram shows the contents of the *Jargoneer* directory after the new project is created.

📁 <J2ME Wireless Toolkit directory>
　📁 apps
　　📁 Jargoneer
　　　📁 bin
　　　📁 lib
　　　📁 res
　　　📁 src

Save the source code as `Jargoneer.java` in the project's *src* directory. You can simply click the **Build** button in the J2ME Wireless Toolkit tool bar to compile the open project.

Behind the scenes, the J2ME Wireless Toolkit uses J2SE's compiler. Normally, when you're compiling J2SE source code, the `CLASSPATH` environment variable points to all the classes that your source code needs to know about. When you use javac to compile a file, there are some implied APIs that get included, like the classes in `java.lang`. With MIDlets, however, the situation is a little more complicated. Say that you use the `java.lang.System` class in your MIDlet. How do you (or how does the J2ME Wireless Toolkit) let the compiler know that you want to use the MIDP version of this class, not the J2SE version?

The answer is a command line option, `-bootclasspath`. This option lets you point to a classpath that describes the fundamental APIs against which you will be compiling your source code. In our case, this option should be used to specify the *classes* directory in the MIDP reference implementation installation. If you install the MIDP reference implementation, the command line looks like this:

```
javac -bootclasspath \midp\classes Jargoneer.java
```

You will need to adjust the path to *classes* if you installed the MIDP reference implementation in a different location.

Preverifying Class Files

Now comes an entirely new step in building your program, *preverifying*. Because the memory on small devices is so scarce, MIDP (actually, CLDC) specifies that bytecode verification be split into two pieces. Somewhere off the device, a pre-verify step is performed. The device itself is only required to do a lightweight second verification step before loading classes.

If you are using the J2ME Wireless Toolkit, you don't have to worry about preverifying class files and you may not even notice that it's happening when you click the **Build** button. If you'd like to understand more about preverifying, read the rest of this section. Otherwise you can just skip ahead.

As you may recall, bytecode verification is one of the foundation stones of Java's runtime security model. Before a classloader dynamically loads a class, the bytecode verifier checks the class file to make sure it behaves well and won't do nasty things to the JVM. Unfortunately, the code that implements the bytecode verifier is bulky, too large to fit on a small device like a mobile phone. The CLDC dictates a two-step bytecode verification:

1. Off the device, class files are preverified. Certain checks are performed, and the class file is massaged into a format that the lightweight second-step verifier can easily handle.

2. On the device, the second step of verification is performed as classes are loaded. If a class file has not been preverified, it is rejected.

The MIDP reference implementation and the J2ME Wireless Toolkit contain a tool called preverify that performs the first step.

The preverify tools takes, as input, a class file. It produces a preverified class file. You need to specify a classpath so that the tool can find the class you want to preverify as well as any referenced classes. Finally, you can specify an output directory using the -d option. To overwrite an existing class file with a preverified version, you could do something like this:

```
preverify -classpath .;\ midp\ classes -d . Jargoneer
```

In this example, the -d option tells preverify to write the preverified class file to the current directory. Don't forget about inner classes, which must also be pre-verified.

 NOTE *Splitting bytecode verification into two pieces like this has important security ramifications. Devices should only download code from trusted sources, using a secure method because some bytecode verification is performed off the device. (See Chapter 3 for more information on MIDlet suite security.) An attacker could supply malicious code that appeared to be preverified, even if it violated the rules of the full J2SE bytecode verifier. To the MIDP second-step verifier, the code would look okay and it would be loaded and run.*

Sun's J2ME Wireless Toolkit Emulators

The J2ME Wireless Toolkit includes several different emulators that you can use to test your applications. When you click the **Run** button in the J2ME Wireless Toolkit, your application is launched in the currently selected emulator.

The Wireless Toolkit Devices

The J2ME Wireless Toolkit 2.0 (in its beta 2 release) contains four main device emulators:

- DefaultColorPhone is a device with a 180×208-pixel color screen. This is the device shown in Figure 2-2 and is used for most of the screen shots in the remainder of this book.

- DefaultGrayPhone is the same as DefaultColorPhone but has a grayscale screen.

- MediaControlSkin looks like the default phone emulator but its buttons are labeled with controls like a music player: a square for stop, a triangle for play, volume control buttons, etc.

- QwertyDevice is a smartphone with a 640×240-color screen and a miniature qwerty keyboard.

Running MIDlets

If you're using the J2ME Wireless Toolkit, you can simply choose an emulator from the Device combo box and click the **Run** button to fire up your application.

Sun's MIDP reference implementation includes an emulator named midp. It emulates an imaginary MID, a mobile telephone with some standard keys and a 182×210-pixel screen. The J2ME Wireless Toolkit includes an almost identical emulator, as well as several others.

Once you've got a preverified class file, you can use the midp emulator to run it. The emulator is an application that runs under J2SE and acts just like a MIDP device. It shows itself on your screen as a representative device, a generic mobile phone. You can run your MIDlet by typing the following at the command line, assuming you added *midp\bin* to your PATH:

```
midp Jargoneer
```

If all goes well, you'll see something like the window shown in Figure 2-2. Congratulations! You've just built and run your first MIDlet.

Using the Emulator Controls

The J2ME Wireless Toolkit emulator appears as a generic mobile phone, as shown in Figure 2-2.

Figure 2-2. Buttons on the J2ME Wireless Toolkit emulator

Sun's J2ME Wireless Toolkit emulator exhibits several qualities that you are likely to find in real devices:

- The device has a small screen size and limited input capabilities. (It's not as small as the J2ME Wireless Toolkit 1.0 emulators, which included emulated devices with 96×128 and 96×54-pixel screens.)

- Two *soft buttons* are available. A soft button does not have a fixed function. Generally, the function of the button at any given time is shown on the screen near the button. In MIDlets, the soft buttons are used for commands.

- *Navigation buttons* are provided to allow the user to browse through lists or other sets of choices.

- A *select button* allows the user to make a choice after moving to it with the navigation buttons. (Think "Yes, that's my final answer.")

Tour of MIDP Features

Now that you have run your first MIDlet, take a moment to admire it. There are several salient features, even in such a small example.

It's Java

First of all, Jargoneer is written in the Java language, the same language you'd use to code servlets, Enterprise JavaBeans, or J2SE client applications. If you're already a J2SE developer, you'll be extremely comfortable developing MIDlets.

Not only is the Java language familiar, but also many core APIs are very similar to J2SE. Notice, for example, that multithreading in Jargoneer is just the same as it might be in any other Java code. The MIDlet class Jargoneer implements java.lang.Runnable, and the technique for kicking off a new thread is the same as it always was:

```
Thread t = new Thread(this);
t.start();
```

Significant parts of java.lang are essentially unchanged from J2SE, as are parts of java.io and java.util. The code that reads the result from the server in lookUp() is familiar stream handling, just like what you might see in J2SE.

MIDlet Life Cycle

Jargoneer also demonstrates the basic structure of MIDlets. Like all good MIDlets, it extends javax.microedition.midlet.MIDlet, the base class for all MIDP applications. Special software on the device, called the Java Application Manager (JAM), Application Management Software (AMS), or MIDlet management software, controls the process of installing, running, and removing MIDlets. When a user chooses to run your MIDlet, it is the JAM that creates an instance of the MIDlet class and runs methods on it.

The sequence of methods that will be called in your MIDlet subclass is defined by the MIDlet life cycle. MIDlets, like applets and servlets, have a small set of well-defined states. The JAM will call methods in the MIDlet to signify changes from one state to another. You can see these methods in Jargoneer—startApp(), pauseApp(), destroyApp(), and Jargoneer's constructor are all part of the MIDlet life cycle.

Generalized User Interface

Jargoneer's user-interface code may take you by surprise. Later on, I'll spend several chapters on user interface. For now, the important thing to notice is how Jargoneer's user interface is flexible enough to run on devices with different screen sizes and different input capabilities. A big part of MIDP's appeal, after all, is the concept of writing one set of source code that runs on multiple devices.

One example of MIDP's generalized user interface is the TextBox that is initially shown when Jargoneer is launched. Figure 2-3 shows this TextBox.

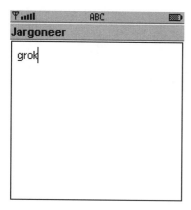

Figure 2-3. Jargoneer's TextBox

TextBox is a text input field. It has a title and an area for entering text. It has a simple design and can easily be shown on screens of different sizes. Even more interesting are the commands that appear at the bottom of the TextBox. These are Exit and Find. The code that creates the TextBox and its commands is in Jargoneer's constructor:

```
mExitCommand = new Command("Exit", Command.EXIT, 0);
mFindCommand = new Command("Find", Command.SCREEN, 0);
// ...
mSubmitBox = new TextBox("Jargoneer", "", 32, 0);
mSubmitBox.addCommand(mExitCommand);
mSubmitBox.addCommand(mFindCommand);
mSubmitBox.setCommandListener(this);
```

Notice how the commands are created. You specify only a label and a type, and you register an event listener to find out when the commands are invoked. This is purposely vague—it leaves the implementation considerable latitude in deciding how commands should be displayed and invoked. In Sun's J2ME Wireless Toolkit emulator, for example, TextBox shows its commands at the bottom of the screen and allows the user to invoke them using soft buttons. Another device might put both commands in a menu and allow the user to invoke them using a selector wheel or some other mechanism.

The Likelihood of Server-Side Components

The Jargoneer example connects to a Web server, sends a request, and receives a response. The Web server is actually an intermediary—it connects to the real Jargon File server, makes a request, parses the result, and sends the stripped-down definition back to the MIDP device.

In the first edition of this book, Jargoneer connected directly to the Jargon File server. In response to its query, it received a lot of information it didn't need. The original Jargoneer went to considerable trouble to parse through the HTML response to extract the definition it wanted. Architecturally, the old Jargoneer looked like Figure 2-4.

The new architecture is shown in Figure 2-5.

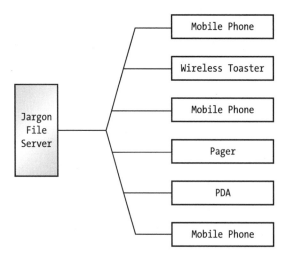

Figure 2-4. Jargoneer *architecture*

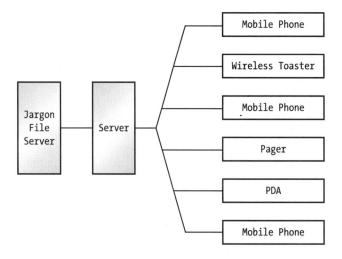

Figure 2-5. A cleaner architecture for Jargoneer

Instead of hitting the web server directly, Jargoneer goes through a different server hosted by Apress. This server queries the Jargon File, parses the result, and returns the definition to the device. This is advantageous from several stand-points:

- Bandwidth is expensive in terms of both time and money. Today's wireless networks are relatively slow, so less data passing through the air means less waiting time for your users. Also, wireless service tends to be pricey, so less data passing through the air means smaller bills for your users.

- Small devices have limited memory and processing power. It is unwise to spend these limited resources on tasks like parsing HTML. In general, you will be able to place most of the processing burden of your application on a server component, making your client MIDlet's life very easy.

- In this particular application, the HTML parsing is not very stable. Suppose the server we are using decides to return its Jargon File definitions in a different format; if four million users are running Jargoneer, then four million copies of our code have just broken. Performing this task on a server gives it a single point of failure and a single point of update. If we fix the parsing code on the server, the interface between the server and the client devices can remain unchanged. This makes it easy to upgrade or fix Jargoneer.

Network MIDP applications are likely to need a server component. If you're planning to do much MIDP development, you might like to study up on Java servlets.

Packaging Your Application

You won't pass class files directly to a MIDP to deploy an application. Instead, you'll package them in a Java Archive (JAR) using the jar tool that comes with the Java 2 SDK.

If you're using the J2ME Wireless Toolkit, you won't ever have to perform these steps manually; the toolkit automatically packages your MIDlets when you choose **Project ➤ Package ➤ Create Package** from the menu. (You don't have to do this if you just want to test your application in the emulator, but you need to create a package if you're going to distribute the MIDlet suite.) Even if you use the J2ME Wireless Toolkit, you might want to read through this section so that you understand exactly what's going on.

If you're using the MIDP reference implementation, you should follow these steps to package your MIDlets. I'll only sketch the steps here; in the next chapter you'll learn all the gory details of MIDlets and MIDlet suites.

Manifest Information

Every JAR includes a manifest file, *META-INF\MANIFEST.MF*, that describes the contents of the archive. For MIDlet JARs, the manifest file should contain extra information. The extra information is stuff that's important to the MIDP runtime environment, like the MIDlet's class name and the versions of CLDC and MIDP that the MIDlet expects.

You can specify extra manifest information in a simple text file and tell the `jar` utility to include that information in the manifest when the JAR is created. To package Jargoneer, for example, save the following text in a file named *extra.mf*:

```
MIDlet-1: Jargoneer, , Jargoneer
MIDlet-Name: Jargoneer
MIDlet-Vendor: Jonathan Knudsen
MIDlet-Version: 1.0
MicroEdition-Configuration: CLDC-1.0
MicroEdition-Profile: MIDP-1.0
```

Now assemble the MIDlet classes and the extra manifest information into a JAR with the following command:

```
jar cvmf extra.mf Jargoneer.jar Jargoneer.class
```

With the J2ME Wireless Toolkit, the toolkit automatically assembles your application into a MIDlet suite JAR when you press the **Build** button. It's very convenient, and it saves you from the effort of learning the `jar` tool.

Creating a MIDlet Descriptor

One additional file is needed before your MIDlet is ready to go out the door. An *application descriptor* file must be created. This file contains a lot of the same information that's in the MIDlet JAR manifest file. However, it lives outside the JAR and enables application management software to learn about a MIDlet JAR without installing it.

The application descriptor is a text file with a *.jad* extension. Type in the following and save it as *Jargoneer.jad*:

```
MIDlet-1: Jargoneer, , Jargoneer
MIDlet-Jar-Size: 3853
MIDlet-Jar-URL: Jargoneer.jar
MIDlet-Name: Jargoneer
MIDlet-Vendor: Jonathan Knudsen
MIDlet-Version: 1.0
```

If your MIDlet suite JAR is a different size, enter the actual size for the `MIDlet-Jar-Size` entry. The MIDlet descriptor is automatically generated when you press the **Build** button in the J2ME Wireless Toolkit. If you're using the J2ME Wireless Toolkit, you won't need to create the application descriptor yourself.

Using an Obfuscator

Because MIDP devices have so little memory, MIDlet suites should be as compact as possible. An *obfuscator* is a useful tool for minimizing the size of MIDlet suite JARs. Obfuscators, originally designed to foil attempts to reverse engineer compiled bytecode, perform any combination of the following functions:

- Renaming classes, member variables, and methods to more compact names

- Removing unused classes, methods, and member variables

- Inserting illegal or questionable data to confuse decompilers

Except for the last point, obfuscators can significantly reduce the size of compiled classes in a MIDlet suite JAR.

There's a wide spectrum of obfuscators, with a variety of licenses, costs, and features. For a comprehensive list, see `http://proguard.sourceforge.net/alternatives.html`.

Using an obfuscator requires some finesse. The trick is to obfuscate the classes before they are preverified. The J2ME Wireless Toolkit, starting with version 1.0.4, includes support for inserting an obfuscator into the build cycle. Support for RetroGuard is built in 1.0.4, with ProGuard supported in 2.0, and you can write adapter code to use other obfuscators. If you're using the 2.0 version of the toolkit, you just need to download ProGuard and copy the *proguard.jar* file into the toolkit's *bin* directory. Then choose **Project ➤ Package ➤ Create Obfuscated Package** and the toolkit handles all the details.

This article describes how to use the ProGuard obfuscator with the J2ME Wireless Toolkit 1.0.4 and outlines how to add support for any obfuscator to the toolkit.

`http://wireless.java.sun.com/midp/ttips/proguard/`

Obfuscators tend to be a little finicky, but once you get them configured correctly, they can provide significant size savings.

Using Ant

Ant is a powerful build tool that is useful for automating MIDlet suite builds. It's similar in concept to `make`, but it is cleaner and easier to use. Ant is open source software, part of the Apache Jakarta project, at `http://jakarta.apache.org/ant/`.

Ant is a tool for serious developers. If you believe you've exhausted the possibilities of the J2ME Wireless Toolkit, Ant is probably the next tool you should learn. Ant provides considerable flexibility in structuring your build cycle and lets you easily automate tasks like generating documentation or packaging source code. For an introduction to Ant and MIDP, see http://wireless.java.sun.com/midp/articles/ant/.

The code download for this book includes an Ant build script. A simplified version of the build script is shown in Listing 2-2.

Listing 2-2. An Example Ant Build Script

```
<project name="wj2" default="dist" basedir="..">
  <property name="project" value="wj2"/>

  <property name="midp" value="/WTK20"/>
  <property name="midp_lib" value="${midp}/lib/midpapi.zip"/>

  <target name="run">
    <exec executable="${midp}/bin/emulator">
      <arg line="-classpath build/bin/${project}.jar"/>
      <arg line="-Xdescriptor build/bin/${project}.jad"/>
    </exec>
  </target>

  <target name="dist" depends="preverify">
    <mkdir dir="build/bin"/>
    <jar basedir="build/preverified"
        jarfile="build/bin/${project}.jar"
        manifest="bin/MANIFEST.MF">
      <fileset dir="res"/>
    </jar>
    <copy file="bin/${project}.jad"
        tofile="build/bin/${project}.jad"/>
  </target>

  <target name="preverify" depends="obfuscate_null">
    <mkdir dir="build/preverified"/>
    <exec executable="${midp}/bin/preverify">
      <arg line="-classpath ${midp_lib}"/>
      <arg line="-d build/preverified"/>
      <arg line="build/obfuscated"/>
    </exec>
  </target>
```

```
<target name="obfuscate_null" depends="compile">
  <mkdir dir="build/obfuscated"/>
  <copy todir="build/obfuscated">
    <fileset dir="build/classes"/>
  </copy>
</target>

<target name="compile" depends="init">
  <mkdir dir="build/classes"/>
  <javac destdir="build/classes" srcdir="src"
      bootclasspath="${midp_lib}" target="1.1"/>
</target>

<target name="init">
  <tstamp/>
</target>
</project>
```

This build script contains targets that correspond to the steps of MIDlet suite development: compile, preverify, and dist (which packages the application). An obfuscate_null target is also included; it serves as a placeholder for inserting obfuscation in the build cycle. (The actual build script in the source download includes a target for obfuscating using ProGuard.)

Several developers have created specialized Ant tasks to help with MIDlet suite builds. One such project is here:

```
http://antenna.sourceforge.net/
```

Running on a Real Device

As of this writing, millions of MIDP-enabled phones are deployed worldwide. A comprehensive list of MIDP devices is available at http://wireless.java.sun.com/device/. How do you actually put MIDlets on a device? There are two possibilities: either you'll transfer MIDlet suites to the phone from your computer via a serial cable, or you'll transfer MIDlet suites over the wireless network. (Another possibility serves as a hybrid—a device in its cradle, attached to your computer via a serial cable, can use the desktop computer's network connection as though it were a wireless connection, and applications can be transferred this way.) This second possibility is called *over the air* (OTA) *provisioning*. There's a standard protocol for OTA, which is described as an addendum to the MIDP 1.0 specification. (The OTA addendum is included in the MIDP 2.0 specification.)

Installing MIDlets via serial cable or OTA provisioning is specific to whatever device you're using. You'll have to check the documentation for your device to see exactly how to install MIDlet suites.

Summary

This chapter took you on a tour of MIDP development. Creating source code is much the same as in J2SE development, but the build process is different. First, the source code must be compiled against the MIDP classes using javac's -bootclasspath option. Second, the class files must be preverified using the preverify command line tool. With the J2ME Wireless Toolkit, these steps are conveniently automated. Just press the **Build** button to build and preverify. Applications can be easily tested in emulators using the J2ME Wireless Toolkit.

CHAPTER 3

All About MIDlets

In Chapter 2, you got a quick introduction to the process of building and running MIDlets. In this chapter, you'll explore the details. I'll cover the subjects that I skimmed in last chapter, starting with the MIDlet life cycle and continuing through to a full discussion of MIDlet packaging. The chapter concludes with a look at MIDP 2.0's security architecture.

The MIDlet Life Cycle

MIDP applications are represented by instances of the `javax.microedition.midlet.MIDlet` class. MIDlets have a specific life cycle, which is reflected in the methods and behavior of the `MIDlet` class.

A piece of device software outside the realm of Java, the *application manager*, controls the installation and execution of MIDlets. A MIDlet is installed by moving its class files to a device. The class files will be packaged in a Java Archive (JAR), while an accompanying descriptor file (with a *.jad* extension) describes the contents of the JAR.

A MIDlet goes through the following states:

1. When the MIDlet is about to be run, an instance is created. The MIDlet's constructor is run, and the MIDlet is in the *Paused* state.

2. Next, the MIDlet enters the *Active* state after the application manager calls `startApp()`.

3. While the MIDlet is Active, the application manager can suspend its execution by calling `pauseApp()`. This puts the MIDlet back in the Paused state. A MIDlet can place itself in the Paused state by calling `notifyPaused()`.

4. The application manager can terminate the execution of the MIDlet by calling `destroyApp()`, at which point the MIDlet is *destroyed* and patiently awaits garbage collection. A MIDlet can destroy itself by calling `notifyDestroyed()`.

Figure 3-1 shows the states of a MIDlet and the transitions between them.

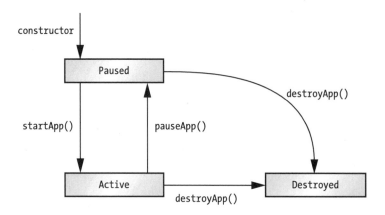

Figure 3-1. MIDlet life cycle

There is one additional method in the MIDlet class related to the MIDlet life cycle: resumeRequest(). A MIDlet in the Paused state can call this method to signal to the application manager that it wants to become Active. It might seem weird to think about a MIDlet in the Paused state running any code at all. However, Paused MIDlets are still able to handle timer events or other types of callbacks and thus have some chances to call resumeRequest(). If the application manager does decide to move a MIDlet from the Paused to the Active state, it will do so through the normal mechanism of calling startApp().

Requesting a Wakeup Call

MIDP 2.0 allows MIDlets to request to be launched at a later time, in essence requesting a wakeup call from the implementation. The method is defined in javax.microedition.io.PushRegistry, which is kind of a weird place for it. All of PushRegistry's other methods have to do with launching MIDlets in response to incoming network connections; the class is fully described in Chapter 9. The following method in PushRegistry requests that a named MIDlet be woken up at a specific time:

```
public static long registerAlarm(String midlet, long time)
    throws ClassNotFoundException, ConnectionNotFoundException
```

You need to supply the class name of a MIDlet in the MIDlet suite, and `time` specifies exactly when you want the MIDlet to be launched, in the standard form as the number of milliseconds since January 1, 1970. (Chapter 4 contains a discussion of MIDP's classes and methods pertaining to time.)

If you supply a class name that is not found in the current MIDlet suite, a `ClassNotFoundException` is thrown. If the implementation is unable to launch MIDlets at specified times, a `ConnectionNotFoundException` is thrown.

If the MIDlet for which you are requesting a timed launch was previously registered for timed launch, this method returns the previous wakeup time.

A Bridge to the Outside World

Many MIDP devices, especially mobile phones, have WAP browsers. A new method in MIDP 2.0's `MIDlet` class supplies a bridge to these browsers and other capabilities:

```
public final boolean platformRequest(String URL)
    throws ConnectionNotFoundException
```

On a sophisticated device, the browser and the MIDlet suite may be able to run at the same time, in which case the browser will be launched and pointed to the specified URL. In this case the method returns `true`.

On smaller devices, the browser may not be able to run until the MIDlet is destroyed. In this case, `platformRequest()` returns `false` and it's the MIDlet's responsibility to terminate. After the MIDlet terminates, it's the implementation's responsibility to launch the browser and point it at the specified URL.

In either case, `platformRequest()` is a nonblocking method.

There are two special possibilities for the supplied URL. If you supply a telephone number URL of the form `tel:<number>` as specified in RFC 2806 (http://ietf.org/rfc/rfc2806.txt), the implementation should initiate a voice call.

If you supply the URL of a MIDlet suite descriptor or JAR, the implementation should interpret this as a request to install the given MIDlet suite.

Packaging MIDlets

MIDlets are deployed in *MIDlet suites*. A MIDlet suite is a collection of MIDlets with some extra information; it is composed of two files. One is an *application descriptor*, which is a simple text file. The other is a JAR file that contains the class files and resource files that make up your MIDlet suite. Like any JAR file, a MIDlet suite's JAR file has a manifest file. Figure 3-2 shows a diagram of a MIDlet suite.

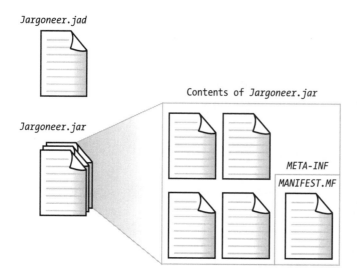

Figure 3-2. Anatomy of a MIDlet suite

If you're using a tool like the J2ME Wireless Toolkit, you don't need to worry much about MIDlet suite packaging because most of the details are handled automatically. If you want to understand things at a lower level, or if you're just curious, keep reading for a complete description of MIDlet suite packaging.

Packaging a MIDlet suite consists of three steps:

1. The class files and resource files that make up the MIDlets are packaged into a JAR file. Usually, you'll use the `jar` command line tool to accomplish this.

2. Additional information that's needed at runtime is placed in the JAR's manifest file. All JARs include a manifest; a MIDlet suite JAR contains some extra information needed by application management software.

3. An application descriptor file must also be generated. This is a file with a *.jad* extension that describes the MIDlet suite JAR. It can be used by the application management software to decide whether a MIDlet suite JAR should be downloaded to the device.

MIDlet Manifest Information

The information stored in a MIDlet's manifest file consists of name and value pairs, like a properties file. For example, an unadorned JAR manifest might look like this:

```
Manifest-Version: 1.0
Created-By: 1.3.0 (Sun Microsystems Inc.)
```

A MIDlet JAR manifest for `Jargoneer` looks like this:

```
Manifest-Version: 1.0
MIDlet-1: Jargoneer, Jargoneer.png, Jargoneer
MIDlet-Name: Jargoneer
MIDlet-Version: 1.0
MIDlet-Vendor: Sun Microsystems
Created-By: 1.3.0 (Sun Microsystems Inc.)
MicroEdition-Configuration: CLDC-1.0
MicroEdition-Profile: MIDP-1.0
```

The extra attributes describe software versions, class names, and other information about the MIDlet suite. The following attributes must be included:

MIDlet-Name: Despite the moniker, this attribute actually refers to the name of the entire MIDlet suite, not just one MIDlet.

MIDlet-Version: This describes the version of the MIDlet suite. It's a number you pick yourself in the form *major.minor.micro*.

MIDlet-Vendor: This is your name or the name of your company.

MIDlet-*n*: For each MIDlet in the MIDlet suite, the displayable name, icon file, and class name are listed. The MIDlets should be numbered starting from 1 and counting up. For example, several MIDlets in a single MIDlet suite could be listed like this:

```
MIDlet-1: Sokoban, /icons/Sokoban.png, example.sokoban.Sokoban
MIDlet-2: Tickets, /icons/Auction.png, example.lcdui.TicketAuction
MIDlet-3: Colors, /icons/ColorChooser.png, example.chooser.Color
MIDlet-4: Stock, /icons/Stock.png, example.stock.StockMIDlet
```

MicroEdition-Configuration: This attribute describes the J2ME configurations upon which this MIDlet suite can run. Multiple configuration names should be separated by spaces.

MicroEdition-Profile: This describes the set of profiles upon which this MIDlet suite can run. For MIDP 1.0 applications, this is MIDP-1.0. For applications that can run on MIDP 1.0 or MIDP 2.0, use "MIDP-2.0 MIDP-1.0".

In addition to the required manifest attributes, the following attributes may also be defined:

MIDlet-Description: The description of the MIDlet suite goes in this attribute.

MIDlet-Icon: Icons for individual MIDlets are described in the MIDlet-n attributes. This attribute specifies an icon to represent the entire MIDlet suite.

MIDlet-Info-URL: If additional information about the MIDlet suite is available online, use this attribute to list the URL.

MIDlet-Data-Size: If you know how many bytes of persistent data are required by the MIDlet suite, you can specify the number with this attribute.

TIP *Don't get tripped up by the attribute names. Many of them appear to refer to a single MIDlet, like MIDlet-Name and MIDlet-Description. In fact, these attributes describe an entire MIDlet suite. The only attribute that applies to a specific MIDlet is the MIDlet-n attribute, which is used to list each MIDlet in the suite.*

In MIDP 2.0, several additional attributes may be included. MIDP 2.0 protects network APIs from unauthorized access using a permission scheme, which will be fully discussed later in this chapter. MIDlets can list necessary permissions and optional permissions in the MIDlet JAR manifest as follows:

MIDlet-Permissions: Use this attribute to list permissions that are critical to the operation of the MIDlet suite. Multiple permissions are separated by commas.

MIDlet-Permissions-Opt: This attribute lists permissions that may be used but are not critical for this MIDlet suite.

Finally, MIDP 2.0 also provides a way for MIDlet suites to signal their dependence on optional APIs:

MIDlet-Extensions: List the optional APIs used by this MIDlet suite in this attribute. The exact names are determined by the individual optional API specifications.

Application Descriptor

The attributes in a MIDlet suite JAR are used by the application management software to run MIDlets within a suite. The application descriptor, by contrast, contains information that helps a device decide whether or not to load a MIDlet suite. Because an application descriptor is a file separate from the MIDlet suite JAR, it is easy for a device to load and examine the file before downloading the MIDlet suite.

As it happens, a lot of the information in the application descriptor is the same as the information that's in the MIDlet suite JAR. For example, the application descriptor must contain the MIDlet-Name, MIDlet-Version, and MIDlet-Vendor attributes. In addition, it should include the following:

MIDlet-Jar-URL: This is the URL where the MIDlet suite JAR can be found.

MIDlet-Jar-Size: This is the size, in bytes, of the MIDlet suite JAR.

The application descriptor can optionally contain the MIDlet-Description, MIDlet-Icon, MIDlet-Info-URL, and MIDlet-Data-Size attributes.

Devices and emulators vary widely in their handling of MIDlet suite descriptors. Some will fail installation if any fields in the descriptor are incorrect while others are more lenient. A tool like the J2ME Wireless Toolkit is extremely useful in creating well-formed descriptors.

The application descriptor is useful in over the air (OTA) deployment. A device can download and inspect the descriptor, a relatively short file, before deciding whether or not the entire MIDlet suite JAR should be downloaded and installed. For OTA provisioning, the server's returned MIME type for the application descriptor should be text/vnd.sun.j2me.app-descriptor. This and more (a whole protocol) is described in the *Over the Air User Initiated Provisioning Specification* section of the MIDP 2.0 specification.

MIDlet Properties

There's one other possibility for attributes in the manifest or application descriptor. You can add attributes that have meaning to your MIDlets. MIDlets can retrieve the values of these attributes using the getAppProperty() in the javax.microedition.midlet.MIDlet class. An attribute can be listed in the application descriptor, JAR manifest, or both; if it is listed in both, the value from the application descriptor will be used. In general, it makes sense to store application properties in the application descriptor file. Because it's distinct from the MIDlet suite JAR, the application descriptor can easily be changed to modify the behavior of your MIDlets. You might, for example, store a URL or other configuration information in the application descriptor.

For example, suppose you put an application-specific attribute in the application descriptor, like this:

```
Jargoneer.url: http://www.dict.org/bin/Dict
```

Inside the MIDlet, you can retrieve the value of the attribute like this:

```
String url = getAppProperty("Jargoneer.url");
```

Changing the URL is as easy as changing the application descriptor, a simple text file. None of your code needs to be recompiled. This could be useful if you were expecting to distribute many copies of a MIDlet and wanted to share the server load among a group of servers. You could distribute the same MIDlet suite JAR with a group of different application descriptors, each one using a MIDlet attribute to point to a different server.

MIDlet Suite Security

Wireless application security is important to almost everyone involved in the wireless industry:

- Carriers want to be sure that viruses do not bring down their customers' devices or their networks.

- Device manufacturers don't want customer-installed software crashing their devices.

- Users want to be able to run downloaded code without threatening the stability of their device or the safety of their personal information. Additionally, they may want control over the network usage of their applications, as network usage often costs money.

MIDP 1.0 does not directly address these issues in the text of the specification, but the JVM-based architecture makes it an attractive platform from a security standpoint. The design of the Java Virtual Machine (JVM) ensures that MIDlets cannot escape the confines of the JVM, so even a rogue MIDlet can do no worse than crash or immobilize the JVM, leaving the rest of the device's software unharmed. Furthermore, the MIDP 1.0 APIs do not expose any sensitive features, with the possible exception of the networking APIs.

Permissions

MIDP 2.0 brings an explicit security architecture to the table. MIDlets must have *permission* to perform sensitive operations. In MIDP 2.0, the only parts of the API that are protected by permissions are the network connections. Optional APIs are free to define additional permissions to protect sensitive data or functionality.

Permission names use the same prefix and class or interface name as the API that they protect. In Chapter 9, I'll explain the names of the network permissions in MIDP 2.0 in detail. For the moment, suppose that you write a MIDlet that needs to make a socket connection. This MIDlet would need the permission of `javax.microedition.io.Connector.socket`. The MIDlet itself needs no knowledge of permissions. It simply attempts the connection, which either succeeds or throws a `java.lang.SecurityException`.

MIDP 2.0 adds a new method to the `MIDlet` class that programmers can use to check if a permission will be granted or denied:

```
public final int checkPermission(String permission)
```

This method returns 1 if the permission is granted and 0 if the permission is denied. A special return value, -1, indicates that the implementation cannot determine whether the permission will be granted or denied, which might be the case if the user will be asked about the given permission.

Protection Domains

In MIDP 2.0, MIDlet suites belong to *protection domains* that determine which permissions are granted, which are denied, and which ones must be deferred to the user's judgment. A protection domain is kind of like a secret club and comprises two parts:

1. The set of permissions that are allowed and those for which the user must be consulted.

2. The rules for how a MIDlet suite can get into this protection domain.

A very simple protection domain, "SimplePD," might contain the permission `javax.microedition.io.Connector.http`. The rules for membership in SimplePD could be something as simple as verifying the origin IP address of the MIDlet suite. For example, if the MIDlet suite is downloaded from `www.bigcarrier.com`, then the application management software on the device would know to place the MIDlet suite in the SimplePD protection domain. At runtime, any MIDlet that tries to make an HTTP connection will be granted the permission. Attempts to make other connection types will be denied.

The simple IP-origin criterion for SimplePD is pretty weak. MIDlet suites in SimplePD are susceptible to many attacks, including data modification, data replacement, man-in-the-middle attacks, and DNS spoofing. More robust rules are based on cryptographic solutions for data integrity and authentication. In the MIDP 2.0 specification, the section "Trusted MIDlet Suites Using X.509 PKI" describes one such scheme, including additional manifest attributes.

MIDlet suites whose contents and origin cannot be verified are placed in a kind of default protection domain, the *untrusted* domain. The only restriction that the MIDP 2.0 specification places on the untrusted domain is that, given explicit confirmation from the user, it must allow MIDlets access to HTTP and HTTPS connections.

The concept of protection domains is deliberately vague, leaving implementations considerable latitude in their implementation. My guess is that many implementations will choose to have a single untrusted domain and a single trusted domain, with entry to the trusted domain limited to cryptographically signed (and verified) MIDlet suites.

Permission Types

The protection domain contains the permissions that will be granted to MIDlets (*allowed* permissions) as well as the permissions for which the user must be consulted (*user* permissions). There are several varieties of user permissions. *Blanket* means that the user is only required to grant or deny the permission once for a MIDlet suite. *Session* means that the user must grant or deny permission once per invocation of a MIDlet suite. Finally, *oneshot* indicates that the user must be consulted each time the necessary permission is needed.

Permissions in MIDlet Suite Descriptors

MIDP 2.0 defines additional attributes for MIDlet suite descriptors. If your MIDlet suite absolutely, positively needs certain permissions, use the MIDlet-Permissions attribute. For example, if your MIDlet suite needs to make HTTP connections to function correctly, you would have a line in your descriptor file like this:

```
MIDlet-Permissions: javax.microedition.io.Connector.http
```

Multiple permission types are placed on the same line, separated by commas.

If your MIDlet suite does not need certain permissions to function, but it may use them for enhanced functionality, these permissions can be placed in the MIDlet-Permissions-Opt attribute.

At installation time, the application management software will compare the permissions requested in the descriptor with the permissions in the destination protection domain. If there are irreconcilable differences, the MIDlet suite will not be installed.

Summary

MIDP applications are called MIDlets. Like applets or servlets, MIDlets have a specific life cycle; they are managed by device software. This chapter details the entries that may be in the MIDlet suite manifest file and the application descriptor. Application properties can be used as a way to store information in the application descriptor instead of hard-coding values into the MIDlet source code. A tool like the J2ME Wireless Toolkit automatically handles many of the details of MIDlet attributes packaging. MIDP 2.0 includes a comprehensive security architecture based on protection domains.

CHAPTER 4

Almost the Same Old Stuff

As I DISCUSSED in Chapter 1, one of the reasons you might be interested in MIDP as a platform is that it's based on the Java programming language and the Java APIs. You'll also recall that MIDP is built on top of the Connected, Limited Device Configuration (CLDC). The CLDC contains most of the APIs that will look familiar to experienced Java programmers. As of this writing, CLDC 1.0 is the current version, but the finishing touches are just being applied to the CLDC 1.1 specification. I'll mention the changes between CLDC 1.0 and CLDC 1.1 throughout this chapter.

In this chapter, we'll explore the java.lang, java.io, and java.util packages as defined in the CLDC. I'll assume you're already familiar with the basic APIs of J2SE; I'll walk through what's the same and what's different.

At the time of this writing (first quarter 2003), CLDC 1.1 and MIDP 2.0 have not yet been implemented on real devices. Although MIDP 2.0 will eventually be implemented on top of CLDC 1.1, the first wave of MIDP 2.0 implementations will use CLDC 1.0.

No Floating Point in CLDC 1.0

One overarching change is that CLDC 1.0 does not support floating-point types at all. That means there are no float or double primitive types. The corresponding wrapper types, java.lang.Float and java.lang.Double, have also been eliminated.

Floating point support is absent in CLDC 1.0 because most small devices don't have hardware support for floating-point operations. If calculations involving fractional numbers are important to your application, you can perform them in software. One implementation (using fixed-point integers) can be found at http://home.rochester.rr.com/ohommes/MathFP/.

CLDC 1.1 includes floating point support, the primitive types double and float, and the wrapper types Double and Float. Various other classes have been modified for floating-point support in CLDC 1.1, but the changes are minor.

java.lang

Table 4-1 and Table 4-2 list the classes and interfaces of java.lang and java.lang.ref in both J2SE (SDK version 1.4.0) and CLDC. The CLDC columns indicate whether the class is identical to its J2SE counterpart, is present with API differences, or is not present at all.

Table 4-1. The java.lang *Package*

INTERFACES

J2SE SDK 1.4.0	CLDC 1.0	CLDC 1.1
CharSequence	–	–
Cloneable	–	–
Comparable	–	–
Runnable	Same	Same

CLASSES

J2SE SDK 1.4.0	CLDC 1.0	CLDC 1.1
Boolean	Different	Different
Byte	Different	Same as CLDC 1.0
Character	Different	Same as CLDC 1.0
Character.Subset	–	–
Character.UnicodeBlock	–	–
Class	Different	Same as CLDC
ClassLoader	–	–
Compiler	–	–
Double	–	Different
Float	–	Different
InheritableThreadLocal	–	–
Integer	Different	Different
Long	Different	Different
Math	Different	Different
Number	–	–
Object	Different	Same as CLDC 1.0
Package	–	–
Process	–	–
Runtime	Different	Same as CLDC 1.0
RuntimePermission	–	–
SecurityManager	–	–
Short	Different	Same as CLDC 1.0
StackTraceElement	–	–
StrictMath	–	–
String	Different	Different

(Continued)

Table 4-1. The `java.lang` *Package (Continued)*

CLASSES

J2SE SDK 1.4.0	*CLDC 1.0*	*CLDC 1.1*
StringBuffer	Different	Different
System	Different	Same as CLDC 1.0
Thread	Different	Different
ThreadGroup	–	–
ThreadLocal	–	–
Throwable	Different	Same as CLDC 1.0
Void	–	–

Table 4-2. The `java.lang.ref` *Package*

CLASSES

J2SE SDK 1.4.0	*CLDC 1.0*	*CLDC 1.1*
PhantomReference	–	–
Reference	–	Different
ReferenceQueue	–	–
SoftReference	–	–
WeakReference	–	Different

`java.lang.Object`, as always, is the root of every Java class. It remains mostly unchanged from J2SE, but there are some important differences.

No User Classloading

As I discussed in Chapter 1, one of the strengths of the Java platform is the ability to load classes at runtime. Unfortunately, because of resource constraints and security concerns, CLDC does not allow you to define your own classloaders. The application manager that runs MIDlets has a classloader, but you cannot access it or use it yourself in any way.

No Object Finalization

Object finalization is not available in CLDC (and, by extension, MIDP). *Finalization* is a mechanism by which objects can clean up after themselves just before they are garbage collected. In J2SE, an `Object`'s `finalize()` method is called before the object is reclaimed by the garbage collector. No such mechanism exists in CLDC. If you need to clean up resources, you will need to do it explicitly instead of placing cleanup code in finalize(). This is a good idea anyhow, particularly in a small device with limited resources. Explicitly cleaning up resources means that the memory and processing power they consume will be reclaimed sooner rather than later. Cleanup code in finalize() methods doesn't get executed until the garbage collector runs, and you never know exactly when that's going to happen.

No Reflection

CLDC does not support the Reflection API. The target devices of CLDC/MIDP are simply too small to allow it. Although most developers don't need to use reflection directly, this omission has important implications. Without reflection, no Remote Method Invocation (RMI) is possible. Without RMI, JINI is not possible. Therefore, bare bones CLDC/MIDP implementations cannot run JINI. If you want to run JINI, you'll need to investigate one of the larger J2ME profiles, most likely the Personal Profile (see Chapter 1), and the RMI Optional API (JSR 66).

No Native Methods

Native methods are not supported in CLDC (and, by extension, MIDP). The specification does not support a way to access native device methods from Java. Although the MIDP implementation does, of course, include native methods, they are compiled into the implementation itself. Applications cannot define new native methods.

Don't worry about losing access to platform-specific features, however, because device vendors are likely to implement proprietary APIs in addition to MIDP. For details, check the developer web site of the manufacturer or network carrier of your device. Bear in mind that your use of vendor- or device-specific APIs will limit the audience of your application. In certain instances (games, mostly), it makes sense to distribute multiple versions of an application targeted at specific devices.

Multithreading

Using threads is much as you remember it from J2SE, as long as you keep things simple. Creating new threads, starting them, and using the handy java.lang.Runnable interface are the same as in J2SE. One important omission in CLDC 1.0 is the interrupt() method, which is not present in the java.lang.Thread class. In CLDC 1.1, the interrupt() method is available.

The pause(), resume(), and stop() methods (which are deprecated in the J2SE SDK) are also absent. Thread groups and daemon threads are not supported in CLDC/MIDP; thread naming is not supported in CLDC 1.0 but is available in CLDC 1.1.

String and StringBuffer

Both String and StringBuffer are present in the CLDC java.lang package. They are largely unchanged from their J2SE counterparts.

The largest change in the String class in CLDC 1.0 is the elimination of valueOf() static methods that convert between floating-point primitives and Strings, although these are present in CLDC 1.1. A few other obscure methods are absent from CLDC's String class, but you probably won't miss them. For example, although CLDC's String includes the compareTo(String str) method, it doesn't have either the compareTo(Object o) or compareToIgnoreCase(String str) methods that are found in the J2SE SDK. (CLDC 1.1 does include an equalsIgnoreCase() method in the String class.)

StringBuffer's append() and insert() methods do not include overrides for floating-point types in the CLDC 1.0 version of the class, but these are available in CDLC 1.1. Also, the substring() method has been pruned. Other than that, however, StringBuffer should be very familiar for seasoned J2SE programmers.

Math

The Math class contains static methods for performing mathematical calculations. In J2SE, many of these methods involve trigonometric functions on floating-point numbers. In CLDC 1.0, these are all gone, leaving only a handful of methods. CLDC 1.1, because it supports floating-point types, includes several more methods in java.lang.Math, but CLDC's java.lang.Math is still a subset of the J2SE version of the class. In the API listing below, the plus signs (+) indicate new variables or methods in CLDC 1.1.

```
  public final class Math
      extends java.lang.Object {
    // Constants
+   public static final double E;
+   public static final double PI;
      // Static methods
    public static int abs(int a);
    public static long abs(long a);
```

```
+   public static float abs(float a);
+   public static double abs(double a);
+   public static native double ceil(double a);
+   public static native double cos(double a);
+   public static native double floor(double a);
    public static int max(int a, int b);
    public static long max(long a, long b);
+   public static float max(float a, float b);
+   public static double max(double a, double b);
    public static int min(int a, int b);
    public static long min(long a, long b);
+   public static float min(float a, float b);
+   public static double min(double a, double b);
+   public static native double sin(double a);
+   public static native double sqrt(double a);
+   public static native double tan(double a);
+   public static double toDegrees(double angrad);
+   public static double toRadians(double angdeg);
  }
```

Runtime and System

Runtime and System provide access to the Java Virtual Machine (JVM) and system-wide resources. These two classes are greatly reduced from their J2SE counterparts, so much so that it makes sense to reproduce their entire public API here. First, let's take a look at Runtime:

```
public class Runtime
    extends java.lang.Object {
  // Static methods
  public static Runtime getRuntime();

  // Methods
  public void exit(int status);
  public native long freeMemory();
  public native void gc();
  public native long totalMemory();
}
```

To get the single Runtime instance, call getRuntime(). You can tell the JVM to run its garbage collector by calling gc(). If you try to call exit(), a SecurityException will be thrown; the application life cycle is managed entirely through the methods of the MIDlet class. The other two methods, totalMemory() and freeMemory(), allow you to examine the amount of memory that is available for your application's data.

Note that Runtime does not support running external processes with the exec() method. MIDlets cannot step outside the bounds of the JVM.

System provides static methods for performing various common tasks:

```
public final class System
    extends java.lang.Object {
    // Constants
    public static final PrintStream err;
    public static final PrintStream out;

    // Static methods
    public static native void arraycopy(Object src, int src_position,
        Object dst, int dst_position, int length);
    public static native long currentTimeMillis();
    public static void exit(int status);
    public static void gc();
    public static String getProperty(String key);
    public static native int identityHashCode(Object x);
}
```

The first thing you might notice is that while the err and out PrintStreams are defined, there is no System.in. This makes sense—System.in represents the console input; on a MIDP device, there really isn't any console. In fact, it may seem weird to have System.out and System.err defined. If you print information to System.out, it may not come out anywhere on a device; however, on a device emulator, you may be able to view System.out in a console window.

The gc() and exit() methods are shortcuts for calling the corresponding methods in the Runtime class.

All of System's methods are static. The arraycopy() method provides a fast implementation of array copying.

Finally, identityHashCode() is a default used by Object's hashCode() method.

The getProperty() method returns system properties, which are different than the MIDlet properties returned by MIDlet's getAppProperty() method. The following standard system properties are supported and their values can be retrieved at runtime:

microedition.platform: This property contains the name of the device or host platform. If the implementation does not supply a value, the default is null.

microedition.encoding: This property contains the default character encoding, which specifies how Unicode characters are represented in a byte stream.

microedition.configuration: This property contains the name of the implemented configuration, e.g., "CLDC-1.1".

microedition.profiles: Implemented profiles are contained in this system property.

Streams in java.io

The java.io package in the CLDC/MIDP world is a stripped down version of java.io in J2SE. Table 4-3 summarizes the classes of java.io in both J2SE and CLDC/MIDP. As you can see, many of the java.io classes you normally find in J2SE are missing from CLDC/MIDP.

Table 4-3. The java.io *Package*

INTERFACES		
J2SE SDK 1.4.0	*CLDC 1.0*	*CLDC 1.1*
DataInput	Different	Different
DataOutput	Different	Different
Externalizable	–	–
FileFilter	–	–
FilenameFilter	–	–
ObjectInput	–	–
ObjectInputValidation	–	–
ObjectOutput	–	–
ObjectStreamConstants	–	–
Serializable	–	–

(Continued)

Table 4-3. The java.io *Package (Continued)*

CLASSES		
J2SE SDK 1.4.0	**CLDC 1.0**	**CLDC 1.1**
BufferedInputStream	-	-
BufferedOutputStream	-	-
BufferedReader	-	-
BufferedWriter	-	-
ByteArrayInputStream	Same	Same
ByteArrayOutputStream	Different	Same as CLDC 1.0
CharArrayReader	-	-
CharArrayWriter	-	-
DataInputStream	Different	Different
DataOutputStream	Different	Different
File	-	-
FileDescriptor	-	-
FileInputStream	-	-
FileOutputStream	-	-
FilePermission	-	-
FileReader	-	-
FileWriter	-	-
FilterInputStream	-	-
FilterOutputStream	-	-
FilterReader	-	-
FilterWriter	-	-
InputStream	Same	Same
InputStreamReader	Different	Same as CLDC 1.0
LineNumberInputStream	-	-
LineNumberReader	-	-
ObjectInputStream	-	-
ObjectInputStream.GetField	-	-
ObjectOutputStream	-	-
ObjectOutputStream.PutField	-	-
ObjectStreamClass	-	-
ObjectStreamField	-	-
OutputStream	Same	Same
OutputStreamWriter	Different	Same as CLDC 1.0
PipedInputStream	-	-
PipedOutputStream	-	-
PipedReader	-	-
PipedWriter	-	-
PrintStream	Different	Different
PrintWriter	-	-

(Continued)

Table 4-3. The `java.io` *Package (Continued)*

CLASSES

J2SE SDK 1.4.0	CLDC 1.0	CLDC 1.1
PushbackInputStream	–	–
PushbackReader	–	–
RandomAccessFile	–	–
Reader	Same	Same
SequenceInputStream	–	–
SerializablePermission	–	–
StreamTokenizer	–	–
StringBufferInputStream	–	–
StringReader	–	–
StringWriter	–	–
Writer	Same	Same

Although the differences between the J2SE and CLDC classes appear large, they can be easily grouped into three categories:

1. Because CLDC/MIDP has no concept of a local file system, all the classes having to do with files have been pruned from the `java.io` package. This includes `File`, `FileInputStream`, `FileOutputStream`, the corresponding `Reader` and `Writer` classes, `RandomAccessFile`, and various supporting classes. If you need to store data persistently on a device, you'll need to use the `javax.microedition.rms` package API, described in Chapter 8.

2. Object serialization is not supported in CLDC. This means that the `Serializable` interface and various object stream classes are not present.

3. Finally, J2SE includes a handful of utility stream classes—things you might want someday but shouldn't include on a device with a small amount of memory. These classes include piped streams, pushback streams, sequence streams, line numbering streams, and a few other gems like `StreamTokenizer`. If you really need one of these in your MIDlet, you may be able to package it with your application.[1] Bear in mind that there are licensing restrictions and technical problems with using classes directly from J2SE; be sure you understand the legal implications before you start copying files.

---

1. A better idea would be to redesign your application so that complicated stream processing isn't necessary on the device. In general, you should make your server do as much work as possible and your MIDlet do as little as possible.

Character Encodings

MIDP includes the Reader and Writer character streams for working with Unicode characters. InputStreamReader and OutputStreamWriter handle the conversion between byte streams and character streams, just as in J2SE. An *encoding* determines how translation occurs between byte streams and character streams. A default encoding is used if you don't specify one. You can pass an encoding name to the constructors for InputStreamReader and OutputStreamWriter, if you wish. So far, this is all the same as in J2SE. In MIDP, though, you will likely find many fewer available encodings than in J2SE.

The default encoding for a MIDP implementation can be obtained by calling System.getProperty("microedition.encoding")—by default, ISO8859_1.

Resource Files

As described in Chapter 8, you can retrieve resource files from your MIDlet suite's JAR file. Use the getResourceAsStream() method in Class; it returns an InputStream that you can use as you please.

java.util

CLDC includes only a dozen classes from J2SE's java.util package. Many of the missing classes are part of the Collections API, which is too bulky for small devices. Table 4-4 lists the classes and interfaces of java.util in both J2SE and CLDC/MIDP.

Table 4-4. The java.util *Package*

INTERFACES		
J2SE SDK 1.4.0	**CLDC 1.0**	**CLDC 1.1**
Collection	–	–
Comparator	–	–
Enumeration	Same	Same
EventListener	–	–
Iterator	–	–
List	–	–
ListIterator	–	–
Map	–	–

(Continued)

Table 4-4. The `java.util` *Package (Continued)*

INTERFACES

J2SE SDK 1.4.0	CLDC 1.0	CLDC 1.1
Map.Entry	–	–
Observer	–	–
RandomAccess	–	–
Set	–	–
SortedMap	–	–
SortedSet	–	–

CLASSES

J2SE SDK 1.4.0	CLDC 1.0	CLDC 1.1
AbstractCollection	–	–
AbstractList	–	–
AbstractMap	–	–
AbstractSequentialList	–	–
AbstractSet	–	–
ArrayList	–	–
Arrays	–	–
BitSet	–	–
Calendar	–	–
Collections	–	–
Currency	–	–
Date	Different	Same as CLDC 1.0
Dictionary	–	–
EventListenerProxy	–	–
EventObject	–	–
GregorianCalendar	–	–
HashMap	–	–
HashSet	–	–
Hashtable	Different	Same as CLDC 1.0
IdentityHashMap	–	–
LinkedHashMap	–	–
LinkedHashSet	–	–
LinkedList	–	–
ListResourceBundle	–	–
Locale	–	–
Observable	–	–
Properties	–	–
PropertyPermission	–	–
PropertyResourceBundle	–	–
Random	Different	Different

(Continued)

Table 4-4. The `java.util` *Package (Continued)*

CLASSES		
J2SE SDK 1.4.0	*CLDC 1.0*	*CLDC 1.1*
ResourceBundle	–	–
SimpleTimeZone	–	–
Stack	Same	Same
StringTokenizer	–	–
Timer	Same (MIDP)	Same (MIDP)
TimerTask	Same (MIDP)	Same (MIDP)
TimeZone	Different	Same as CLDC 1.0
TreeMap	–	–
TreeSet	–	–
Vector	Different	Same as CLDC 1.0
WeakHashMap		

Collections

Although the full J2SE Collections API is not supported by CLDC, the old familiar Vector and Hashtable classes remain, as well as the lesser-known Stack. If you are familiar with the J2SE SDK Vector and Hashtable classes, you should have no trouble with them in MIDP.

Timers

MIDP includes the Timer and TimerTask classes that were introduced into J2SE in the 1.3 version of the SDK. These are the only J2SE classes that are not included in the CLDC but are included in MIDP.

Timer's API is identical to the J2SE version with one exception. The constructor that specifies whether the thread is a daemon is missing, as daemon threads are not supported in MIDP. The TimerTask API is exactly the same in the J2SE SDK and MIDP.

Telling Time

J2SE has an impressive array of classes that can be used for specifying dates and times and translating to and from human-readable representations of dates and times. The J2SE time classes have four distinct responsibilities:

- *Points in time* are represented by instances of java.util.Date. If you think of time as a line graph, then an instance of Date is just a point on the line.

- *Calendars* are used for representing points in time with calendar fields like year, month, and day. If you're using a Gregorian calendar, for example, then you can translate from a single point in time to a set of calendar values like month, day, and hours, minutes, and seconds. In J2SE, `java.util.Calendar` is a parent class for calendars, while the `java.util.GregorianCalendar` class represents the Gregorian calendar system that is familiar to most of the world.

- *Formatting* classes translate between points in time and human-readable strings. In J2SE, `java.text.DateFormat` is the parent for classes that can both generate and parse human-readable strings representing points in time. Formatting classes are very likely to make use of a calendar. For example, a typical `DateFormat` implementation might use a `GregorianCalendar` to translate a point in time to a set of calendar values, which it would then format in a string.

- *Time zone* classes represent the time zones of the world. The calendar and format classes use a time zone to create a localized representation of a particular point in time. In J2SE, `java.util.TimeZone` is the parent class of all time zones, with `java.util.SimpleTimeZone` as a concrete implementation.

Understanding these classes and their interactions is a little tricky, and it's complicated by the fact that the APIs changed considerably between JDK 1.0 and JDK 1.1. The `java.util.Date` class used to have extra functionality in it; although the methods are deprecated, they're still present and may be confusing. Fortunately, you don't have to deal with this in the CLDC/MIDP world.

The situation is somewhat simpler in CLDC/MIDP. There are fewer classes, for one thing, and the `Date` class API has been cleaned up. In MIDP, the four responsibilities I just discussed are assigned to classes as follows:

- *Points in time* are represented by instances of `java.util.Date`, just like before. The `Date` class, in essence, is just a wrapper for a `long` value that indicates the number of milliseconds since midnight on January 1, 1970. (This is a standard way of representing time. It will work for about another 290 million years, so don't worry about another millennium bug.)

- *Calendars* are still represented by instances of `java.util.Calendar`. However, the `GregorianCalendar` class is no longer part of the public API. To get a `Calendar` instance, you can use the `getInstance()` factory method. Chances are you won't need to do this.

- *Formatting* classes are hidden from view in MIDP. One of the user interface classes, javax.microedition.lcdui.DateField, can convert a Date to a human-readable display, eliminating the need for you to mess around with date formatters yourself. Essentially DateField is a graphic wrapper around a Date instance. It also allows the user to edit calendar and clock fields to produce a new Date value. See Chapter 6 for a full discussion of DateField.

- *Time zone*s are still represented by instances of java.util.TimeZone. TimeZone offers several static methods for examining the available time zones and getting an instance representing a particular time zone.

Summary

Developers are bombarded with information, and the best developers are the ones who can learn new material fast. Every once in a while, though, something you already know can be used again. This is one of those cases—something you already know about, the J2SE APIs, comes in very handy as you learn MIDP programming. MIDP's java.lang, java.io, and java.util packages contain classes that look and act a lot like the corresponding classes in J2SE.

CHAPTER 5

Creating a User Interface

MIDP APPLICATIONS ARE built to run on many different devices without modification. This is particularly difficult in the area of the user interface because devices have screens of all sizes, in grayscale and in color. Furthermore, devices vary widely in their input capabilities, from numeric keypads to alphabetic keyboards, soft keys, and even touch screens. The minimum screen size mandated by MIDP is 96×54 pixels, with at least one bit of color depth.[1] As for input, MIDP is fairly open-ended: devices are expected to have some type of keyboard, or a touch screen, or possibly both.

Given the wide variety of devices that are compliant with MIDP, there are two ways to create applications that work well on all devices:

- *Abstraction*: Specify a user interface in abstract terms, relying on the MIDP implementation to create something concrete. Instead of saying something like, "Display the word 'Next' on the screen above the soft button," you say, "Give me a **Next** command somewhere in this interface."

- *Discovery*: The application learns about the device at runtime and tailors the user interface programmatically. You might, for example, find out how big the device's screen was in order to scale your user interface appropriately.

The MIDP APIs support both methods. Abstraction is the preferred method because it involves less code in your application and more work by the MIDP implementation. In some cases, like games, you need to be more specific about the user interface; these types of applications will discover the capabilities of a device and attempt to tailor their behavior appropriately. MIDP's user-interface APIs are designed so that it's easy to mix the two techniques in the same application.

---

1. Color depth is the number of bits that determine the color of a pixel on the screen. One bit allows for two colors (usually black and white). Four bits allows for 16 colors, which could be different levels of gray or a palette of other colors.

The View from the Top

MIDP contains user-interface classes in the javax.microedition.lcdui and javax.microedition.lcdui.game packages. The device's display is represented by an instance of the Display class, accessed from a factory method, getDisplay(). Display's main purpose in life is to keep track of what is currently shown, which is an instance of Displayable. If you think of Display as an easel, a Displayable instance is akin to a canvas on that easel.

MIDlets can change the contents of the display by passing Displayable instances to Display's setCurrent() method. This is the basic function of a typical MIDlet:

1.   Show a Displayable.

2.   Wait for input.

3.   Decide what Displayable should be next.

4.   Repeat.

Displayable has a small family of subclasses that represent various types of user interfaces. Figure 5-1 shows the lineage.

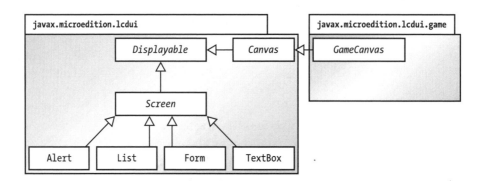

Figure 5-1. Displayables in the javax.microedition.lcdui *and* javax.microedition.lcdui.game *package*

Displayable's progeny are split between two branches that correspond to the two methods for creating generalized user interfaces, abstraction and discovery. The Screen class represents displays that are specified in abstract terms.

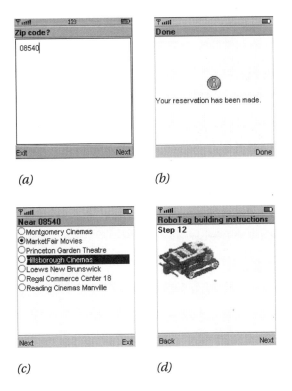

(a)   *(b)*

(c)   *(d)*

Figure 5-2. The four children of Screen: *(a)* TextBox, *(b)* Alert, *(c)* List, *and*
(d) Form

These screens contain standard user-interface items like combo boxes, lists,
menus, and buttons. Four subclasses provide a wide range of functionality, as
illustrated in Figure 5-2.

The remainder of this chapter is devoted to explaining the simplest of these
four classes: TextBox and Alert. The next chapter explores the more flexible List
and Form.

For particularly demanding or idiosyncratic displays, you'll have to create a
subclass of Canvas. Your MIDlet will assume responsibility for most of the drawing,
but you get much finer control over what is shown and how user input is handled.
Canvas supplies methods that allow your MIDlet to learn about its environment—
the size of the display, for example, and which kinds of events are supported by
the device. User interfaces built on Canvas discover the attributes of a device and
attempt to create something that looks reasonable. Chapter 10 explains Canvas-
based user interfaces in detail.

GameCanvas, new in MIDP 2.0, provides user interface functionality specifically
for game displays. Chapter 11 explains this new API.

Using Display

Display manages a device's screen. You can get a reference to the device's display by supplying a MIDlet reference to the static getDisplay() method. Typically, you'll do this in the startApp() method of a MIDlet:

```
public void startApp() {
  Display d = Display.getDisplay(this);
  // ...
}
```

You may be tempted to call getDisplay() in a MIDlet's constructor, but according to the specification, getDisplay() can only be called after the beginning of the MIDlet's startApp() method.

Once you've got a reference to a device's Display, you'll just need to create something to show (an instance of Displayable) and pass it to one of Display's setCurrent() methods:

```
public void setCurrent(Displayable next)
public void setCurrent(Alert alert, Displayable nextDisplayable)
```

The second version is used when you want to show a temporary message (an Alert) followed by something else. I'll talk more about Alerts at the end of this chapter.

Display's getCurrent() method returns a reference to what's currently being shown. Note that a MIDlet may return a valid object from getCurrent() even if it is not visible to the user. This could happen on a device running multiple MIDlets simultaneously, for example. Note that the Displayable interface has a method called isShown() that indicates whether the given object is actually being shown on the device screen.

You can also query a Display to determine its capabilities, which is helpful for applications that need to adapt themselves to different types of displays. The numColors() method returns the number of distinct colors supported by this device, while the isColor() method tells whether the device supports color or grayscale. A Display for a device supporting 16 levels of gray, for example, would return false from isColor() and 16 from numColors(). In MIDP 2.0, you can also find out whether the device supports transparency by calling numAlphaLevels(), which returns the number of transparency levels. The minimum return value is two, indicating that image pixels with full transparency and full opacity are supported. Return values greater than two indicate that alpha blending is supported. In MIDP 2.0, Display contains two additional pairs of methods. The first methods, getColor() and getBorderStyle(), are used for finding out colors and line styles from the system user interface scheme. These methods are useful for drawing custom items, a topic that is covered in Chapter 7. The other method pair, flashBacklight() and vibrate(), invoke the corresponding features of the device. These are more fully discussed in Chapter 11.

Event Handling with Commands

Displayable, the parent of all screen displays, supports a very flexible user interface concept, the command. A *command* is something the user can invoke—you can think of it as a button. Like a button, it has a title, like "OK" or "Cancel," and your application can respond appropriately when the user invokes the command. The premise is that you want a command to be available to the user, but you don't really care how it is shown on the screen or exactly how the user invokes it—keypad button, soft button, touch screen, whatever.

Every Displayable keeps a list of its Commands. You can add and remove Commands using the following methods:

```
public void addCommand(Command cmd)
public void removeCommand(Command cmd)
```

Creating Commands

In MIDP, commands are represented by instances of the Command class. To create a Command, just supply a name, a type, and a priority. The name is usually shown on the screen. The type can be used to signify a commonly used command. It should be one of the values defined in the Command class. Table 5-1 shows the type values and their meanings.

Table 5-1. Command Types

NAME	MEANING
OK	Confirms a selection.
CANCEL	Cancels pending changes.
BACK	Moves the user back to a previous screen.
STOP	Stops a running operation.
HELP	Shows application instructions.
SCREEN	Generic type for specific application commands.

To create a standard **OK** command, for example, you would do this:

```
Command c = new Command("OK", Command.OK, 0);
```

To create a command specific to your application, you might do this:

```
Command c = new Command("Launch", Command.SCREEN, 0);
```

It's up to the MIDP implementation to figure out how to show the commands. In the Sun J2ME Wireless Toolkit emulator, commands are assigned to the two soft buttons. A *soft button* is a button on the device keypad with no predefined function. A soft button can serve a different purpose at different times. If there are more commands than there are soft buttons, the commands that don't fit will be grouped into a menu that is assigned to one of the soft buttons.

A simple priority scheme determines who wins when there are more commands than available screen space. Every command has a priority that indicates how hard the display system should try to show the command. Lower numbers indicate a higher priority. If you add a command with priority 0, then several more with priority 1, the priority 0 command will show up on the screen directly. The other commands will most likely end up in a secondary menu.

MIDP 2.0 adds support for long labels on commands. The MIDP implementation decides which label it will use based on the available screen space and the size of the labels. You can create a command with a short and long label like this:

```
Command c = new Command("Run", "Run simulation", Command.SCREEN, 0);
```

The Command class provides getLabel(), getLongLabel(), and getCommandType() methods for retrieving information about commands.

Responding to Commands

By themselves, Commands aren't very exciting. They'll show up on the screen, but nothing happens automatically when a user invokes a command. An object called a *listener* is notified when the user invokes any command in a Displayable. This follows the basic form of the JavaBeans event model; a Displayable is a *unicast event source*. A Displayable fires off an event every time the user invokes one of its Commands.

The listener is an object that implements the CommandListener interface. To register the listener with a Displayable, use the following method:

```
public void setListener(CommandListener l)
```

Displayable is a unicast event source because it can only have one listener object. (*Multicast* event sources can have multiple listeners and use an add... method for adding listeners rather than a set... method.)

Implementing a CommandListener is a matter of defining a single method:

```
public void commandAction(Command c, Displayable s)
```

When a command is invoked, the Displayable that contains it calls the commandAction() method of the registered listener.

 TIP *Event listeners should not perform lengthy processing inside the event-handling thread. The system uses its own thread to call* commandAction() *in response to user input. If your implementation of* commandAction() *does any heavy thinking, it will tie up the system's event-handling thread. If you have anything complicated to do, use your own thread.*

A Simple Example

By way of illustration, consider the following class:

```
import javax.microedition.midlet.*;
import javax.microedition.lcdui.*;

public class Commander extends MIDlet {
  public void startApp() {
    Displayable d = new TextBox("TextBox", "Commander", 20, TextField.ANY);
    Command c = new Command("Exit", Command.EXIT, 0);
    d.addCommand(c);
    d.setCommandListener(new CommandListener() {
      public void commandAction(Command c, Displayable s) {
        notifyDestroyed();
      }
    } );

    Display.getDisplay(this).setCurrent(d);
  }

  public void pauseApp() { }

  public void destroyApp(boolean unconditional) { }
}
```

This MIDlet creates a TextBox, which is a kind of Displayable, and adds a single command to it. The listener is created as an anonymous inner subclass. In Sun's toolkit, this MIDlet appears as shown in Figure 5-3.

Figure 5-3. A simple MIDlet with a single command, **Exit**

Figure 5-3 shows the **Exit** command being mapped to one of the MIDP simulator's soft buttons. If you add another command to this MIDlet, it will be mapped to the other soft button. If you continue adding commands, the ones that don't fit on the screen will be put into an off-screen menu. For example, a screen with four commands shows up in the MIDP simulator as illustrated in Figure 5-4a.

If you press the soft button for **Menu**, you'll see the remainder of the commands as shown in Figure 5-4b. Menu items can now be selected by pressing a number or using the arrow keys for navigation. In the example shown in Figure 5-4, the **Exit** command is given a higher priority (lower number) than the other commands, which insures that it appears directly on the screen. The other commands, with a lower priority, are relegated to the command menu.

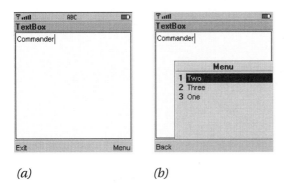

(a)   *(b)*

Figure 5-4. This MIDlet has more commands than the device has soft buttons. Invoking the (a) system-generated **Menu** *command brings up the (b) remaining commands.*

Screens and Tickers

The remainder of this chapter and all of Chapter 6 are devoted to Screen and its subclasses, which is the left branch of the hierarchy shown in Figure 5-1. Screen is the base class for all classes that represent generalized user interfaces.

Canvas, by contrast, is a base class for specialized interfaces, such as those for games. Canvas will be fully covered later, in Chapter 10.

In the coming sections, we'll explore each of Screen's child classes. Here, I'll briefly describe what all Screens have in common: a title and a ticker. The *title* is just what you expect: a string that appears at the top of the screen. A *ticker* is simply a bit of text that scrolls across the top of a Screen; it is named after old-fashioned stock tickers.

In MIDP 2.0, the four methods I'm about to describe are moved from Screen to Displayable. Thus, MIDP 2.0 extends the concept of title and ticker to all Displayables, not just Screens. In MIDP 2.0, the Screen class has no methods.

The title is a text string displayed at the top of the screen. As you saw in Figure 5-3, the title of the screen is "TextBox." Subclasses of Screen have constructors that set the title, but the title may also be accessed using the following methods:

```
public void setTitle(String newTitle)
public String getTitle()
```

The ticker is just as easy to access:

```
public void setTicker(Ticker newTicker)
public Ticker getTicker()
```

The Ticker class is a simple wrapper for a string. To add a ticker to a screen, you would do something like this:

```
// Displayable d = ...
Ticker ticker = new Ticker("This is the ticker message!");
d.setTicker(ticker);
```

Figure 5-5 shows a ticker in action.

Figure 5-5. A ticker scrolls across the top of a screen.

TextBox, the Simplest Screen

The simplest type of screen is the TextBox, which you've already seen in action. TextBox allows the user to enter a string. Keep in mind that on a garden-variety MIDP device, text input is a tedious process. Many devices only have a numeric keypad, so entering a single character is a matter of one, two, or three button presses. A good MIDlet requires minimal user input.

That said, your MIDlet may need some kind of input—perhaps a zip code, or a short name, or some kind of password. In these cases, you'll probably want to use a TextBox.

A TextBox is created by specifying four parameters:

```
public TextBox(String title, String text, int maxSize, int constraints)
```

The title is used as the screen title, while text and maxSize determine the initial text and maximum size of the text box. Finally, constraints can be used to restrict the user's input. Constants from the TextField class are used to specify the type of input required:

- ANY allows any type of input.

- NUMERIC restricts the input to integers.

- DECIMAL (new in MIDP 2.0) allows numbers with fractional parts.

- PHONENUMBER requires a telephone number.

- EMAILADDR input must be an e-mail address.

- URL input must be a web address.

It's up to the implementation to determine how these constraints are enforced. The toolkit emulators simply don't allow invalid input; for example, a NUMERIC TextBox doesn't allow you to enter alphabetic characters.

The constraints above may be combined with the flags listed below. Constraints limit the behavior of users, while flags define the behavior of the TextBox. All the flags except PASSWORD are new in MIDP 2.0.

- PASSWORD characters are not shown when entered; generally, they are represented by asterisks.

- UNEDITABLE indicates text that cannot be edited.

- SENSITIVE is used to flag text that the implementation should not store. Some input schemes store input from the user for later use in autocompletion. This flag indicates that the text is off-limits and should not be saved or cached.

- NON_PREDICTIVE indicates that you are expecting the user to enter text that any text-predicting input scheme will probably not be able to guess. For example, if you're expecting the user to enter an order number like Z51002S, you would use this flag to tell the input scheme to not bother trying to predict the input.

- INITIAL_CAPS_WORD is used for input where each word should be capitalized.

- INITIAL_CAPS_SENTENCE indicates input where the first character of each sentence should be capitalized.

If you don't want the TextBox to perform any validation, use ANY or its numerical equivalent, 0, for the constraints parameter in the constructor.

The flags may be combined with any of the other constraints using the OR operator. For example, to create a TextBox that constrains input to an e-mail address but keeps the entered data hidden, you would do something like this:

```
Displayable d = new TextBox("Email", "", 64,
        TextField.EMAILADDR | TextField.PASSWORD);
```

If you think about it, though, PASSWORD is probably more trouble than it's worth. The point of PASSWORD fields, at least on desktop machines, is to keep someone walking past your computer screen from seeing your secret password. For every character you enter, the password field shows an asterisk or some other symbol. As you type your secret password, all that shows up on the screen is a line of asterisks. On mobile phones and other small devices, this is less of a concern because the screens are smaller and much more difficult to read than a typical desktop monitor.

Furthermore, the difficulty of entering data on a small device means that it will be hard to correctly enter passwords if you are typing blind. Mobile phones, for example, typically require you to press keys several times to enter a single letter. On Sun's toolkit emulator, pressing the '7' key twice enters the letter 'Q.' On a real device, you would have to enter a password "gandalf" with the following sequence of key presses: 4, 2, 6, 6, 3, 2, 5, 5, 5, 3, 3, 3. Without visual feedback, it would be extremely easy to make a mistake when entering a password. ("Did I press the 5 key two times or three times?") The J2ME Wireless Toolkit emulator shows the current character but previously typed characters are shown as asterisks. Good passwords typically have mixed case, numbers, and possibly punctuation; these would be hard to enter correctly.

In MIDP 2.0 applications, password fields (whether or not they use the PASSWORD flag) should be protected with the SENSITIVE flag so that the password doesn't show up in any system dictionaries or pop up unexpectedly when the user is entering other text.

MIDP 2.0 includes a single new method in the TextBox class called setInitialInputMode(String characterSubset). This method is used to suggest to the implementation what input mode would be best suited to the expected text. You can only suggest the input mode, and you have no way of knowing whether the implementation has honored the request. The string passed to the method can be one of the constants from the J2SE java.lang.Character.UnicodeBlock class, prepended with "UCB_". For example, you might pass "UCB_BASIC_LATIN" or "UCB_KATAKANA" to this method. You can also use input subsets defined by java.awt.im.InputSubset by prepending them with "IS_". For example, "IS_LATIN" or "IS_KANJI" would be valid. Finally, MIDP 2.0 also defines the character subsets "MIDP_UPPERCASE_LATIN" and "MIDP_LOWERCASE_LATIN".

The input mode is complementary to the text constraints and flags. You might specify ANY for the constraints, then call setInitialInputMode("MIDP_LOWERCASE_LATIN") to request that the implementation begin by allowing lowercase input. This doesn't prevent the user from changing the input mode, it just starts things off on the right foot.

Using Alerts

An *alert* is an informative message shown to the user. In the MIDP universe, there are two flavors of alert:

- A *timed* alert is shown for a certain amount of time, typically just a few seconds. It displays an informative message that does not need to be acknowledged, like "Your transaction is complete," or "I can't do that right now, Dave."

- A *modal* alert stays up until the user dismisses it. Modal alerts are useful when you need to offer the user a choice of actions. You might display a message like "Are you ready to book these tickets?" and offer **Yes** and **No** commands as options.

MIDP alerts can have an associated icon, like a stop sign or question mark. Alerts may even have an associated sound, although this depends on the implementation. MIDP alerts are very much the same concept as modal dialogs in windowing systems like MacOS and Windows. Figure 5-6 shows a typical Alert.

Figure 5-6. Alerts are similar to modal dialogs in a desktop windowing system.

Alerts are represented by instances of the javax.microedition.lcdui.Alert class, which offers the following constructors:

```
public Alert()
public Alert(String title, String alertText, Image alertImage, AlertType alertType)
```

Any or all of the parameters in the second constructor may be null. (Don't worry about the Image class right now; I'll discuss it in the next chapter in the section on Lists.)

By default, timed Alerts are created using a default timeout value; you can find out the default value by calling getDefaultTimeout(). To change the Alert's timeout, call setTimeout() with the timeout value in milliseconds. A special value, FOREVER, may be used to indicate that the Alert is modal.

You could create a simple timed Alert with the following code:

```
Alert alert = new Alert("Sorry", "I'm sorry, Dave...", null, null);
```

To explicitly set the timeout value to five seconds, you could do this:

```
alert.setTimeout(5000);
```

If, instead, you wanted a modal alert, you would use the special value FOREVER:

```
alert.setTimeout(Alert.FOREVER);
```

The MIDP implementation will automatically supply a way to dismiss a modal alert. Sun's reference implementation, for example, provides a **Done** command mapped to a soft button. MIDP 2.0 exposes this command as the static member DISMISS_COMMAND, allowing you to register your own command listener and explicitly recognize this command. You can add your own commands to an Alert using the usual addCommand() method. The first time you call addCommand(), the system's dismiss command is removed.

The default behavior for Alerts automatically advances to the next screen when the Alert is dismissed or times out. You can specify the next screen by passing it and the Alert to the two-argument setCurrent() method in Display. If you call the regular one-argument setCurrent() method, the previous screen is restored when the Alert is dismissed. Alert types serve as hints to the underlying MIDP implementation. The implementation may use the alert type to decide what kind of sound to play when the alert is shown. The AlertType class provides five types, accessed as static member variables: ALARM, CONFIRMATION, ERROR, INFO, and WARNING.

MIDP 2.0 adds an indicator to an Alert. By default, no indicator is present, but you can add one by passing a Gauge to Alert's setIndicator() method. (Gauge is presented in the next chapter in the section on Forms.) The indicator is handy for showing progress in a network connection or a long computation.

The following example, TwoAlerts, shows both types of alert. It features a main TextBox that is displayed when the MIDlet begins. Two commands, **Go** and **About**, provide access to the alerts. The **Go** command shows a timed alert that contains a message about a fictitious network error. The **About** command displays a modal alert that could contain copyright information. A third command, **Exit**, provides a way to exit the MIDlet. Keep in mind that all three commands may not fit on the screen; some of them may be accessible from a secondary menu.

```
import javax.microedition.midlet.*;
import javax.microedition.lcdui.*;

public class TwoAlerts
    extends MIDlet
    implements CommandListener {
  private Display mDisplay;

  private TextBox mTextBox;
  private Alert mTimedAlert;
  private Alert mModalAlert;

  private Command mAboutCommand, mGoCommand, mExitCommand;

  public TwoAlerts() {
    mAboutCommand = new Command("About", Command.SCREEN, 1);
    mGoCommand = new Command("Go", Command.SCREEN, 1);
    mExitCommand = new Command("Exit", Command.EXIT, 2);

    mTextBox = new TextBox("TwoAlerts", "", 32, TextField.ANY);
    mTextBox.addCommand(mAboutCommand);
    mTextBox.addCommand(mGoCommand);
    mTextBox.addCommand(mExitCommand);
    mTextBox.setCommandListener(this);

    mTimedAlert = new Alert("Network error",
        "A network error occurred. Please try again.",
        null,
        AlertType.INFO);
```

```
        mModalAlert = new Alert("About TwoAlerts",
            "TwoAlerts is a simple MIDlet that demonstrates the use of Alerts.",
            null,
            AlertType.INFO);
        mModalAlert.setTimeout(Alert.FOREVER);
    }

    public void startApp() {
      mDisplay = Display.getDisplay(this);

      mDisplay.setCurrent(mTextBox);
    }

    public void pauseApp() {
    }

    public void destroyApp(boolean unconditional) {}

    public void commandAction(Command c, Displayable s) {
      if (c == mAboutCommand)
        mDisplay.setCurrent(mModalAlert);
      else if (c == mGoCommand)
        mDisplay.setCurrent(mTimedAlert, mTextBox);
      else if (c == mExitCommand)
        notifyDestroyed();
    }
}
```

Summary

MIDP's main user-interface classes are based on abstractions that can be adapted to devices that have different display and input capabilities. Several varieties of prepackaged screen classes make it easy to create a user interface. Screens have a title and an optional ticker. Most importantly, screens can contain Commands, which the implementation makes available to the user. Your application can respond to commands by acting as a listener object. This chapter described TextBox, a screen for accepting user input, and Alert, a simple screen for displaying information. In the next chapter, we'll get into the more complex List and Form classes.

CHAPTER 6

Lists and Forms

IN THE LAST chapter, you learned about MIDP's simpler screen classes. Now we're getting into deeper waters, with screens that show lists and screens with mixed types of controls.

Using Lists

After TextBox and Alert, the next simplest Screen is List, which allows the user to select items (called *elements*) from a list of choices. A text string or an image is used to represent each element in the list. List supports the selection of a single element or of multiple elements.

There are two main types of List, denoted by constants in the Choice interface:

- MULTIPLE designates a list where multiple elements may be selected simultaneously.

- EXCLUSIVE specifies a list where only one element may be selected. It is akin to a group of radio buttons.

Understanding List Types

For both MULTIPLE and EXCLUSIVE lists, selection and confirmation are separate steps. In fact, List does not handle confirmation for these types of lists—your MIDlet will need to provide some other mechanism (probably a Command) that allows users to confirm their choices. MULTIPLE lists allow users to select and de-select various elements before confirming the selection. EXCLUSIVE lists permit users to change their minds several times before confirming the selection.

Figure 6-1a shows an EXCLUSIVE list. The user navigates through the list using the arrow up and down keys. An element is selected by pressing the select button on the device. Figure 6-1b shows a MULTIPLE list. It works basically the same way as an EXCLUSIVE list, but multiple elements can be selected simultaneously. As before, the user moves through the list with the up and down arrow keys. The select key toggles the selection of a particular element.

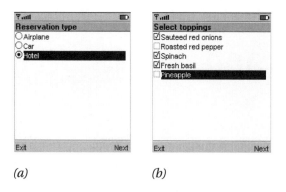

(a)   *(b)*

Figure 6-1. List types: (a) EXCLUSIVE *and (b)* MULTIPLE

A further refinement of EXCLUSIVE also exists: IMPLICIT lists combine the steps of selection and confirmation. The IMPLICIT list acts just like a menu. Figure 6-2 shows an IMPLICIT list with images and text for each element. When the user hits the select key, the list immediately fires off an event, just like a Command. An IMPLICIT list is just like an EXCLUSIVE list in that the user can only select one of the list elements. But with IMPLICIT lists, there's no opportunity for the user to change his or her mind before confirming the selection.

Figure 6-2. IMPLICIT *lists combine selection and confirmation.*

Event Handling for IMPLICIT Lists

When the user makes a selection in an IMPLICIT List, the commandAction() method of the List's CommandListener is invoked. A special value is passed to commandAction() as the Command parameter:

```
public static final Command SELECT_COMMAND
```

For example, you can test the source of command events like this:

```
public void commandAction(Command c, Displayable s) {
  if (c == nextCommand)
    // ...
  else if (c == List.SELECT_COMMAND)
    // ...
}
```

There's an example at the end of this chapter that demonstrates an IMPLICIT List.

In MIDP 2.0, the setSelectCommand() offers you the opportunity to specify your own Command to be used for selections instead of having to use the SELECT_COMMAND.

Creating Lists

To create a List, specify a title and a list type. If you have the element names and images available ahead of time, you can pass them in the constructor:

```
public List(String title, int type)
public List(String title, int type,
    String[] stringElements, Image[] imageElements)
```

The stringElements parameter cannot be null; however, stringElements or imageElements may contain null array elements. If both the string and image for a given list element are null, the element is displayed blank. If both the string and the image are defined, the element will display using the image and the string.

Some Lists will have more elements than can be displayed on the screen. Indeed, the actual number of elements that will fit varies from device to device. But don't worry: List implementations automatically handle scrolling up and down to show the full contents of the List.

About Images

Our romp through the List class yields a first look at images. Instances of the javax.microedition.lcdui.Image class represent images in MIDP. The specification dictates that implementations be able to load images files in PNG format.[1] This format supports both a transparent color and lossless compression.

Image has no constructors, but the Image class offers a handful of createImage() factory methods for obtaining Image instances. The first are for loading images from PNG data.

```
public static Image createImage(String name)
public static Image createImage(byte[] imagedata, int imageoffset,
    int imagelength)
```

The first method attempts to create an Image from the named file, which should be packaged inside the JAR that contains your MIDlet. You should use an absolute pathname or the image file may not be found. The second method creates an Image using data in the supplied array. The data starts at the given array offset, imageoffset, and is imagelength bytes long. In MIDP 2.0, you can also create an Image from an InputStream:

```
public static Image createImage(InputStream stream)
```

Images may be *mutable* or *immutable*. Mutable Images can be modified by calling getGraphics() and using the returned Graphics object to draw on the image. (For full details on Graphics, see Chapter 10.) If you try to call getGraphics() on an immutable Image, an IllegalStateException will be thrown.

The createImage() methods described above return immutable Images. To create a mutable Image, use the following method:

```
public static Image createImage(int width, int height)
```

Typically you would create a mutable Image for off-screen drawing, perhaps for an animation or to reduce flicker if the device's display is not double buffered.

---

1.   MIDP implementations are not required to recognize all varieties of PNG files. The documentation for the Image class has the specifics.

Any Image you pass to Alert, ChoiceGroup, ImageItem, or List should be immutable. To create an immutable Image from a mutable one, use the following method:

```
public static Image createImage(Image image)
```

In MIDP 2.0, you can also create an Image from a portion of another Image using the following method:

```
public static Image createImage(Image image,
    int x, int y, int width, int height, int transform)
```

This method takes the part of the original image described by x, y, width, and height, applies the specified transformation, and returns the result as an immutable Image. The possible transformations are described by constants in the javax.microedition.lcdui.game.Sprite class and include things like mirroring and 90-degree rotation.

Image also includes methods that handle image data as an int array. I'll talk about these methods later in Chapter 10.

How do you figure out what size Images you need? In MIDP 2.0, Display provides methods that return information about the optimal width and height for various types of images:

```
public int getBestImageHeight(int imageType);
public int getBestImageWidth(int imageType);
```

The imageType parameter should be one of Display's constants LIST_ELEMENT, ALERT, or CHOICE_GROUP_ELEMENT. (You'll learn all about ChoiceGroup later in this chapter.) If you were building a List, you could query Display to find the best size for element images. Assuming you had packaged icons of various sizes in your application, you could select the best-sized images at runtime.

Editing a List

List provides methods for adding items, removing elements, and examining elements. Each element in the List has an index. The first element is at index 0, the next at index 1, and so forth. You can replace an element with set() or add an element to the end of the list with append(). The insert() method adds a new element to the list at the given index; this bumps all elements at that position and higher up by one.

```
public void set(int elementNum, String stringPart, Image imagePart)
public void insert(int elementNum, String stringPart, Image imagePart)
public int append(String stringPart, Image imagePart)
```

You can examine the string or image for a given element by supplying its index. Similarly, you can use delete() to remove an element from the List.

```
public String getString(int elementNum)
public Image getImage(int elementNum)
public void delete(int elementNum)
```

MIDP 2.0 also features a deleteAll() method that removes every element from the List.

Finally, the size() method returns the number of elements in the List.

Although you usually give the MIDP implementation the responsibility of displaying your List, new methods in MIDP 2.0 give you some control over the appearance of a List. The first method, setFitPolicy(), tells the List how it should handle elements whose text is wider than the screen. The possible values (from the Choice interface) are

- TEXT_WRAP_ON denotes that long elements will be wrapped to multiple lines.

- TEXT_WRAP_OFF denotes that long elements will be truncated at the edge of the screen.

- TEXT_WRAP_DEFAULT indicates that the implementation should use its default fit policy.

Another new method is setFont(), which allows you to specify the font that will be used for a specific List element. (Fonts will be fully discussed in Chapter 10.) The current Font for an element can be retrieved by calling getFont(). Calls to setFitPolicy() and setFont() only serve as hints; it's up to the implementation to decide how to display the List and whether the requested fit policy or font can be honored.

Working with List Selections

You can find out whether a particular element in a List is selected by supplying the element's index to the following method:

```
public boolean isSelected(int index)
```

For EXCLUSIVE and IMPLICIT lists, the index of the single selected element is returned from the following method:

```
public int getSelectedIndex()
```

If you call getSelectedIndex() on a MULTIPLE list, it will return –1.

To change the current selection programmatically, use setSelectedIndex().

```
public void setSelectedIndex(int index, boolean selected)
```

Finally, List allows you to set or get the selection state *en masse* with the following methods. The supplied arrays must have as many array elements as there are list elements.

```
public int getSelectedFlags(boolean[] selectedArray_return)
public void setSelectedFlags(boolean[] selectedArray)
```

An Example

The example in Listing 6-1 shows a simple MIDlet that could be part of a travel reservation application. The user chooses what type of reservation to make. This example uses an IMPLICIT list, which is essentially a menu.

Listing 6-1. The TravelList *Source Code*

```
import java.io.*;
import javax.microedition.midlet.*;
import javax.microedition.lcdui.*;

public class TravelList
    extends MIDlet
    implements CommandListener {
  private List mList;
  private Command mExitCommand, mNextCommand;

  public TravelList() {
    String[] stringElements = { "Airplane", "Car", "Hotel" };
    Image[] imageElements = { loadImage("/airplane.png"),
        loadImage("/car.png"), loadImage("/hotel.png") };
    mList = new List("Reservation type", List.IMPLICIT,
        stringElements, imageElements);
```

```
    mNextCommand = new Command("Next", Command.SCREEN, 0);
    mExitCommand = new Command("Exit", Command.EXIT, 0);
    mList.addCommand(mNextCommand);
    mList.addCommand(mExitCommand);
    mList.setCommandListener(this);
  }

  public void startApp() {
    Display.getDisplay(this).setCurrent(mList);
  }

  public void commandAction(Command c, Displayable s) {
    if (c == mNextCommand || c == List.SELECT_COMMAND) {
      int index = mList.getSelectedIndex();
      Alert alert = new Alert("Your selection",
          "You chose " + mList.getString(index) + ".",
          null, AlertType.INFO);
      Display.getDisplay(this).setCurrent(alert, mList);
    }
    else if (c == mExitCommand)
      notifyDestroyed();
  }

  public void pauseApp() {}

  public void destroyApp(boolean unconditional) {}

  private Image loadImage(String name) {
    Image image = null;
    try {
      image = Image.createImage(name);
    }
    catch (IOException ioe) {
      System.out.println(ioe);
    }

    return image;
  }
}
```

To see images in this example, you'll need to either download the examples from the book's Web site or supply your own images. With the J2ME Wireless Toolkit, image files should go in the *res* directory of your toolkit project directory. TravelList expects to find three images named *airplane.png*, *car.png*, and *hotel.png*.

Construction of the List itself is very straightforward. Our application also includes a **Next** command and an **Exit** command, which are both added to the List. The TravelList instance is registered as the CommandListener for the List. If the **Next** command or the List's IMPLICIT command is fired off, we simply retrieve the selected item from the List and show it in an Alert.

The **Next** command, in fact, is not strictly necessary in this example since you can achieve the same result by clicking the select button on one of the elements in the List. Nevertheless, it might be a good idea to leave it there. Maybe all of the other screens in your application have a **Next** command, so you could keep it for user interface consistency. It never hurts to provide the user with more than one way of doing things.

The difference between EXCLUSIVE and IMPLICIT lists can be subtle. Try changing the List in this example to EXCLUSIVE to see how the user experience is different.

Creating Advanced Interfaces with Forms

A Form is a screen that can include an arbitrary collection of user-interface controls, called items. In a movie ticket reservation MIDlet, you might use a form to allow the user to enter a date and a Zip code on one screen.

Keep in mind that the minimum screen size for a MID is 96 × 54 pixels. You can't fit a whole lot on a screen this size, nor should you try to. Forms that don't fit on the screen will automatically scroll as needed, so your MIDlet will be able to show forms, regardless of the screen size. Scrolling forms tend to be confusing to users, however, so you should keep your forms as small as possible.

The javax.microedition.ldcui.Form class itself is fairly simple. One way to create a Form is by specifying a title:

```
public Form(String title)
```

In essence, a Form is a collection of items. Each item is represented by an instance of the Item class. If you have all the items ahead of time, you can pass them to Form's other constructor:

```
public Form(String title, Item[] items)
```

As a subclass of Screen and Displayable, Form inherits both a title and a ticker. Given the small screen size of a typical MIDP device, however, you may want to avoid using a ticker with your forms.

Form's grandparent class, Displayable, gives Form the capabilities of displaying commands and firing command events. Again, you should probably keep commands simple with forms; in many cases a **Next** and a **Back** will probably be sufficient.

As with any Displayable, the basic strategy for showing a Form is to create one and pass it to Display's setCurrent() method. MIDP 2.0 offers an additional option, the setCurrentItem() method in Display. This method makes the form containing the item visible, then it scrolls the form so the item is visible and has input focus.

Managing Items

Items may be added and removed, even while the Form is showing. The order of items is important, as well; most MIDP implementations will display a form's items top to bottom and possibly left to right, scrolling the form vertically as needed if there are more items than available screen space.

To add an Item to the bottom of a form, use one of the append() methods. The first one can be used to add any Item implementation. The second two append() methods are strictly for convenience; behind the scenes, a StringItem or an ImageItem will be created for you.

```
public int append(Item item)
public int append(String str)
public int append(Image image)
```

Every item in a form has an index. You can place an item at a specific index (replacing the previous item at that index) using the method:

```
public void set(int index, Item item)
```

Alternately, if you'd like to add an item somewhere in the middle of the form, just supply the desired index for the new item to the insert() method. Subsequent items will move up by one index.

```
public void insert(int index, Item item)
```

To remove an item from a form, use delete().

```
public void delete(int index)
```

MIDP 2.0 also includes a deleteAll() method, which removes all of a Form's Items.

If you forget what you put in a form, you can find out the number of items and retrieve them with the following methods:

```
public int size()
public Item get(int index)
```

Understanding Form Layout

In MIDP 1.0 implementations, Forms are mostly vertical beasts. In general, items added to a form will appear in a vertical stack. If the items don't all fit on the screen, the form allows the user to scroll as needed.

The exceptions to this rule are StringItems and ImageItems. These items may be laid out left-to-right if there is enough space on the screen. However, it's up to the implementation to decide exactly how a form is laid out. In the J2ME Wireless Toolkit 1.0.1 emulator, StringItems and ImageItems are always stacked vertically.

MIDP 2.0 acknowledges the ever-expanding screens of MIDP devices by adding support for more specific layout. There's an exhaustive description of the layout algorithm in the documentation for javax.microedition.lcdui.Form, in the section titled "Layout." Stated briefly, Form attempts to lay out items left-to-right in rows, stacking rows top-to-bottom, just like English text on a page. The Item class, as you'll see, includes extra plumbing in MIDP 2.0 that allows some control over the layout of individual items.

The Item Pantry

The MIDP specification includes a handy toolbox of items that can be used to build forms. I'll cover each of them briefly in this section and show how some of them look in Sun's MIDP reference implementation.

The Item Class

All of the items that can be added to forms descend from the class javax.microedition.lcdui.Item. In MIDP 1.0, Item doesn't specify much, just a getLabel() and setLabel() method. All Items have a string label, although it may or may not be shown by the specific subclass.

MIDP 2.0 expands the Item class considerably in two areas. The first is command handling. In MIDP 2.0, Items can have commands, just like Displayables. When an Item is selected in a form, the Item's commands are shown along with the commands in the form. Figure 6-3 shows a form with four string items, cunningly named "one," "two," "three," and "four." The form itself has one command, "Exit." None of the string items has commands, except for "three," which has one command named "Details."

Figure 6-3. Item "three" has a command.

Note how the toolkit emulator indicates the presence of one or more commands on the item with a light underline. When you navigate through the form to the item with the additional command, it shows up just like any other command, as shown in Figure 6-4.

Figure 6-4. When an item is selected, its commands are shown.

The semantics for managing item commands are nearly identical to the semantics for managing form commands. You can manage the commands on an Item using addCommand() and removeCommand(). Note that the command type should be ITEM for commands added to Item, although no exception will be thrown if this is not true. A command listener may be assigned using the setItemCommandListener() method. The ItemCommandListener interface contains a single method, similar to CommandListener's single method:

```
public void commandAction(Command c, Item item)
```

It's up to the implementation to figure out how to show commands for an item. All you do in a MIDlet is add commands, set a listener, and wait for command events.

Items also support a *default command*. This command may be invoked if the runtime device has a button or knob or other user interface control that is appropriate for a default command. You can set an Item's default command by calling setDefaultCommand().

Item's greatest API changes in MIDP 2.0 are related to layout control. Items have a *minimum size* and a *preferred size* that can be used to control how large an item appears in a form. The minimum size is computed by the implementation and can be retrieved using getMinimumWidth() and getMinimumHeight(). The minimum size depends on the contents of the Item and can be changed by the implementation every time the contents change. There's no way to change an item's minimum size, but examining the minimum size may be useful to your application in deciding how to lay out a form.

The preferred size, by contrast, can either be computed by the implementation or specified by you. The default values for preferred width and height are -1, a special value that tells the implementation "I don't care, you go ahead and figure out the best size for this item." If you pass a specific positive value for the width or height in setPreferredSize(), that dimension is said to be *locked* and the implementation will attempt to use it during layout.

The getPreferredWidth() and getPreferredHeight() methods don't always return the values you've passed to setPreferredSize(). For example, if you've unlocked the width and height by calling setPreferredSize(-1, -1) the values returned from getPreferredWidth() and getPreferredHeight() are the preferred sizes that the implementation has computed.

Finally, the MIDP 2.0 Item class includes a layout directive, accessed using getLayout() and setLayout(). Represented by an integer, the layout value is usually a combination of LAYOUT_2 (a flag indicating MIDP 2.0 layout), a horizontal value and a vertical value. LAYOUT_2 is a flag to the implementation that the item should be laid out using MIDP 2.0 rules. The horizontal values are

- LAYOUT_LEFT

- LAYOUT_RIGHT

- LAYOUT_CENTER

The vertical values are

- LAYOUT_TOP

- LAYOUT_BOTTOM

- LAYOUT_VCENTER

In addition, a layout value may include *shrinking* or *expanding*. Shrinking means that an item's minimum width or height is used, while expanding means that an item's size is stretched to fill the available width or row height. The constants for shrinking and expanding are

- LAYOUT_SHRINK (for width)

- LAYOUT_EXPAND (for width)

- LAYOUT_VSHRINK (for height)

- LAYOUT_VEXPAND (for height)

Finally, an Item's layout may include a request for a new line before or after the item using the LAYOUT_NEWLINE_BEFORE or LAYOUT_NEWLINE_AFTER constants. Items are laid out in Forms much like text flows on a page, so these constants allow you to request a new row before or after an item.

Figure 6-5 shows a simple example, three components with the following layouts:

- LAYOUT_2 | LAYOUT_LEFT | LAYOUT_NEWLINE_AFTER

- LAYOUT_2 | LAYOUT_CENTER | LAYOUT_NEWLINE_AFTER

- LAYOUT_2 | LAYOUT_RIGHT | LAYOUT_NEWLINE_AFTER

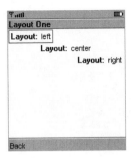

Figure 6-5. Form layout example

StringItem

StringItem represents a simple text label. For example, consider the following code:

```
Form form = new Form("Form Title");
StringItem stringItem = new StringItem("Label: ", "Value");
form.append(stringItem);
```

The form produced by this code (plus a **Back** command) is shown in Figure 6-6.

Figure 6-6. A form with a single `StringItem` *and a* **Back** *command*

You can use `null` for the `StringItem`'s label or value to indicate that it should not be shown on the screen. (Better yet, you could just use Form's `append(String)` method.) `StringItem` inherits `setLabel()` and `getLabel()` methods from `Item`. It also includes `getText()` and `setText()` methods for accessing and adjusting the string value.

MIDP 2.0 adds support for *appearance modes* for both `StringItem` and `ImageItem`. The appearance mode allows the item to look like a URL link or a button, although in all other respects the item behaves the same as a regular `StringItem` or `ImageItem`. The three appearance modes (which are defined in the `Item` class) are

- `PLAIN` shows the item in its normal state.

- `HYPERLINK` shows the item as a URL. A typical action would be to attempt to open the link using `MIDlet`'s `platformRequest()` method.

- `BUTTON` shows the item as a button. Note that this may be clumsy, especially on devices without pointer events, and you should generally use a `Command` where you feel tempted to use an item with a `BUTTON` appearance mode.

As with almost everything else in the `javax.microedition.lcdui` package, it's the implementation's responsibility to show different appearance modes, and your application may look different on different devices. Furthermore, it is your application's responsibility to implement appropriate behavior. For example, you might want to add a command to a `HYPERLINK` `StringItem` that calls `MIDlet`'s `platformRequest()` method to open the link.

NOTE *The J2ME Wireless Toolkit beta release emulators don't show* HYPERLINK *or* BUTTON StringItem*s any differently from* PLAIN *ones, except for one special case. If the* StringItem *has a* BUTTON *type and it has an associated item command, it is shown with a beveled border.*

Finally, MIDP 2.0 offers getFont() and setFont() methods in the StringItem class. I'll describe the Font class in Chapter 10.

Spacer in MIDP 2.0

MIDP 2.0 introduces a new Item, Spacer, that represents empty space in a Form. It may be used for layout purposes. All you need to do is specify a minimum width and height:

```
public Spacer(minWidth, minHeight)
```

TextField

TextField represents an editable string. Figure 6-7 shows a TextField with a label of "TextFieldTitle" and a value of "text".

Figure 6-7. A form with a single TextField *and a* **Back** *command*

In Sun's MIDP 2.0 emulator, text can be entered directly into a TextField either by clicking on the number buttons in the emulator or by typing on the keyboard. Of course, it's up to the implementation to decide exactly how to allow editing. Some implementations may even show a separate screen for editing.

TextFields can limit input. The following constants are defined:

- ANY allows any type of input.

- NUMERIC restricts the input to numbers.

- DECIMAL (new in MIDP 2.0) allows numbers with fractional parts.

- PHONENUMBER requires a telephone number.

- EMAILADDR input must be an e-mail address.

- URL input must be a URL.

These input constraints might look familiar; they're the same ones used by TextBox, which I covered in the previous chapter. As with TextBox, the flags PASSWORD, SENSITIVE, UNEDITABLE, NON_PREDICTIVE, INITIAL_CAPS_WORD, and INITIAL_CAPS_SENTENCE can be combined with constraints using the OR operator.

To create a TextField, you need to supply the label, text value, maximum length, and input constraints.

```
public TextField(String label, String text, int maxSize, int constraints)
```

For an initially empty TextField, pass null for the text parameter.

As with TextBox, the TextField class in MIDP 2.0 includes a setInitialInputMode() method for suggesting to the implementation an appropriate input mode.

ImageItem

Forms can also contain images, which are represented by instances of ImageItem. ImageItems have several pieces of associated data:

- A *label* may be displayed with the image.

- The *layout* determines the placement of the image.

- *Alternate text* is displayed if the image cannot be shown.

To create an ImageItem, just supply the Image that is to be displayed, the label, layout, and alternate text.

ImageItem defines constants for the layout parameter. The simplest thing is to specify the default value, LAYOUT_DEFAULT. If you need more control, combine a horizontal value with a vertical value. The horizontal values are LAYOUT_LEFT, LAYOUT_CENTER, and LAYOUT_RIGHT. The vertical values are LAYOUT_NEWLINE_BEFORE and LAYOUT_NEWLINE_AFTER. In MIDP 2.0, layout is controlled with the layout constants in the Item class. The constants in the ImageItem class are present for backward compatibility.

ImageItem supports appearance modes in MIDP 2.0, just like StringItem. ItemItem includes a new constructor that allows you to set the appearance mode.

Figure 6-8 shows a form containing a single ImageItem.

Figure 6-8. An ImageItem

DateField

DateField is an extremely handy mechanism by which users can enter dates, times, or both. It's up to the implementation to determine some reasonable way for users to enter dates and times; you, as the MIDlet programmer, can simply use DateField and not worry about the implementation.

To create a DateField, specify a label and a type. Three constants in the DateField class describe the different types:

- DATE displays an editable date.

- TIME displays an editable time.

- DATE_TIME displays both a date and a time.

DateField provides two constructors. The first uses the default time zone, while the second allows you to specify a TimeZone explicitly:

```
public DateField(String label, int mode)
public DateField(String label, int mode, TimeZone timeZone)
```

In essence, a DateField is an editor for a java.util.Date. As you saw in Chapter 4, Dates represent points in time. DateField takes the role of translating between a Date and strings that humans can read, much like the Calendar class. You can set or get the Date represented by the DateField using the following methods:

```
public Date getDate()
public void setDate(Date date)
```

In the J2ME Wireless Toolkit emulator, a DateField appears as shown in Figure 6-9a. Note that if you do not supply a Date to setDate() before showing the DateField, it will appear unitialized, as shown in Figure 6-9b.

When the user selects either the date or time portion of the DateField and selects it for editing, the MIDP implementation provides some kind of appropriate editor. Sun's emulator provides the editors shown in Figure 6-9c and Figure 6-9d.

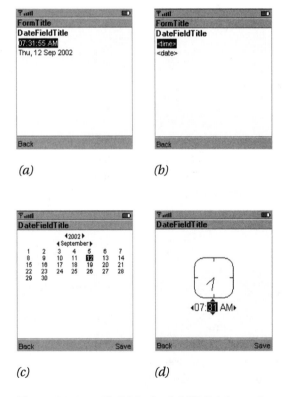

Figure 6-9. DateField *in Sun's MIDP 2.0 emulator*

Gauge

A Gauge represents an integer value. It's up to the implementation to decide how to display it. In Sun's MIDP implementation, a Gauge appears as shown in Figure 6-10.

Figure 6-10. A Gauge

The value of the Gauge can be retrieved and modified with the getValue() and setValue() methods. This value runs from 0 to a variable maximum value. The maximum for the Gauge can be retrieved and modified with the getMaxValue() and setMaxValue() methods.

The visual appearance of the Gauge is an approximation of the Gauge's value. The Gauge shown in Figure 6-10 could, for example, have a value of 7 and a maximum of 10, or perhaps a value of 42 and a maximum of 61.

In an *interactive* Gauge, the user can modify the value. Again, it's up to the implementation to decide exactly how this works. In Sun's reference implementation, the left and right navigation buttons can be used to modify a Gauge's value.

Gauge's constructor is straightforward:

```
public Gauge(String label, boolean interactive,
    int maxValue, int initialValue)
```

For example, the following code creates an interactive Gauge with a maximum value of 24 and an initial value of 2:

```
Gauge g = new Gauge("Power", true, 24, 2);
```

MIDP 2.0 expands Gauge's role. Interactive gauges are the same as before, but there are three varieties of noninteractive gauges that can be useful as progress indicators. You can use a regular noninteractive gauge with a known maximum value to show the progress of a download or a calculation. For example, if you were going to run through a loop 20 times, you could create a Gauge with a maximum of 20 and update its value each time through the loop.

There are two kinds of noninteractive gauges with no maximum value. In this case, you use the special value INDEFINITE for the maximum. Such gauges can be either *incremental* or *continuous*. An incremental gauge shows an operation with measurable steps; your application will update the gauge every time it does something significant. For example, if you were downloading a file, but you didn't know how big it was, you could use an incremental gauge and update the gauge whenever you read some data. A continuous gauge shows progress, probably using an animation, with no prodding needed from the application. This type of gauge is useful for operations where you can't measure the progress.

The gauge value itself can be set to one of the following:

- INCREMENTAL_UPDATING indicates that you have just accomplished something and the gauge should be updated to reflect it.

- INCREMENTAL_IDLE means that you want the gauge to be incremental but nothing is currently happening.

- CONTINUOUS_RUNNING indicates a continuous gauge in its running mode.

- CONTINUOUS_IDLE is used for a continuous gauge, indicating that no progress is currently being made.

The following example shows interactive, continuous, and incremental gauges. Commands (**Update** and **Idle**) set the appropriate values on the continuous and incremental gauges. Normally you would set these from separate threads, but using commands makes it easy to understand what's going on in this example.

In Sun's MIDP 2.0 emulator, the continuous and idle gauges use simple Duke animations to show progress. See Figure 6-11 for a screen shot. Listing 6-2 contains the source code for a MIDlet that demonstrates different kinds of Gauges.

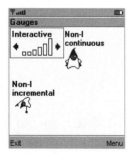

Figure 6-11. Three kinds of Gauges in MIDP 2.0

Listing 6-2. GaugeMIDlet *Source Code*

```java
import javax.microedition.midlet.*;
import javax.microedition.lcdui.*;

public class GaugeMIDlet
    extends MIDlet
    implements CommandListener {
  private Display mDisplay;

  private Form mGaugeForm;
  private Command mUpdateCommand, mIdleCommand;

  private Gauge mInteractiveGauge;
  private Gauge mIncrementalGauge;
  private Gauge mContinuousGauge;

  public GaugeMIDlet() {
    mGaugeForm = new Form("Gauges");
    mInteractiveGauge = new Gauge("Interactive", true, 5, 2);
    mInteractiveGauge.setLayout(Item.LAYOUT_2);
    mGaugeForm.append(mInteractiveGauge);
    mContinuousGauge = new Gauge("Non-I continuous", false,
        Gauge.INDEFINITE, Gauge.CONTINUOUS_RUNNING);
    mContinuousGauge.setLayout(Item.LAYOUT_2);
    mGaugeForm.append(mContinuousGauge);
    mIncrementalGauge = new Gauge("Non-I incremental", false,
        Gauge.INDEFINITE, Gauge.INCREMENTAL_UPDATING);
    mIncrementalGauge.setLayout(Item.LAYOUT_2);
    mGaugeForm.append(mIncrementalGauge);

    mUpdateCommand = new Command("Update", Command.SCREEN, 0);
    mIdleCommand = new Command("Idle", Command.SCREEN, 0);
    Command exitCommand = new Command("Exit", Command.EXIT, 0);
    mGaugeForm.addCommand(mUpdateCommand);
    mGaugeForm.addCommand(mIdleCommand);
    mGaugeForm.addCommand(exitCommand);
    mGaugeForm.setCommandListener(this);
  }

  public void startApp() {
    if (mDisplay == null) mDisplay = Display.getDisplay(this);
    mDisplay.setCurrent(mGaugeForm);
  }
```

```
  public void pauseApp() {}

  public void destroyApp(boolean unconditional) {}

  public void commandAction(Command c, Displayable s) {
    if (c.getCommandType() == Command.EXIT)
      notifyDestroyed();
    else if (c == mUpdateCommand) {
      mContinuousGauge.setValue(Gauge.CONTINUOUS_RUNNING);
      mIncrementalGauge.setValue(Gauge.INCREMENTAL_UPDATING);
    }
    else if (c == mIdleCommand) {
      mContinuousGauge.setValue(Gauge.CONTINUOUS_IDLE);
      mIncrementalGauge.setValue(Gauge.INCREMENTAL_IDLE);
    }
  }
}
```

ChoiceGroup

The final class in the Form arsenal of Items is ChoiceGroup. ChoiceGroup offers a list of choices. It is very similar to javax.microedition.lcdui.List, which was described at the beginning of this chapter. This similarity is more than coincidental; ChoiceGroup and List both implement the Choice interface, which is the wellspring of all of the instance methods in both classes.

If you read the section about List, you already know almost everything you need to know to use ChoiceGroup because the instance methods work exactly the same way.

ChoiceGroup features the following constructors:

```
public ChoiceGroup(String label, int choiceType)
public ChoiceGroup(String label, int choiceType, String[] stringElements,
    Image[] imageElements)
```

The choiceType should look familiar; it can be either EXCLUSIVE or MULTIPLE, the constants defined in the Choice interface. In fact, ChoiceGroup's constructors work exactly like List's constructors, except that IMPLICIT is not allowed. This makes sense, since a ChoiceGroup is one item in a form, not an entire screen. MIDP 2.0 also adds a POPUP type for ChoiceGroup that makes it appear like a combo box or a drop-down menu. The ChoiceGroup appears like any other element in the Form; Figure 6-12 shows examples.

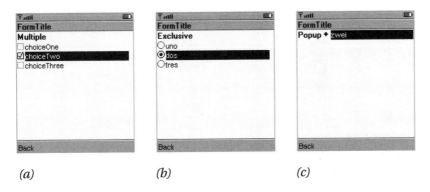

(a)   *(b)*   *(c)*

Figure 6-12. ChoiceGroup *examples: (a)* MULTIPLE, *(b)* EXCLUSIVE *and (c)* POPUP

Responding to Item Changes

Most items in a Form fire events when the user changes them. Your application can listen for these events by registering an ItemStateListener with the Form using the following method:

```
public void setItemStateListener(ItemStateListener iListener)
```

ItemStateListener is an interface with a single method. This method is called every time an item in a Form is changed:

```
public void itemStateChanged(Item item)
```

Listing 6-3 creates a Form with two items, an interactive Gauge and a StringItem. As you adjust the Gauge, its value is reflected in the StringItem using the ItemStateListener mechanism.

Listing 6-3. GaugeTracker *Source Code*

```
import javax.microedition.midlet.*;
import javax.microedition.lcdui.*;

public class GaugeTracker
    extends MIDlet
    implements ItemStateListener, CommandListener {
  private Gauge mGauge;
  private StringItem mStringItem;
```

```
public GaugeTracker() {
  int initialValue = 3;
  mGauge = new Gauge("GaugeTitle", true, 5, initialValue);
  mStringItem = new StringItem(null, "[value]");
  itemStateChanged(mGauge);
}

public void itemStateChanged(Item item) {
  if (item == mGauge)
    mStringItem.setText("Value = " + mGauge.getValue());
}

public void commandAction(Command c, Displayable s) {
  if (c.getCommandType() == Command.EXIT)
    notifyDestroyed();
}

public void startApp() {
  Form form = new Form("GaugeTracker");
  form.addCommand(new Command("Exit", Command.EXIT, 0));
  form.setCommandListener(this);
  // Now add the selected items.
  form.append(mGauge);
  form.append(mStringItem);
  form.setItemStateListener(this);

  Display.getDisplay(this).setCurrent(form);
}

public void pauseApp() {}

public void destroyApp(boolean unconditional) {}
}
```

Summary

This chapter described MIDP's advanced user-interface screens, List and Form. A List is a list of elements that allows for single or multiple selections. You supply the items—it's up to the implementation to figure out how to show them, how the user navigates through them, and how the user selects items. Forms are generalized screens that are built up from a collection of Items. The MIDP API supplies a handy toolbox of Items—everything from simple string and image Items to the more complex DateField and ChoiceGroup classes.

Even though List and Form are very capable, you should use them sparingly, particularly Form. Small devices have small screens, so you don't want to put much information in each screen, especially if it's going to force the user to scroll up and down a lot. Furthermore, ease of use is crucial on consumer devices like mobile phones and pagers. Make sure your interface is clean, intuitive, and as simple as it can possibly be.

CHAPTER 7

Custom Items

IN THE LAST chapter, you learned about Forms, the most flexible and powerful descendents of javax.microedition.lcdui.Screen. Forms are essentially collections of Items. The MIDP APIs include a complete toolbox of Item subclasses, everything from text and image display to interactive date fields and gauges.

MIDP 2.0 provides even more power, through the opportunity to define your own items. In this chapter, you'll learn how to create items that do their own drawing and respond to user input.

Introducing CustomItem

The class that makes custom items possible is appropriately named CustomItem. Like all items that live in a Form, it is a subclass of Item. To create your very own item, all you have to do is define a subclass of CustomItem by implementing five abstract methods. The first four, listed below, have to do with the size of the item's *content area*, which is the area for which your code has responsibility. The total area of the custom item includes a label and perhaps borders, but these are the responsibility of the implementation. Your CustomItem subclass is only responsible for the content area.

```
protected int getPrefContentWidth(int height)
protected int getPrefContentHeight(int width)
protected int getMinContentWidth()
protected int getMinContentHeight()
```

The first two methods should return values that define how big your item *wants* to be. When the MIDP implementation lays out a Form containing your item, it may not be able to honor your preferred size, but it will try. The implementation passes a proposed height and width into these methods to give your item class an idea of what its dimensions might eventually be. For example, the implementation might call your item's getPrefContentWidth() method and pass a value of 18 for the height parameter. This is the implementation asking your item, "What width would you like to be if I make your height 18?"

The second pair of methods should return information about the minimum size of the item. This is the smallest size that your item believes it can tolerate.

The fifth method that must be defined by a concrete `CustomItem` subclass is the paint() method, which the implementation calls to render the item.

```
protected void paint(Graphics g, int w, int h)
```

The Graphics object can be used to draw lines, shapes, text, and images on the content area of the item. The Graphics class is fully covered in Chapter 10; for now, I'll just use a few simple methods to demonstrate how to draw custom items. The w and h parameters indicate the current width and height of the content area.

Armed with this knowledge, you can create a simple `CustomItem` by implementing the five abstract methods described above and providing a constructor. Listing 7-1 shows one such class, `SimpleItem`. This class returns hardcoded values for the minimum and preferred content dimensions and provides a paint() method that draws a simple pattern of triangles.

Listing 7-1. A Simple Custom Item

```
import javax.microedition.lcdui.*;

public class SimpleItem
    extends CustomItem {
  public SimpleItem(String title) { super(title); }

  // CustomItem abstract methods.

  public int getMinContentWidth() { return 100; }
  public int getMinContentHeight() { return 60; }

  public int getPrefContentWidth(int width) {
    return getMinContentWidth();
  }

  public int getPrefContentHeight(int height) {
    return getMinContentHeight();
  }

  public void paint(Graphics g, int w, int h) {
    g.drawRect(0, 0, w - 1, h - 1);
    g.setColor(0x000000ff);
    int offset = 0;
```

```
    for (int y = 4; y < h; y += 12) {
      offset = (offset + 12) % 24;
      for (int x = 4; x < w; x += 24) {
        g.fillTriangle(x + offset,      y,
                        x + offset - 3, y + 6,
                        x + offset + 3, y + 6);
      }
    }
  }
}
```

I won't make you write your own MIDlet to see your new item. Listing 7-2 shows a MIDlet that uses SimpleItem:

Listing 7-2. A MIDlet That Demonstrates SimpleItem

```
import javax.microedition.midlet.*;
import javax.microedition.lcdui.*;

public class SimpleItemMIDlet
    extends MIDlet
    implements CommandListener {
  public void startApp() {
    Form form = new Form("SimpleItemMIDlet");
    form.append(new SimpleItem("SimpleItem"));

    Command c = new Command("Exit", Command.EXIT, 0);
    form.addCommand(c);
    form.setCommandListener(this);

    Display.getDisplay(this).setCurrent(form);
  }

  public void pauseApp() {}

  public void destroyApp(boolean unconditional) {}

  public void commandAction(Command c, Displayable s) {
    if (c.getCommandType() == Command.EXIT)
      notifyDestroyed();
  }
}
```

Figure 7-1 shows this MIDlet in action.

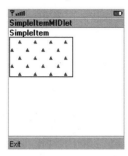

Figure 7-1. A simple custom item

CustomItem Painting

As you've seen, a CustomItem is drawn on the screen in its paint() method. This method is passed a Graphics object that serves two purposes. First, it represents the drawing surface of the CustomItem's content area. Second, it provides numerous methods for drawing shapes, images, and text. I won't cover all of these methods until Chapter 10, but you'll see a couple of them in the examples in this chapter: for instance, drawString() renders text, while drawLine() renders a straight line.

The paint() method is an example of a *callback*, a method in your code that is called by the MIDP implementation. The implementation calls paint() whenever it needs to show your custom item on the screen. It calls other methods to find out the minimum and preferred sizes of your component when its containing form is being laid out. It's the implementation's job to show the whole screen; it just calls your paint() method to show the part of the screen occupied by your custom item. You don't tell the implementation when to draw your item; you just tell it that your item is part of a form and then it figures out how to show everything.

If something needs to change in your custom item's appearance, you can request a refresh by calling the repaint() method. This method signals to the implementation that your item needs to be drawn. In response, the implementation will soon call the paint() method again. For optimized drawing, you may only wish to redraw part of the item. In this case, use repaint(int x, int y, int width, int height) to describe a rectangular region of the item that needs to be drawn.

Two methods return information that can help you make your item's appearance consistent with the device's look and feel. The first is getColor() in the Display class. This method returns an int representing a color when you supply one of the following constants:

- COLOR_BACKGROUND

- COLOR_BORDER

- COLOR_FOREGROUND

- COLOR_HIGHLIGHTED_BACKGROUND

- COLOR_HIGHLIGHTED_BORDER

- COLOR_HIGHLIGHTED_FOREGROUND

For example, you could set the current drawing color to the system's high-lighted foreground color with the following code:

```
public void paint(Graphics g) {
  // Display mDisplay = ...
  int fhc = mDisplay.getColor(
      Display.COLOR_HIGHLIGHTED_FOREGROUND);
  g.setColor(fhc);
  // Draw stuff ...
}
```

Similarly, if you want any text drawn by your custom item to harmonize with other items in a Form, you can retrieve an appropriate Font using the following method in the Font class:

```
public static Font getFont(int fontSpecifier)
```

Just pass either FONT_STATIC_TEXT or FONT_INPUT_TEXT and this method returns an appropriate Font object that you can use for drawing text. The following code shows how to use an appropriate font for drawing user-editable text:

```
public void paint(Graphics g) {
  Font f = Font.getFont(Font.FONT_INPUT_TEXT);
  g.setFont(f);
  // Draw text ...
}
```

I'll cover Font in detail in Chapter 10. In brief, a Font determines the appearance of text that is drawn on the screen.

Showing, Hiding, and Sizing

When a CustomItem is made visible, even partially visible, its showNotify() method is called by the MIDP implementation. You can expect subsequent calls to paint() to render the item. Similarly, hideNotify() is called when the item is no longer visible (if the user has scrolled the item off the screen, for example).

The size of your custom item may be changed by the implementation, perhaps if the containing Form gets laid out again in response to changing content. In this case, your item's sizeChanged() method is called with the new width and height of the content area.

Similarly, your custom item may decide that it needs to be a different size. In this case, your item should call the invalidate() method, which signals the implementation that it may need to lay out the containing Form again.

Handling Events

A CustomItem can respond to keyboard and pointer events by overriding any or all of the following methods:

```
protected void keyPressed(int keyCode)
protected void keyReleased(int keyCode)
protected void keyRepeated(int keyCode)
protected void pointerPressed(int x, int y)
protected void pointerReleased(int x, int y)
protected void pointerDragged(int x, int y)
```

These methods are called in response to the user's actions. The keyCode parameter will most likely be one of the constants defined in the Canvas class: KEY_NUM0 through KEY_NUM9, KEY_POUND, or KEY_STAR. The CustomItem class also supports a handy mechanism called *game actions*, which maps device-specific keys to device-independent actions. The getGameAction() method performs this mapping. For a full discussion of game actions, see Chapter 10.

The pointer callback methods supply the location of the pointer event as a pair of coordinates relative to the custom item's content area.

Devices have varying capabilities, and some may not be able to deliver certain types of events to CustomItems. Many phones, for example, will not support pointer events. To find out the capabilities of the device at runtime, custom items use the getInteractionModes() method. This method returns some combination of the following constants (defined in CustomItem):

- KEY_PRESS

- KEY_RELEASE

- KEY_REPEAT

- POINTER_PRESS

- POINTER_RELEASE

- POINTER_DRAG

- TRAVERSE_HORIZONTAL

- TRAVERSE_VERTICAL

Except for the traversal items (which are covered in the next section), the combination of values returned from getInteractionModes() corresponds directly to which callbacks are likely to be invoked in your custom item. You can use this information to build a CustomItem that will work under any circumstances. For example, in the unlikely event that a device was unable to deliver both key and pointer events to a custom item, you could supply a Command on the item to invoke a separate editing screen.

Item Traversal

Forms support a concept of *focus*, where one item in the form is currently selected. *Traversal* refers to the user being able to shift focus from one item to another. In most cases, the MIDP implementation handles the details of Form traversal. In the Sun emulator, for example, you can move the focus through the items in a form by pressing the up and down keys. Focus is indicated by a solid black border around an item. Figure 7-2 shows a form with several items; the third item, an ImageItem, has the focus.

Figure 7-2. The focus is on the third item in this form.

So far, so good—this is all pretty straightforward. As a matter of fact, the default implementation provided in `CustomItem` means you don't even have to think about traversal in many cases.

What makes things a little wonky is the concept of *internal* traversal. Some items support traversal of multiple choices *inside* the item. A good example is the `ChoiceGroup` item. The following sequence shows traversal through a form with three items in the MIDP reference implementation emulator. Figure 7-3 shows the traversal progressing from the text field through the gauge and into the `ChoiceGroup`.

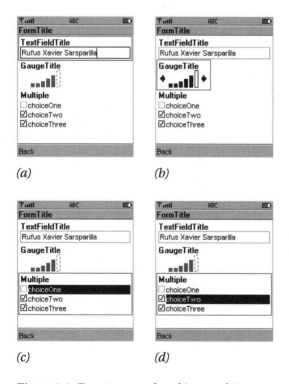

Figure 7-3. Form traversal and internal item traversal

Two methods signal traversal events. The first, traverse(), is called the first time the user traverses into the item. By default this method returns false, indicating that the item does not support internal traversal. The second method, traverseOut(), is called whenever the user leaves the item.

```
protected boolean traverse(int dir, int viewportWidth, int viewportHeight,
    int[] visRect_inout);
protected void traverseOut();
```

NOTE *At first glance, you might expect custom items to receive calls on both the traversal methods and the key event methods when keys are pressed on the device. For example, if the user presses the down arrow key to move into the item, you might expect both the* traverse() *and* keyPressed() *methods to be called. In reality, the implementation should keep key events and traversal events unambiguous. Bear in mind that some devices will have alternate traversal controls (wheels, for example), so the implementation (and your custom item) should treat the events distinctly.*

If you do write a custom item that supports internal traversal, you need to pay attention to the arguments passed to traverse() and you need to return true to indicate that your item supports internal traversal. The information passed to the traverse() method is as follows:

- dir indicates the traversal direction requested by the user. It is one of the following: Canvas.UP, Canvas.DOWN, Canvas.LEFT, Canvas.RIGHT, or CustomItem.NONE.

- viewportWidth and viewportHeight indicate the size available for items in the Form containing this custom item. (In essence, viewportWidth and viewportHeight describe the content area of the Form.) These dimensions may be useful for determining the relationship between an item's choices and the amount of available screen area.

- visRect_inout is kind of weird. It is an integer array with four elements. When the traverse() method is called, visRect_inout describes the region of the custom item's visible content area. When the traverse() method returns, visRect_inout should contain the bounds of the currently selected choice in the item.

If this is starting to sound a little hairy, just wait. The traversal mechanism is flexible enough to support different kinds of traversal. Some devices may only be able to support vertical traversal, while others may only support horizontal, and still others may support both. You can find out the device's traversal capabilities with the getInteractionModes() method, which can return CustomItem.TRAVERSE_ HORIZONTAL, CustomItem.TRAVERSE_VERTICAL, or both. Depending on the nature of the choices contained in your custom item, you may have to be flexible about the traversal directions you're receiving and the actual traversal inside the item.

Remember, the traverse() method is called when focus first comes to your item. If this method returns true, traverse() will be repeatedly called while traversal progresses through your item. When the user traverses out of your item, return false from the traverse() method. This lets the implementation know that internal traversal has ended. Most likely the implementation will call traverseOut(), although this only happens if focus actually moves away from the item. This may not be the case if the user has reached the end or beginning of the form.

All of this is discussed in meticulous detail in the API documentation for CustomItem's traverse() method. If you're planning to implement a custom item with internal traversal, go read the documentation a few times until it all sinks in.

An Example

In this section, I'll show you StationSign, a CustomItem of medium complexity. StationSign has the following features:

- Implements a simple scrolling list of string choices. Pointer events and key events cause the current selection to move to the next choice. The scrolling is animated. StationSign is a Runnable—a separate thread is created in the constructor and used to call the run() method. If there's a difference between the current display state of the item and the current selection, run() reconciles the two by scrolling.

- Conforms to the device's look and feel by using the font for static text and colors returned from Display's getColor() method.

- Does not implement internal traversal.

- Uses the traverse() and traverseOut() methods to recognize focus and paint using highlight colors. When traverse() is called, StationSign sets a boolean member variable, mFocus, to indicate that the item has focus. In the paint() method, mFocus is used to determine what colors are used to draw the item. When traverseOut() is called, mFocus is set to false indicating that focus has been lost.

The entire source code for StationSign is shown in Listing 7-3.

Listing 7-3. The StationSign *Custom Item*

```java
import java.util.Vector;

import javax.microedition.lcdui.*;

public class StationSign
    extends CustomItem
    implements Runnable {
  private Vector mValues;
  private int mSelection;
  private boolean mTrucking;

  private Display mDisplay;
  private Font mFont;
  private int mVisibleIndexTimesTen;
  private boolean mFocus;

  public StationSign(String title, Display display) {
    super(title);
    mDisplay = display;
    mValues = new Vector();
    mSelection = 0;
    mTrucking = true;
    mFont = Font.getFont(Font.FONT_STATIC_TEXT);
    mVisibleIndexTimesTen = mSelection * 10;

    Thread t = new Thread(this);
    t.start();
  }

  public void add(String value) {
    if (value == null) return;
    mValues.addElement(value);
  }

  public void remove(String value) {
    if (value == null) return;
    mValues.removeElement(value);
  }

  public String getSelection() {
    if (mValues.size() == 0) return "";
```

```
    return (String)mValues.elementAt(mSelection);
  }

  public void flip() {
    mSelection++;
    if (mSelection >= mValues.size()) mSelection = 0;
  }

  public void dispose() {
    mTrucking = false;
  }

  // Runnable interface.

  public void run() {
    while (mTrucking) {
      int target = mSelection * 10;
      if (mVisibleIndexTimesTen != target) {
        mVisibleIndexTimesTen++;
        if (mVisibleIndexTimesTen >= mValues.size() * 10)
          mVisibleIndexTimesTen = 0;
        repaint();
      }
      try { Thread.sleep(50); }
      catch (InterruptedException ie) {}
    }
  }

  // CustomItem abstract methods.

  public int getMinContentWidth() {
    // Loop through the values. Find the maximum width.
    int maxWidth = 0;
    for (int i = 0; i < mValues.size(); i++) {
      String value = (String)mValues.elementAt(i);
      int width = mFont.stringWidth(value);
      maxWidth = Math.max(maxWidth, width);
    }
    // Don't forget about the title, although we don't
    // really know what font is used for that.
    int width = mFont.stringWidth(getLabel()) + 20;
    maxWidth = Math.max(maxWidth, width);
    return maxWidth;
  }
```

```java
public int getMinContentHeight() {
  return mFont.getHeight();
}

public int getPrefContentWidth(int width) {
  return getMinContentWidth();
}

public int getPrefContentHeight(int height) {
  return getMinContentHeight();
}

public void paint(Graphics g, int w, int h) {
  int fraction = mVisibleIndexTimesTen % 10;
  int visibleIndex = (mVisibleIndexTimesTen - fraction) / 10;
  String value = (String)mValues.elementAt(visibleIndex);

  g.setFont(mFont);
  int bc = mDisplay.getColor(Display.COLOR_BACKGROUND);
  int fc = mDisplay.getColor(Display.COLOR_FOREGROUND);
  if (mFocus == true) {
    bc = mDisplay.getColor(Display.COLOR_HIGHLIGHTED_BACKGROUND);
    fc = mDisplay.getColor(Display.COLOR_HIGHLIGHTED_FOREGROUND);
  }
  g.setColor(bc);
  g.fillRect(0, 0, w, h);
  g.setColor(fc);

  // Simple case: visibleIndex is aligned on a single item.
  if (fraction == 0) {
    g.drawString(value, 0, 0, Graphics.TOP | Graphics.LEFT);
    return;
  }

  // Complicated case: show two items and a line.
  int lineHeight = mFont.getHeight();
  int divider = lineHeight - lineHeight * fraction / 10;

  // Draw the piece of the visible value.
  g.drawString(value, 0, divider - lineHeight,
      Graphics.TOP | Graphics.LEFT);
  // Now get the next value.
  visibleIndex = (visibleIndex + 1) % mValues.size();
  value = (String)mValues.elementAt(visibleIndex);
```

```
      // Draw the line.
      g.setStrokeStyle(Graphics.DOTTED);
      g.drawLine(0, divider, w, divider);

      g.drawString(value, 0, divider,
          Graphics.TOP | Graphics.LEFT);
    }

    // CustomItem methods.

    protected void keyPressed(int keyCode) { flip (); }

    protected void pointerPressed(int x, int y) { flip(); }

    protected boolean traverse(int dir,
        int viewportWidth, int viewportHeight,
        int[] visRect_inout) {
      mFocus = true;
      repaint();
      return false;
    }

    protected void traverseOut() {
      mFocus = false;
      repaint();
    }
  }
```

The MIDlet in Listing 7-4 displays a form that contains a StationSign.

Listing 7-4. A MIDlet That Demonstrates StationSign

```
import javax.microedition.midlet.*;
import javax.microedition.lcdui.*;

public class StationSignMIDlet
    extends MIDlet
    implements CommandListener {
  public void startApp() {
    Display display = Display.getDisplay(this);
```

```
    Form form = new Form("StationSignMIDlet");
    form.append(new StringItem("StringItem: ", "item one"));
    StationSign ss = new StationSign("Destination", display);
    ss.add("Albuquerque");
    ss.add("Savannah");
    ss.add("Pocatello");
    ss.add("Des Moines");
    form.append(ss);
    form.append(new StringItem("StringItem: ", "item two"));

    Command c = new Command("Exit", Command.EXIT, 0);
    form.addCommand(c);
    form.setCommandListener(this);

    display.setCurrent(form);
  }

  public void pauseApp() {}

  public void destroyApp(boolean unconditional) {}

  public void commandAction(Command c, Displayable s) {
    if (c.getCommandType() == Command.EXIT)
      notifyDestroyed();
  }
}
```

The MIDlet in action appears in Figure 7-4. The figure shows an instance of StationSign sandwiched between two StringItems. You can navigate through the form to see how the appearance of StationSign changes when it has input focus. If you press the select key on StationSign, you'll see the next choice scroll into view.

Figure 7-4. StationSign *in action in a* Form

Summary

This chapter describes one of MIDP 2.0's exciting new features, custom items. The CustomItem class is the basis of items you can write to include in Forms. You can determine the custom item's appearance in the paint() method by drawing using a Graphics object. Callback methods throughout CustomItem let you know when the item is shown or hidden and deliver key, pointer, and traversal events. Two examples, SimpleItem and StationSign, provide a foundation of working code that you can adapt to build your own items.

CHAPTER 8

Persistent Storage

MIDP APPLICATIONS HAVE to run seamlessly on many devices. You've already seen how this can be a challenge in the user-interface arena. The trick there was to use abstract concepts that would be mapped to the screen by a device-specific implementation.

MIDP's approach to persistent storage is basically the same. Your application could run on a device with flash ROM, battery-backed RAM, or even a small hard disk. MIDP applications don't really care; all they know about are small databases called record stores. It's up to the device's MIDP implementation to map record stores in some reasonable manner to whatever persistent storage is available.

These are *small* amounts of data we're talking about; the MIDP specification dictates that the minimum amount of persistent storage is only 8KB.

Overview

Persistent storage in MIDP is centered around record stores. A *record store* is a small database that contains pieces of data called *records*. Record stores are represented by instances of javax.microedition.rms.RecordStore. In MIDP 1.0, the scope of a record store is limited to a single MIDlet suite. Said another way, a MIDlet can only access record stores that were created by a MIDlet in the same suite. Figure 8-1 shows the relationship between MIDlet suites and record stores. MIDP 2.0 allows optional sharing of record stores. See the section on "Sharing Record Stores in MIDP 2.0" later in this chapter.

Record stores are identified by a name. Within a MIDlet suite's record stores, the names must be unique.

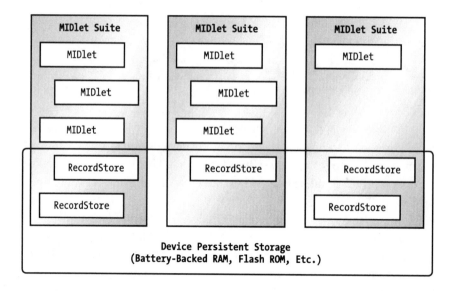

Figure 8-1. Record stores belong to MIDlet suites.

Managing Record Stores

The RecordStore class serves two purposes. First, it defines an API for manipulating individual records. Second, it defines an API (mostly static methods) for managing record stores.

Opening, Closing, and Removing Record Stores

To open a record store, you simply need to name it.

```
public static RecordStore openRecordStore(String recordStoreName,
    boolean createIfNecessary) throws RecordStoreException,
    RecordStoreFullException, RecordStoreNotFoundException
```

If the record store does not exist, the createIfNecessary parameter determines whether a new record store will be created or not. If the record store does not exist, and the createIfNecessary parameter is false, then a RecordStoreNotFoundException will be thrown.

The following code opens a record store named "Address."

```
RecordStore rs = RecordStore.openRecordStore("Address", true);
```

The record store will be created if it does not already exist.

An open record store can be closed by calling the `closeRecordStore()` method. As with anything that can be opened and closed, it's a good idea to close record stores when you're finished with them. Memory and processing power are in short supply on a small device, so you should remember to clean up after yourself as much as possible. You probably shouldn't even keep a record store open over the lifetime of the MIDlet; after all, your MIDlet may be paused by the device's application manager, and it would be unwise to have open resources while the MIDlet is paused.

To find out all the record stores available to a particular MIDlet suite, call the `listRecordStores()` method:

```
public static String[] listRecordStores()
```

Finally, to remove a record store, call the static `deleteRecordStore()` method. The record store and its contained records will be deleted.

NOTE *Record store operations, particularly opening and closing, may be time-consuming on actual devices. You probably won't notice the delays using a desktop MIDP emulator, but on a real device, it may slow down applications noticeably. (See* http://www.poqit.com/midp/bench/ *for some sobering measurements from real devices.) For many applications, it may be appropriate to place record store access in its own thread, just as network access goes in its own thread.*

Sharing Record Stores in MIDP 2.0

In MIDP 2.0, record stores also have an *authorization mode*. The default authorization mode is `AUTHMODE_PRIVATE`, which means that a record store is only accessible from MIDlets in the MIDlet suite that created the record store. This is exactly as described earlier.

Record stores can be shared by changing their authorization mode to `AUTHMODE_ANY`, which means that any other MIDlet on the device can access the record store. Be careful with this! Don't put any secrets in an `AUTHMODE_ANY` record store. In addition, you can also decide if you want a shared record store to be writable or read-only.

You can create a shared record store using a new `openRecordStore()` method in the `RecordStore` class:

```
public static RecordStore openRecordStore(String recordStoreName,
    boolean createIfNecessary, byte authMode, boolean writable)
    throws RecordStoreException, RecordStoreFullException,
    RecordStoreNotFoundException
```

The `authMode` and `writable` parameters are only used if the record store is created, which implies that the record store doesn't exist and `createIfNecessary` is true. You can change the authorization mode and writable flag of an open record store using the following method:

```
public void setMode(byte authmode, boolean writable)
    throws RecordStoreException
```

Note that only a MIDlet belonging to the suite that created the record store can change its authorization mode and writable flag.

How do you access a shared record store? One final `openRecordStore()` method provides the answer:

```
public static RecordStore openRecordStore(String recordStoreName,
    String vendorName, String suiteName)
    throws RecordStoreException, RecordStoreNotFoundException
```

To access a shared record store, you need to know its name, the name of the MIDlet suite that created it, and the name of the MIDlet suite's vendor. These names should be the `MIDlet-Name` and `MIDlet-Vendor` attributes in the MIDlet suite JAR manifest or the application descriptor.

Record Store Size

Record stores consist of records; each record is simply an array of bytes. On space-constrained devices, you'll probably want to keep a close eye on the size of your record stores. To find out the number of bytes used by a record store, call the following method on a `RecordStore` instance:

```
public int getSize()
```

You can find out how much more space is available by calling the following method:

```
public int getSizeAvailable()
```

Note that this method returns the total space available in the record store, which is not the same as the amount of record data that is available. That is, there is some overhead associated with each record in the record store; the getSizeAvailable() method returns the amount of space available for both record data and overhead.

Version and Timestamp

Record stores maintain both a version number and a timestamp. The version number is updated every time the record store is modified. It is represented by an integer and can be retrieved by calling getVersion().

The record store also remembers the last time it was modified. This moment in time is represented by a long, which can be retrieved with getLastModified(). The long represents the number of milliseconds since midnight on January 1, 1970. You may recall (from Chapter 4) that this is the same way that Date uses a long to represent a moment in time. If you need to examine the timestamp of a record store, you can create a Date from the long timestamp. Then you could use a Calendar to translate from a Date to calendar fields like month, day, hour, and minute.

Working with Records

A *record* is simply an array of bytes. Each record in a RecordStore has an integer identification number. Figure 8-2 shows a diagram of a RecordStore with four records.

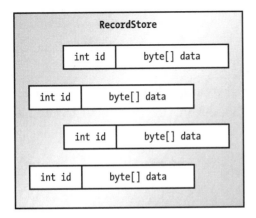

Figure 8-2. Inside a RecordStore

Adding Records

To add a new record, supply the byte array to the addRecord() method:

```
public int addRecord(byte[] data, int offset, int numBytes)
    throws RecordStoreNotOpenException,
           RecordStoreException,
           RecordStoreFullException
```

The added record will be numBytes long, taken from the data array starting at offset. The new record's ID is returned. Most other record operations need this ID to identify a particular record.

There's no explicit maximum record length, although of course there will be limits based on the amount of space that is available on the device for record stores.

The following code fragment illustrates adding a new record to a record store named rs. It creates a byte array from a String, and then writes the entire byte array into a new record.

```
String record = "This is a record";
byte[] data = record.getBytes();
int id = rs.addRecord(data, 0, data.length);
```

Retrieving Records

You can retrieve a record by supplying the record ID to the following method:

```
public byte[] getRecord(int recordId)
    throws RecordStoreNotOpenException,
           InvalidRecordIDException,
           RecordStoreException
```

This method returns a freshly created byte array containing the record with the requested ID. An alternate version of this method puts the record data into an array that you supply:

```
public int getRecord(int recordId, byte[] buffer, int offset)
    throws RecordStoreNotOpenException,
           InvalidRecordIDException,
           RecordStoreException
```

This method returns the number of bytes that were copied into your array. If the array you supply is not large enough to hold the record, an ArrayOutOfBoundsException will be thrown. You can find out the size of a particular record ahead of time by calling getRecordSize().

Given a RecordStore rs and a record ID id, here is one way to retrieve a record's data:

```
byte[] retrieved = new byte[rs.getRecordSize(id)];
rs.getRecord(id, retrieved, 0);
String retrievedString = new String(retrieved);
```

If you're going to be pulling many records out of the record store, you probably won't want to create a new byte array each time. For efficiency, you would create one array and use it over and over again to pull records out of the record store. One way to create the buffer is to make it as large as the largest record in the record store. If that's not practical, or if you don't know how large the largest record will be, you can simply check the size of each record before you retrieve it. If you come across a record that's larger than the buffer, you could create a larger buffer.

If you're not worried about memory usage or speed, then you might as well use the other form of getRecord(), which is essentially the same as the previous code example:

```
byte[] retrieved = rs.getRecord(id);
```

Deleting and Replacing Records

So far you've seen how to add new records and retrieve them. There are two more record operations supported by RecordStore. First, you can remove a record by passing its ID to deleteRecord(). Second, you can replace the data of an existing record by calling the following method:

```
public void setRecord(int recordId, byte[] newData, int offset, int numBytes)
    throws RecordStoreNotOpenException,
            InvalidRecordIDException,
            RecordStoreException,
            RecordStoreFullException
```

Getting RecordStore Record Information

The RecordStore keeps an internal counter that it uses to assign record IDs. You can find out what the next record ID will be by calling getNextRecordID(). And you can find out how many records exist in the RecordStore by calling getNumRecords().

Saving User Preferences

Let's put some of this knowledge to work. This section details a simple MIDlet that saves a user name and password in a RecordStore. Each time the MIDlet is used, it can load the user name and password from the RecordStore instead of requiring the user to enter the same information over and over.

The MIDlet itself is very simple. Its only screen is a Form that contains fields for entering the user name and password. It uses a helper class, Preferences, to do all the RecordStore work. Listing 8-1 shows the source code for the MIDlet.

Listing 8-1. Source Code for RecordMIDlet

```java
import javax.microedition.midlet.*;
import javax.microedition.lcdui.*;
import javax.microedition.rms.RecordStoreException;

public class RecordMIDlet
    extends MIDlet
    implements CommandListener {
  private static final String kUser = "user";
  private static final String kPassword = "password";

  private Preferences mPreferences;
  private Form mForm;
  private TextField mUserField, mPasswordField;

  public RecordMIDlet() {
    try {
      mPreferences = new Preferences("preferences");
    }
    catch (RecordStoreException rse) {
      mForm = new Form("Exception");
      mForm.append(new StringItem(null, rse.toString()));
      mForm.addCommand(new Command("Exit", Command.EXIT, 0));
```

```
    mForm.setCommandListener(this);
    return;
  }

  mForm = new Form("Login");
  mUserField = new TextField("Name",
      mPreferences.get(kUser), 32, 0);
  mPasswordField = new TextField("Password",
      mPreferences.get(kPassword), 32, 0);
  mForm.append(mUserField);
  mForm.append(mPasswordField);

  mForm.addCommand(new Command("Exit", Command.EXIT, 0));
  mForm.setCommandListener(this);
}

public void startApp() {
  Display.getDisplay(this).setCurrent(mForm);
}

public void pauseApp() {}

public void destroyApp(boolean unconditional) {
  // Save the user name and password.
  mPreferences.put(kUser, mUserField.getString());
  mPreferences.put(kPassword, mPasswordField.getString());
  try { mPreferences.save(); }
  catch (RecordStoreException rse) {}
}

public void commandAction(Command c, Displayable s) {
  if (c.getCommandType() == Command.EXIT) {
    destroyApp(true);
    notifyDestroyed();
  }
}
}
```

All the RecordStore work is encapsulated in the Preferences class shown in Listing 8-2. Preferences is a wrapper for a map of string keys and values, stored internally as mHashtable. When a Preferences object is created, key and value pairs are loaded from the record store. A key and value pair is stored in a single record using a pipe character separator (|).

Preferences uses a RecordEnumeration to walk through all the records in the record store. I'll talk about RecordEnumeration soon; for now, just trust me when I tell you it gives you a way to paw through the data in the record store.

Listing 8-2. A Class That Encapsulates RecordStore Access

```java
import java.util.*;
import javax.microedition.lcdui.*;
import javax.microedition.rms.*;

public class Preferences {
  private String mRecordStoreName;

  private Hashtable mHashtable;

  public Preferences(String recordStoreName)
      throws RecordStoreException {
    mRecordStoreName = recordStoreName;
    mHashtable = new Hashtable();
    load();
  }

  public String get(String key) {
    return (String)mHashtable.get(key);
  }

  public void put(String key, String value) {
    if (value == null) value = "";
    mHashtable.put(key, value);
  }

  private void load() throws RecordStoreException {
    RecordStore rs = null;
    RecordEnumeration re = null;

    try {
      rs = RecordStore.openRecordStore(mRecordStoreName, true);
      re = rs.enumerateRecords(null, null, false);
      while (re.hasNextElement()) {
        byte[] raw = re.nextRecord();
        String pref = new String(raw);
```

```
      // Parse out the name.
      int index = pref.indexOf('|');
      String name = pref.substring(0, index);
      String value = pref.substring(index + 1);
      put(name, value);
    }
  }
  finally {
    if (re != null) re.destroy();
    if (rs != null) rs.closeRecordStore();
  }
}

public void save() throws RecordStoreException {
  RecordStore rs = null;
  RecordEnumeration re = null;
  try {
    rs = RecordStore.openRecordStore(mRecordStoreName, true);
    re = rs.enumerateRecords(null, null, false);

    // First remove all records, a little clumsy.
    while (re.hasNextElement()) {
      int id = re.nextRecordId();
      rs.deleteRecord(id);
    }

    // Now save the preferences records.
    Enumeration keys = mHashtable.keys();
    while (keys.hasMoreElements()) {
      String key = (String)keys.nextElement();
      String value = get(key);
      String pref = key + "|" + value;
      byte[] raw = pref.getBytes();
      rs.addRecord(raw, 0, raw.length);
    }
  }
  finally {
    if (re != null) re.destroy();
    if (rs != null) rs.closeRecordStore();
  }
}
```

RecordMIDlet saves the updated values back to the RecordStore in its destroyApp() method. It saves the user name and password from the user interface in the Preferences object, then calls the save() method to write the new values out to the RecordStore. The save() method removes all records from the record store, then adds each key and value pair.

To test out the MIDlet, enter some text into the user name and password fields. Then exit the MIDlet and restart it. You will see the same values loaded into the text fields.

Note that Preferences only deals with String values, but records can contain any data packed into a byte array. By using stream classes from the java.io package, it's possible to store complex data types in records. For example, you could use a DataOutputStream wrapped around a ByteArrayOutputStream to generate data to be written into the record store. To extract data values, you would use a DataInputStream wrapped around a ByteArrayInputStream based on the record data.

Listening for Record Changes

RecordStores support a JavaBeans-style listener mechanism. Interested objects can listen for changes to a record store by registering themselves as listeners.

The listener interface is javax.microedition.rms.RecordListener. You can manage a RecordStore's listeners with the following two methods:

```
public void addRecordListener(RecordListener listener)
public void removeRecordListener(RecordListener listener)
```

The RecordListener interface has three methods: recordAdded(), recordChanged(), and recordDeleted(). These are called whenever a record is added, changed, or deleted. Each method is passed the RecordStore involved and the ID of the record in question.

Performing RecordStore Queries

The real power of a database is being able to pull out just the record or records you want. In a larger database, this is called *performing a query*. In the RecordStore world, you use the enumerateRecords() method:

```
public RecordEnumeration enumerateRecords(RecordFilter filter,
    RecordComparator comparator, boolean keepUpdated)
    throws RecordStoreNotOpenException
```

This single method in RecordStore involves three different interfaces that you've never seen before. Let's start with the big picture first, and then drill down into the new interfaces.

The enumerateRecords() method returns a sorted subset of the records in a RecordStore. The RecordFilter determines which records will be included in the subset, while the RecordComparator is used to sort them. The returned RecordEnumeration allows you to navigate through the returned records.

RecordFilter

The simplest interface is RecordFilter. When you call enumerateRecords() on a RecordStore, each record's data is retrieved. RecordFilter has a single method, matches(), which is called for each record. A record filter should examine the record data and return true if the record should be included in the results returned from enumerateRecords().

Here's a simple RecordFilter implementation that will only select records whose first byte of data is 7:

```
public class SevenFilter
    implements javax.microedition.rms.RecordFilter {
  public boolean matches(byte[] candidate) {
    if (candidate.length == 0) return false;
    return (candidate[0] == 7);
  }
}
```

RecordComparator

The job of a RecordComparator implementation is to determine the order of two sets of record data. RecordComparator is similar to the java.util.Comparator interface in J2SE.

To implement the RecordComparator interface, you just need to define one method:

```
public int compare(byte[] rec1, byte[] rec2)
```

This method examines the data contained in rec1 and rec2 and determines which of them should come first in a sorted list. It should return one of the following constants defined in RecordComparator:

- PRECEDES indicates that rec1 should come before rec2.

- FOLLOWS indicates that rec1 should come after rec2.

- EQUIVALENT signals that rec1 and rec2 are the same, at least as far as sorting is concerned.

The following simple implementation compares each byte of the given records and sorts them numerically. If the two records have the same data, up to the length of the shorter one, then they are deemed EQUIVALENT.

```
public class SimpleComparator
    implements javax.microedition.rms.RecordComparator {
  public int compare(byte[] rec1, byte[] rec2) {
    int limit = Math.min(rec1.length, rec2.length);

    for (int index = 0; index < limit; index++) {
      if (rec1[index] < rec2[index])
        return PRECEDES;
      else if (rec1[index] > rec2[index])
        return FOLLOWS;
    }
    return EQUIVALENT;
  }
}
```

Working with RecordEnumeration

RecordStore's enumerateRecords() method returns an implementation of the RecordEnumeration interface. RecordEnumeration is surprisingly complicated. Its basic function is to allow you to iterate through the records retrieved from the RecordStore. Unlike a regular J2SE Enumeration or Iterator, however, RecordEnumeration allows you to scroll through its contents both forward and backward. In addition, you can peek at the next or previous record ID. Finally, RecordEnumeration offers the possibility of keeping its data synchronized with the actual RecordStore. Behind the scenes, this is accomplished by registering the RecordEnumeration as a listener for RecordStore changes.

The basic operation of RecordEnumeration is to iterate through a set of records. You can find out if there's a next record by calling hasNextElement(). If the next record exists, you can retrieve its data by calling the following method:

```
public byte[] nextRecord()
    throws InvalidRecordIDException,
        RecordStoreNotOpenException,
        RecordStoreException
```

Alternately, you can retrieve the next record's ID by calling this method:

```
public int nextRecordId() throws InvalidRecordIDException
```

You can't really have your cake and eat it, though; both nextRecord() and nextRecordId() advance the RecordEnumeration to the next record. If you want to retrieve both the ID and the data for the next record, you'd need to call nextRecordId() and then retrieve the record data directly from the RecordStore.

A typical use of RecordEnumeration would be to walk straight through the selected records, like this:

```
// Open a RecordStore rs
// Create a RecordFilter rf
// Create a RecordComparator rc

RecordEnumeration re = rs.enumerateRecords(rf, rc, false);
while (re.hasNextElement()) {
  byte[] recordBytes = re.nextRecord();
  // Process the retrieved bytes.
}
```

The RecordFilter and RecordComparator can both be null, in which case the RecordEnumeration will iterate through every record in the record store. The Preferences class uses RecordEnumeration in this way.

NOTE RecordEnumeration *makes no guarantees about the order of the returned records if the* RecordComparator *is* null.

As you're moving through the selected records, you can also move backward. RecordEnumeration includes hasPreviousElement(), previousRecord(), and previousRecordId() methods that work just like their next counterparts.

Four out of the five ways to move the current position in the RecordEnumeration are the nextRecord(), nextRecordId(), previousRecord(), or previousRecordId() methods. The fifth method is kind of like a rewind button: reset() moves the record pointer back to the very beginning of the selected records.

When you're finished using a RecordEnumeration, you should release its resources. You can do this by calling destroy(), after which the RecordEnumeration is no longer usable.

Keeping a RecordEnumeration Up-to-Date

In a multithreaded environment, it's entirely possible that a RecordStore will change at the same time you're iterating through a RecordEnumeration for the same RecordStore. There are two ways to deal with this.

The first thing you can do is call rebuild(), which explicitly rebuilds the RecordEnumeration based on the RecordFilter and RecordComparator you originally specified.

The other possibility is to request a RecordEnumeration that is automatically updated with any changes to the underlying RecordStore. You can do this by passing true for the keepUpdated parameter of RecordStore's enumerateRecords() method. You can find out if the RecordEnumeration is automatically updated by calling isKeptUpdated(). Furthermore, you can change its state by calling keepUpdated().

Automatically updated RecordEnumerations register themselves as RecordListeners with the underlying RecordStore. Each time the RecordStore is changed, the RecordEnumeration is rebuilt. Keep in mind that this is an expensive operation (in terms of time), so if there are many RecordStore changes, you'll be paying a price for it.

Using Resource Files

Resource files are another form of persistent storage. Accessing resource files is very simple, but they are important nevertheless. Resource files can be images, text, or other types of files that are stored in a MIDlet suite JAR. These files are read-only.

You can access a resource file as an InputStream by using the getResourceAsStream() method in Class. A typical usage looks like this:

```
InputStream in = this.getClass().getResourceAsStream("/Robotag-t.png");
```

Summary

The MIDP API for persistent storage is deliberately abstract in recognition that small devices will likely have many different methods for storing data. In MIDP, the central concept for persistent storage is the record store, which is a collection of bits of data called records. A record store is really a tiny database, but the details of exactly how it is stored are left to the device implementation. The javax.microedition.rms.RecordStore class encapsulates all access to persistent storage. It provides methods for accessing and manipulating RecordStores, as well as methods for working with individual records. For more advanced RecordStore work, methods and interfaces exist to help keep track of changes to a RecordStore or to perform RecordStore queries.

CHAPTER 9

Connecting to the World

IT'S COOL RUNNING Java on mobile phones and pagers, but the real kicker is getting your MIDlets connected to the Internet. With an Internet connection, you can write applications that allow you to access information and do work from your mobile telephone, from wherever you are in the world.

The Generic Connection Framework

The CLDC defines an extremely flexible API for network connections, the *generic connection framework*. It's all contained in the `javax.microedition.io` package and based around the `Connection` interface. Figure 9-1 details the `Connection` interface and its various child interfaces. Plus signs indicate new interfaces in MIDP 2.0.

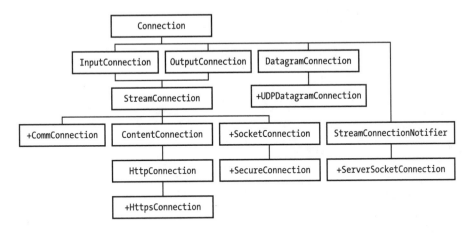

Figure 9-1. The Connection *family tree*

The link between the `Connection` interfaces and reality is a class called `javax.microedition.io.Connector`. The basic idea is that you pass a connection string to one of `Connector`'s static methods and get back some `Connection` implementation. A *connection string* looks something like a URL, but there are various other possibilities. The connection string `socket://apress.com:79` might open a

TCP/IP connection to apress.com on port 79, then return a StreamConnection implementation.

MIDP 1.0 simplifies this generic framework considerably by only requiring one type of connection, Hypertext Transfer Protocol (HTTP). You pass an HTTP URL to Connector and get back an implementation of HttpConnection. Although MIDP 1.0–compliant devices may support additional types of connections, HTTP is the only one you should depend on. MIDP 2.0 adds mandatory support for HTTPS connections (secure HTTP) and standardizes the connection strings for several other types of connections. I'll discuss these new features later in this chapter.

HttpConnection's methods are detailed in Figure 9-2. Most of the methods in HttpConnection have to do with details of HTTP, which I won't cover here. I'll cover everything you need to know to connect to a server here, including both GET and POST requests. If you need to dig deeper, you can read RFC 2616 (one of the Internet standards documents), available at http://www.faqs.org/rfcs/rfc2616.html. Note that MIDP uses a subset of the full HTTP 1.1; only the GET, POST, and HEAD commands are required.

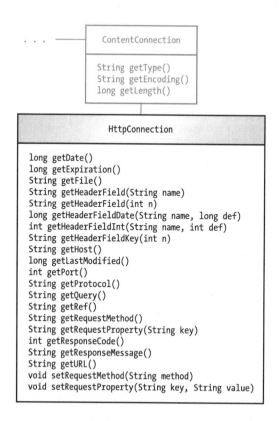

Figure 9-2. The HttpConnection *interface*

Review of HTTP

This section presents a brief review of the Hypertext Transfer Protocol. The whole story is in RFC 2616; this section covers the essentials.

Requests and Responses

HTTP is built around requests and responses. A client sends a request for a server—something like, "Please give me such-and-so HTML page." The server sends back a response—something like, "Here's the file," or "I don't know what you're talking about."

Requests and responses have two parts: headers and content. If you type a URL into your browser, the browser creates an HTTP request (mostly headers) and sends it to a server. The server finds the requested file and sends it back in an HTTP response. The response headers describe things like the type of web server, the file type of the response, the length of the response, and other information. The response content is the data of the file itself.

Parameters

Browsers and other HTTP clients request specific named resources from HTTP servers. In addition, clients can pass parameters to the server. Parameters are simple name and value pairs. For example, a client might send a "userid" parameter with a value of "jonathan" to a server. HTTP also supports passing binary data to the server in the body of a request, and the Java stream classes make it easy to exchange a variety of data types.

When a browser is the HTTP client, parameters are generally collected from HTML forms. You've seen these forms, like the one where you fill in your shipping address and your credit card number. Form values are sent as parameters to a web server when you click the **Submit** or **Next** button on the form.

The client encodes parameters before they are sent to the server. Parameters are passed as name and value pairs; multiple parameters are separated by amper- sands. The exact way that parameters are encoded is documented in the J2SE documentation for `java.net.URLEncoder`. The rules are relatively simple.

- The space character is converted to a plus (+) sign.

- The following characters remain unchanged: lowercase letters a through z, uppercase letters A through Z, the numbers 0 through 9, the period (.), the hyphen (-), the asterisk (*), and the underscore (_).

- All other characters are converted into "%xy", where "xy" is a hexadecimal number that represents the low eight bits of the character.

GET, HEAD, and POST

The simplest HTTP operation is GET. This is what happens when you type a URL into your browser. The browser says, "GET me this URL," and the server responds with the headers and content of the response.

With a GET request, parameters are added to the end of the URL in encoded form. (Some servers have trouble with very long URLs; if you have a lot of parameters, or binary data, you may wish to pass data in the body of the HTTP request.) For example, suppose the following URL maps to a servlet or some other server-side component of your application:

```
http://jonathanknudsen.com/simple
```

Adding a parameter is easy. If you want to pass a parameter with a name of "user" and a value of "jonathan," you would use the following URL:

```
http://jonathanknudsen.com/simple?user=jonathan
```

Additional name and value pairs can be added, separated by ampersands:

```
http://jonathanknudsen.com/simple?user=jonathan&zip=08540&day=saturday
```

The HEAD operation is identical to GET, but the server sends back only the headers of the response.

POST is basically the same as GET, but parameters are handled differently. Instead of being pasted on the end of the URL, as they are with GET, the parameters are passed as the body of the request. They are encoded in the same way.

Making a Connection with HTTP GET

Loading data from a server is startlingly simple, particularly if you're performing an HTTP GET. Simply pass a URL to Connector's static open() method. The returned Connection will probably be an implementation of HttpConnection, but you can just treat it as an InputConnection. Then get the corresponding InputStream and read data to your heart's content.

In code, it looks something like this:

```
String url = "http://jonathanknudsen.com/simple";
InputConnection ic = (InputConnection)Connector.open(url);
InputStream in = ic.openInputStream();
// Read stuff from the InputStream
ic.close();
```

Most of the methods involved can throw a `java.io.IOException`. I've omitted the try and catch blocks from the example for clarity.

That's all there is to it. You can now connect your MIDlets to the world. The story is a little more complicated in MIDP 2.0 because network access is subject to security policies on the device. I'll talk more about this near the end of this chapter.

Passing Parameters

With HTTP GET, all parameters are passed to the server in the body of the URL. This makes it easy to send parameters to the server. The following code fragment shows how two parameters can be passed:

```
String url = "http://localhost/midp/simple?pOne=one+bit&pTwo=two";
InputConnection ic = (InputConnection)Connector.open(url);
InputStream in = ic.openInputStream();
```

The first parameter is named "pOne" and has "one bit" as a value; the second parameter is named "pTwo" and has "two" as a value.

A Simple Example

HTTP isn't all about exchanging HTML pages. It's actually a generic file-exchange protocol. In this section, we'll look at an example that loads an image from the network and displays it. Listing 9-1 shows the source code for `ImageLoader`, a MIDlet that retrieves an image from the Internet and displays it on the screen.

Listing 9-1. Retrieving an Image from the Internet

```java
import java.io.*;

import javax.microedition.io.*;
import javax.microedition.lcdui.*;
import javax.microedition.midlet.*;

public class ImageLoader
    extends MIDlet
    implements CommandListener, Runnable {
  private Display mDisplay;
  private Form mForm;

  public ImageLoader() {
    mForm = new Form("Connecting...");
    mForm.addCommand(new Command("Exit", Command.EXIT, 0));
    mForm.setCommandListener(this);
  }

  public void startApp() {
    if (mDisplay == null) mDisplay = Display.getDisplay(this);
    mDisplay.setCurrent(mForm);

    // Do network loading in a separate thread.
    Thread t = new Thread(this);
    t.start();
  }

  public void pauseApp() {}

  public void destroyApp(boolean unconditional) {}

  public void commandAction(Command c, Displayable s) {
    if (c.getCommandType() == Command.EXIT)
      notifyDestroyed();
  }

  public void run() {
    HttpConnection hc = null;
    DataInputStream in = null;

    try {
      String url = getAppProperty("ImageLoader-URL");
      hc = (HttpConnection)Connector.open(url);
```

```
      int length = (int)hc.getLength();
      byte[] data = null;
      if (length != -1) {
        data = new byte[length];
        in = new DataInputStream(hc.openInputStream());
        in.readFully(data);
      }
      else {
        // If content length is not given, read in chunks.
        int chunkSize = 512;
        int index = 0;
        int readLength = 0;
        in = new DataInputStream(hc.openInputStream());
        data = new byte[chunkSize];
        do {
          if (data.length < index + chunkSize) {
            byte[] newData = new byte[index + chunkSize];
            System.arraycopy(data, 0, newData, 0, data.length);
            data = newData;
          }
          readLength = in.read(data, index, chunkSize);
          index += readLength;
        } while (readLength == chunkSize);
        length = index;
      }
      Image image = Image.createImage(data, 0, length);
      ImageItem imageItem = new ImageItem(null, image, 0, null);
      mForm.append(imageItem);
      mForm.setTitle("Done.");
    }
    catch (IOException ioe) {
      StringItem stringItem = new StringItem(null, ioe.toString());
      mForm.append(stringItem);
      mForm.setTitle("Done.");
    }
    finally {
      try {
        if (in != null) in.close();
        if (hc != null) hc.close();
      }
      catch (IOException ioe) {}
    }
  }
}
```

The run() method contains all of the networking code. It's fairly simple; we pass the URL of an image (retrieved as an application property) to Connector's open() method and cast the result to HttpConnection. Then we retrieve the length of the image file, using the getLength() method. Given the length, we create a byte array and read data into it. Finally, having read the entire image file into a byte array, we can create an Image from the raw data.

If the content length is not specified, the image data is read in 512-byte chunks.

You'll need to specify the MIDlet property "ImageLoader-URL" in order for this example to work correctly. Note that you need to specify the URL of a PNG image, not of a JPEG or GIF. The URL http://65.215.221.148:8080/wj2/res/java2d_sm_ad.png produces the results shown in Figure 9-3.

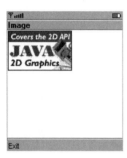

Figure 9-3. The ImageLoader *example*

Posting a Form with HTTP POST

Posting a form is a little more complicated on the MIDlet side. In particular, there are request headers that need to be set in HttpConnection before the server is contacted. The process works like this:

1. Obtain an HttpConnection from Connector's open() method.

2. Modify the header fields of the request. In particular, you need to change the request method by calling setRequestMethod(), and you should set the "Content-Length" header by calling setRequestProperty(). This is the length of the parameters you will be sending.

3. Obtain the output stream for the HttpConnection by calling openOutputStream(). This sends the request headers to the server.

4. Send the request parameters on the output stream returned from the `HttpConnection`. Parameters should be encoded as described earlier (and in the documentation for the J2SE class `java.net.URLEncoder`).

5. Read the response from the server from the input stream retrieved from `HttpConnection`'s `openInputStream()` method.

The following example, Listing 9-2, demonstrates how to send a single parameter to a server using an HTTP POST. Multiple parameters can be assembled by joining them with an ampersand separator. Note that the parameter in this example has been encoded as described above. In this example, the parameter value "Jonathan Knudsen!" has been encoded to "Jonathan+Knudsen%21". Listing 9-3 shows a very simple servlet that can communicate with `PostMIDlet`.

Listing 9-2. A Simple MIDlet Performing an HTTP POST

```java
import java.io.*;

import javax.microedition.io.*;
import javax.microedition.lcdui.*;
import javax.microedition.midlet.*;

public class PostMIDlet
    extends MIDlet
    implements CommandListener, Runnable {
  private Display mDisplay;
  private Form mForm;

  public PostMIDlet() {
    mForm = new Form("Connecting...");
    mForm.addCommand(new Command("Exit", Command.EXIT, 0));
    mForm.setCommandListener(this);
  }

  public void startApp() {
    if (mDisplay == null) mDisplay = Display.getDisplay(this);
    mDisplay.setCurrent(mForm);

    // Do network loading in a separate thread.
    Thread t = new Thread(this);
    t.start();
  }
```

```
public void pauseApp() {}

public void destroyApp(boolean unconditional) {}

public void commandAction(Command c, Displayable s) {
  if (c.getCommandType() == Command.EXIT)
    notifyDestroyed();
}

public void run() {
  HttpConnection hc = null;
  InputStream in = null;
  OutputStream out = null;

  try {
    String message = "name=Jonathan+Knudsen%21";
    String url = getAppProperty("PostMIDlet-URL");
    hc = (HttpConnection)Connector.open(url);
    hc.setRequestMethod(HttpConnection.POST);
    hc.setRequestProperty("Content-Type",
        "application/x-www-form-urlencoded");
    hc.setRequestProperty("Content-Length",
        Integer.toString(message.length()));
    out = hc.openOutputStream();
    out.write(message.getBytes());
    in = hc.openInputStream();
    int length = (int)hc.getLength();
    byte[] data = new byte[length];
    in.read(data);
    String response = new String(data);
    StringItem stringItem = new StringItem(null, response);
    mForm.append(stringItem);
    mForm.setTitle("Done.");
  }
  catch (IOException ioe) {
    StringItem stringItem = new StringItem(null, ioe.toString());
    mForm.append(stringItem);
    mForm.setTitle("Done.");
  }
  finally {
    try {
      if (out != null) out.close();
      if (in != null) in.close();
```

```
        if (hc != null) hc.close();
      }
      catch (IOException ioe) {}
    }
  }
}
```

Listing 9-3. A Simple Servlet That Responds to PostServlet

```
import javax.servlet.http.*;
import javax.servlet.*;
import java.io.*;

public class PostServlet extends HttpServlet {
  public void doPost(HttpServletRequest request,
      HttpServletResponse response)
      throws ServletException, IOException {
    String name = request.getParameter("name");

    String message = "Received name: '" + name + "'";
    response.setContentType("text/plain");
    response.setContentLength(message.length());
    PrintWriter out = response.getWriter();
    out.println(message);
  }
}
```

Using Cookies for Session Tracking

HTTP is a stateless protocol, which means that each request and response pair is a separate conversation. Sometimes, though, you want the server to remember who you are. This can be done with a *session.* On the server side, a session is just a collection of information. When the client sends an HTTP request to the server, it includes a session ID as part of the request. The server can then look up the corresponding session and have some idea of the identity (or at least the state) of the client.

The most common way to store a session ID on the client side is using HTTP *cookies.* A cookie is just a little piece of data that is passed from the server to the client in an HTTP response. Most web browsers automatically store cookies and will send them back to the appropriate server when a new request is made.

In the MIDP world, of course, there's no web browser taking care of cookies for you. You have to do it yourself. Fortunately, it's not very complicated.

Network code that maintains a server session ID needs to do two things:

1. When receiving a response from a server, check for a cookie. If there is a cookie present, save it away for later (perhaps in a member variable). A cookie is just another HTTP response header line. You can check for a cookie by calling getHeaderField() on an HttpConnection object after the request has been sent.

2. When sending a request to the server, send the session ID cookie if it has been previously received. Again, sending a cookie to the server is just a matter of putting it in the request headers, using HttpConnection's setRequestProperty() method.

Each time you send a request to the server, you will be sending a session ID as a request header. The server uses this session ID to look up a session object that can be used, server side, to do useful stuff like retrieve preferences or maintain a shopping cart.

It's not hard to implement this behavior in a MIDlet. If you have a session ID cookie handy, you should send it when you open up an HTTP connection to the same server, like this:

```
HttpConnection hc = (HttpConnection)Connector.open(url);
if (mSession != null)
    hc.setRequestProperty("cookie", mSession);
```

This code assumes you have a session ID cookie saved away in the mSession member variable. The first time you contact the server, of course, you won't have a session ID cookie.

Later, when you receive a response from an HTTP request, look for a cookie. If you find one, parse out the session ID and save it away, like this:

```
InputStream in = hc.openInputStream();

String cookie = hc.getHeaderField("Set-cookie");
if (cookie != null) {
  int semicolon = cookie.indexOf(';');
  mSession = cookie.substring(0, semicolon);
}
```

The cookie string needs to be parsed because it comes in two pieces. The first piece is a path that can be used to determine when the cookie should be sent back to the server. The second part contains the session ID—that's the part we parse out and save.

For more information on the different parts of a cookie string and how they are used, see http://www.ietf.org/rfc/rfc2965.txt and http://www.ietf.org/rfc/rfc2109.txt.

Listing 9-4 shows a class, CookieMIDlet, that uses this technique to maintain a session with a server. It has a very bland user interface—just an empty Form with two commands. If you invoke the **Send** command, the MIDlet sends an HTTP request and receives a response using the cookie handling described earlier.

Listing 9-4. Saving a Server Session ID Cookie

```java
import java.io.*;

import javax.microedition.io.*;
import javax.microedition.midlet.*;
import javax.microedition.lcdui.*;

public class CookieMIDlet
    extends MIDlet
    implements CommandListener, Runnable {
  private Display mDisplay;
  private Form mForm;

  private String mSession;

  public void startApp() {
    mDisplay = Display.getDisplay(this);

    if (mForm == null) {
      mForm = new Form("CookieMIDlet");

      mForm.addCommand(new Command("Exit", Command.EXIT, 0));
      mForm.addCommand(new Command("Send", Command.SCREEN, 0));
      mForm.setCommandListener(this);
    }

    mDisplay.setCurrent(mForm);
  }
```

```
    public void pauseApp() {}

    public void destroyApp(boolean unconditional) {}

    public void commandAction(Command c, Displayable s) {
      if (c.getCommandType() == Command.EXIT) notifyDestroyed();
      else {
        Form waitForm = new Form("Connecting...");
        mDisplay.setCurrent(waitForm);
        Thread t = new Thread(this);
        t.start();
      }
    }

    public void run() {
      String url = getAppProperty("CookieMIDlet-URL");

      try {
        // Query the server and retrieve the response.
        HttpConnection hc = (HttpConnection)Connector.open(url);
        if (mSession != null)
          hc.setRequestProperty("cookie", mSession);
        InputStream in = hc.openInputStream();

        String cookie = hc.getHeaderField("Set-cookie");
        if (cookie != null) {
          int semicolon = cookie.indexOf(';');
          mSession = cookie.substring(0, semicolon);
        }

        int length = (int)hc.getLength();
        byte[] raw = new byte[length];
        in.read(raw);

        String s = new String(raw);
        Alert a = new Alert("Response", s, null, null);
        a.setTimeout(Alert.FOREVER);
        mDisplay.setCurrent(a, mForm);

        in.close();
        hc.close();
      }
      catch (IOException ioe) {
```

```
        Alert a = new Alert("Exception", ioe.toString(), null, null);
        a.setTimeout(Alert.FOREVER);
        mDisplay.setCurrent(a, mForm);
    }
  }
}
```

On the server side, things are much simpler, as you'll see in Listing 9-5. If you're writing Java servlets, you don't even have to worry about cookies. Instead, you just deal with an `HttpSession` object. The code that follows shows a servlet that interacts with `CookieMIDlet`; it implements a session-based hit counter. It's been tested on Tomcat 4.0 but should work fine on other servers. Note that you will have to map the URL used by the MIDlet to this servlet class; for details, see an introductory book on servlets or your server's documentation.

Listing 9-5. A Simple Session Handling Servlet

```java
import javax.servlet.http.*;
import javax.servlet.*;
import java.io.*;
import java.util.*;

public class CookieServlet extends HttpServlet {
  private Map mHitMap = new HashMap();

  public void doGet(HttpServletRequest request,
      HttpServletResponse response)
      throws ServletException, IOException {
    HttpSession session = request.getSession();

    String id = session.getId();

    int hits = -1;

    // Try to retrieve the hits from the map.
    Integer hitsInteger = (Integer)mHitMap.get(id);
    if (hitsInteger != null)
      hits = hitsInteger.intValue();

    // Increment and store.
    hits++;
    mHitMap.put(id, new Integer(hits));
```

```
    String message = "Hits for this session: " + hits + ".";

    response.setContentType("text/plain");
    response.setContentLength(message.length());
    PrintWriter out = response.getWriter();
    out.println(message);
  }
}
```

The servlet retrieves the `HttpSession` object. Then it pulls out the session ID and uses it as a key into a map of hit counts. After retrieving and incrementing the hit count for the session, the servlet sends it as the response back to the MIDlet. You can start up multiple copies of the emulator and run them simultaneously to see how the hit counts are independent of each other and associated with each session.

Design Tips

This section contains some suggestions about creating networked MIDlets.

- Use GET rather than POST. It's simpler, and you won't have to worry about fiddling around with the request headers.

- Don't hard-code URLs. Put them in a MIDlet property in the application descriptor. This will make it possible to change the URL without recompiling your code.

- Put network access in a separate thread. Network access always takes time; it shouldn't hold up the user interface. Furthermore, you must let your users know what's going on. Put up a "loading progress" type of message or some kind of indication that your application is trying to access a network resource.

- Make sure you handle exceptions gracefully. Network connections on wireless devices are not tremendously reliable, so you should make sure you're prepared for the worst. Catch all your exceptions and do something reasonable.

- Clean up after yourself. On a small device, resources are scarce, so be sure to close connections when you are done with them. `try - finally` blocks are especially useful for ensuring that unused streams and connections are closed.[1] The code in `Jargoneer` demonstrates this technique.

Using HTTPS

HTTP is not a secure protocol. It operates on top of TCP/IP sockets. Information exchanged using HTTP is highly susceptible to eavesdroppers. A more secure alternative, HTTPS, runs atop Transport Layer Security (TLS), Secure Sockets Layer (SSL), or a similar protocol. TLS and SSL provide a layer of authentication and encryption between sockets and higher-level protocols like HTTP, POP3, SMTP, and NNTP.

TLS 1.0 is really just an updated version of SSLv3. For more information on these protocols, see `http://wp.netscape.com/eng/ssl3/` and `http://www.ietf.org/rfc/rfc2246.txt`.

In typical TLS interactions, the server sends a certificate to the client to authenticate itself. The client must have Certificate Authority (CA) root certificates on hand to verify the server's certificate. (The J2ME Wireless Toolkit comes with a utility, `MEKeyTool`, that can be used to modify the set of CA root certificates used by the toolkit emulator. Real devices may have similar utilities, but in general, you'll have to make sure that your server certificate is signed by a CA that is widely recognized.) If the client can verify the certificate, the client will then send a secret value to the server, encrypted with the server's public key. The server and the client both derive a *session key* from this secret value, which is used to encrypt all subsequent traffic sent between the client and server.

The generic connection framework makes it very easy to obtain HTTPS connections. All you have to do is construct an HTTPS connection string. So instead of this:

```
HttpConnection hc = (HttpConnection)
    Connector.open("http://www.cert.org/");
```

You would do this:

```
HttpConnection hc = (HttpConnection)
    Connector.open("https://www.cert.org/");
```

---

1. You are probably familiar with the `try - catch` blocks that are used in Java for exception handling. The `finally` clause is not as well known, but it is very useful. Code in the `finally` block will be executed regardless of how control leaves the `try` block.

It's really that simple. HTTPS connections were possible in MIDP 1.0; even though the specification didn't demand support, implementations were free to provide it. In MIDP 2.0, the API also supports HTTPS, so there's a new interface, HttpsConnection, that represents HTTP carried over some secure transport.

HttpsConnection is an extension of HttpConnection; it adds a getPort() method so that you can find out the server's port number. The default port for HTTPS is 443. More importantly, HttpsConnection has a getSecurityInfo() method that returns information about the secure connection. The new SecurityInfo interface encapsulates information about the cipher suite in use, the name and version of the secure protocol, and the server's certificate. The certificate is an implementation of javax.microedition.pki.Certificate and includes standard information like the subject, signer, signature algorithm, and validity dates of the certificate.

The following example shows how you can retrieve the subject of a server certificate from an HTTPS connection:

```
String url = "https://www.cert.org/";
HttpsConnection hc = (HttpsConnection)Connector.open(url);
SecurityInfo si = hc.getSecurityInfo();
Certificate c = si.getServerCertificate();
String subject = c.getSubject();
```

Using Datagram Connections

In this section, I'll briefly describe datagram connections. Although support for datagrams is not mandated by the MIDP specification, certain device implementations may choose to support datagram connections. Unlike stream-oriented connections, datagram connections are *connectionless*. This means that you can fire packets of data around the network, but you have no guarantee that they will reach their destination in the right order, or that they will even arrive at all.

Datagram communications is based on two interfaces in the javax.microedition.io package, DatagramConnection and Datagram. Figure 9-4 shows the methods in DatagramConnection.

The first step is to use the generic connection framework to obtain a DatagramConnection—something like this:

```
String url = "datagram://jonathanknudsen.com:7999";
DatagramConnection dc = (DatagramConnection)Connector.open(url);
```

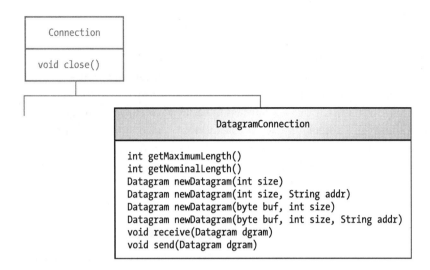

Figure 9-4. The DatagramConnection *interface*

The URL string passed to Connector's open() method contains both the host name and port of the opposite end of the datagram connection. If datagram connections are not supported by a MIDP implementation, an exception will be thrown from the open() method.

All data is exchanged using Datagrams. To send a datagram, first ask the DatagramConnection to create one for you using one of the newDatagram() methods. Then write some data into it and pass it into the send() method of DatagramConnection. Receiving a datagram is almost as easy. You just call receive(), which blocks until a datagram is received.

In essence, Datagram is a wrapper for an array of bytes that are the payload of the datagram. You can retrieve a reference to this byte array by calling getData(). Keep in mind, however, that the data for the Datagram may be only a subset of the data in the array. You can find the array offset and length of the actual data by calling getOffset() and getLength().

Interestingly, Datagram is an extension of both the DataInput and DataOutput interfaces, so it's possible to read and write data in a Datagram as though it were a stream.

In MIDP 2.0, datagram connections are represented by the UDPDatagramConnection interface, an extension of the DatagramConnection interface. UDPDatagramConnection adds two new methods, getLocalAddress() and getLocalPort(). You can use these methods to find out the originating point of datagrams sent using the connection.

Other Connection Types

Although the MIDP 2.0 specification requires only HTTP and HTTPS connections, it suggests that implementations support socket, server socket, and secure socket connections. The API provides appropriate interfaces for these connections. Devices may also choose to implement access to serial ports through the generic connection framework. Table 9-1 details the additional connection types, their supporting connection interfaces, and example connection strings. For more detailed information, see the API documentation for the corresponding interface.

Table 9-1. Optional Connection Types

TYPE	INTERFACE	EXAMPLE
Socket	SocketConnection	socket://jonathanknudsen.com:79
Server socket	ServerSocketConnection	socket://:129
TLS or SSL socket	SecureConnection	ssl://jonathanknudsen.com:79
Serial port	CommConnection	comm:com0;baudrate=19200

Responding to Incoming Connections

You may be used to thinking of mobile phones as client devices, but they may be full-fledged networked citizens, with the ability to receive incoming network connections. Although ServerSocketConnection provides the ability to listen for incoming socket connections, it can only be active while a MIDlet is actually running.

A typical server loop, listening for incoming socket connections on port 80, looks something like this:

```
ServerSocketConnection ssc;
ssc = (ServerSocketConnection)Connector.open("socket://:80");
boolean trucking = true;
while (trucking) {
  SocketConnection sc = (SocketConnection)ssc.acceptAndOpen();
  // Handle the client connection sc.
}
```

MIDP 2.0 goes one step further and allows MIDlets to be launched in response to incoming network connections. The name for this technique is *push*. You could, in theory, create a web server MIDlet, although in practice a mobile phone is probably a poor platform for a web server. A more likely example would be an SMS

MIDlet, something built using JSR 120, the Wireless Messaging API. Assuming the MIDlet was configured correctly, incoming SMS messages would cause the MIDlet to be launched to handle the connection.

A MIDlet may register for push connections in two ways. It can register at runtime, using static methods in `javax.microedition.io.PushRegistry`, or it can register at install time using special entries in the application descriptor (JAD file). The important thing to remember is that the push registry has a lifetime beyond your MIDlet. It is part of the MIDlet management software that runs on the device. When a MIDlet registers for push notifications, the device software is obligated to listen for incoming network connections and launch your MIDlet if the appropriate connection is made.

Inside your MIDlet, you don't have to do anything different to catch the incoming connection. All you do is call `Connector.open()` with the appropriate network listening string.

Let's say, for example, that you had created a web server in a MIDlet and called it `PatchyMIDlet`. (The source code for this book, available from `http://www.apress.com/`, includes `PatchyMIDlet`; it sends a randomly selected text message in response to incoming requests.) This MIDlet responds to incoming socket connections on port 80 (the default HTTP port). If you wanted to register the MIDlet at runtime, you'd do this in the code somewhere:

```
PushRegistry.registerConnection("socket://:80", PatchyMIDlet, "*");
```

The first two parameters are pretty clear—any incoming socket connections on port 80 should launch `PatchyMIDlet`. The third parameter is a filter that will be applied to incoming connections. In this case, we accept all incoming connections with the "*" wildcard. Other possibilities would be to restrict incoming connections to a single IP address or a range of addresses.

Remember, the results of the call to `registerConnection()` persist beyond the lifetime of the MIDlet. Even after the MIDlet has been destroyed, the MIDlet management software on the device is watching out for incoming socket connections on port 80. If a connection is received, `PatchyMIDlet` will be launched. The push registry doesn't actually do anything with the incoming connection; it just detects it and launches a registered MIDlet to respond. It's the MIDlet's responsibility to accept the incoming connection. To find out whether it has been launched by the push registry or the user, the MIDlet can call `PushRegistry`'s `listConnections()` method, passing `true` for the `available` parameter. The method will then return a list of connections that have input available. If this list is empty, then the MIDlet must have been launched by the user, not by an incoming connection.

Instead of a MIDlet registering push connections at runtime, it's much more likely that the push registrations would be contained in the application description for the MIDlet suite containing `PatchyMIDlet`. Thus, the push registration would be performed at installation time so that the user would never need to run the MIDlet manually. In this case, the MIDlet descriptor would contain a line like this:

```
MIDlet-Push-1: socket://:80, PatchyMIDlet, *
```

The parameters are exactly the same. The push registration is made when the MIDlet suite is installed. If the MIDlet cannot be registered (for example, some other application might already be listening for incoming socket connections on port 80), then the MIDlet suite will not be installed. Multiple push registrations are listed in the descriptor using ascending numbers: MIDlet-Push-1, MIDlet-Push-2, and so on.

The J2ME Wireless Toolkit (version 2.0) allows you to register and test push connections easily. Just click on the **Settings...** button, then choose the **Push Registry** tab. If you downloaded the source code for this book, you'll see an entry for PatchyMIDlet. Figure 9-5 shows this entry.

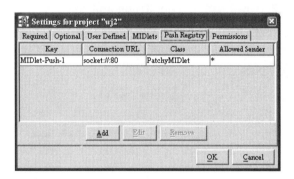

Figure 9-5. The push registry entry for PatchyMIDlet

To test the push notification, you'll have to package the application, then deploy it on the emulator. First choose **Project ➤ Package ➤ Create Package** to package the project into a MIDlet suite JAR. Then choose the **Project ➤ Run via OTA** from the KToolbar menu. You'll see the emulator pop up, showing its Application Management Software (AMS). Select **Install Application**, then accept the URL that is supplied. KToolbar contains a small OTA server; the URL is automatically preloaded when you select **Run via OTA**. You will see a series of other prompts about installing the application; just say yes to everything. Eventually the installation succeeds and you will see the MIDlet suite wj2 listed in the emulator's menu. The emulator is now running, listening for incoming connections, even though no MIDlets are running.

Now test `PatchyMIDlet` by pointing your browser to `http://localhost/`. `PatchyMIDlet` will be launched and will send a response to the browser. (The emulator will ask if it's okay to send data back on the network; you'll have to say yes.) Figure 9-6 shows the emulator running `PatchyMIDlet` and a browser showing its output.

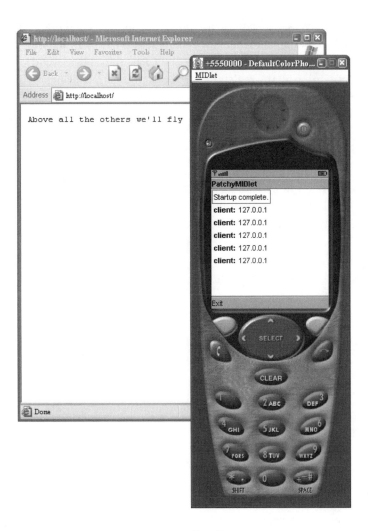

Figure 9-6. `PatchyMIDlet`, *a small web server*

Run via OTA is an excellent tool for testing your MIDlet's installation behavior rather than its runtime behavior. Just remember that you need to package the MIDlet first because the toolkit's small OTA distributes the MIDlet suite JAR file from the project's *bin* directory.

NOTE *The **Run via OTA** feature is not available in the J2ME Wireless Toolkit 2.0 beta 1. It was added in version 2.0 beta 2.*

PushRegistry contains several other static methods that are related to network registrations. The getMIDlet() and getFilter() methods return the MIDlet name and filter for a given network connection string. The listConnections() method returns a string array containing all the registered network connection strings. Finally, to remove a connection-to-MIDlet mapping, use unregisterConnection().

Permissions for Network Connections

MIDP 2.0 includes a security framework that is designed to prevent MIDlets from running up your phone bill by making unauthorized network connections. As I discussed in Chapter 3, network access in MIDP 2.0 is guarded by permissions and protection domains. Here are the permission names defined by MIDP 2.0:

- javax.microedition.io.Connector.http

- javax.microedition.io.Connector.https

- javax.microedition.io.Connector.datagram

- javax.microedition.io.Connector.datagramreceiver

- javax.microedition.io.Connector.socket

- javax.microedition.io.Connector.serversocket

- javax.microedition.io.Connector.ssl

- javax.microedition.io.Connector.comm

- javax.microedition.io.PushRegistry

These permissions have names corresponding to the API that they protect. All of these permissions, except one, protect connection types, which are accessed via the javax.microedition.io.Connector class, hence the prefix on those permission names. The very last permission refers to the push registry and shares its name with the PushRegistry class.

When you run a MIDlet suite in the toolkit, it runs in the untrusted domain by default. In the untrusted domain, HTTP and HTTPS connections are allowed if the user grants permission. You can see this when you run a MIDlet that attempts a network connection. Figure 9-7 shows how the emulator asks the user for permission and allows the user to make the decision stick for the remainder of the session.

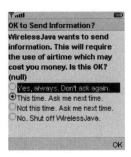

Figure 9-7. The emulator asks for the user's permission for network connections.

You can indicate the necessary and optional permissions used by your MIDlet suite by using the MIDlet-Permissions and MIDlet-Permissions-Opt descriptor attributes. (In the J2ME Wireless Toolkit, you can set permissions in the descriptor by choosing **Settings...**, then clicking the **Permissions** tab.)

Summary

Networking on the MIDP platform is based on a generalized connection framework. The only protocol mandated by the MIDP 1.0 specification is HTTP. You can perform GET, HEAD, or POST requests with just a few lines of code. HTTP session handling is also feasible. Implementations are free to support additional connection types; datagrams, sockets, server sockets, and serial port communications are some of the possibilities. MIDP 2.0 requires support for HTTPS in addition to HTTP and formalizes the connection strings and APIs for handling additional connection types. MIDP 2.0's security architecture protects users from unauthorized network use.

CHAPTER 10

Programming a Custom User Interface

CHAPTERS 5, 6, AND 7 were devoted to MIDP's generalized user-interface APIs. Clever as these APIs are, they are unsuitable for game development and other specialized user interfaces. Games are programmed "closer to the metal" than other applications. MIDP offers a class, `javax.microedition.lcdui.Canvas`, that provides low-level access to a device's screen and input facilities. You can find out exactly which keys a user is pressing and draw whatever you want on the screen.

A further enhancement in MIDP 2.0 is the Game API, contained in the `javax.microedition.lcdui.game` package. It includes a refinement of `Canvas` and classes for layer-based graphics and sprite animations. The Game API is fully discussed in Chapter 11. In this chapter you'll learn the basics of `Canvas` and drawing with the `Graphics` class.

The Canvas Class

`Canvas` is the heart of MIDP's custom user-interface API. To use it, you must create a subclass of `Canvas`. This differs from the `Screen` subclasses, which are ready to use "out of the box."

Aside from that, however, `Canvas` fits in very nicely with the other subclasses of `Displayable`. A MIDlet can mix and match regular screens and `Canvas`es. In a game, for instance, a high score screen might be a `Form`, while the game itself would be played on a `Canvas`.

`Canvas` contains event-handling methods that are invoked by the MIDP implementation whenever something important happens. When the user presses a key, or when the screen needs to be painted, one of `Canvas`'s methods will be called. Most of these methods have empty implementations in `Canvas`. To respond to an event, you need to override the appropriate method and provide an implementation.

The one exception to this rule is the `paint()` method, which is declared `abstract` and thus must be defined in subclasses.

Canvas Information

If you would like to draw your own user interface, you'll need some basic information about the Canvas. You can find out the size of the Canvas by calling getWidth() and getHeight(). As we'll discuss later, you can also find out the color capabilities of the device by calling methods in Display.

MIDP 2.0 offers a full screen mode. Some Canvas implementations won't occupy all the available screen space, reserving areas of the screen for information about the state of the device or other purposes. If the device supports an alternate full screen mode for Canvas, you can use it by calling setFullScreenMode(true). Setting full screen mode on or off may result in calls to the sizeChanged() method Canvas inherits from Displayable.

Canvas also features event handler methods that will be called by the MIDP implementation as your Canvas is displayed and hidden. Each time your Canvas is shown, the showNotify() method will be called. If another Displayable is shown, or the application manager decides to run a different application, hideNotify() is called.

Painting and Repainting

The MIDP implementation calls a Canvas's paint() method when the contents of the Canvas need to be shown. This paint() method should look familiar to anyone who has ever implemented a custom Swing or AWT component.

The MIDP implementation passes a Graphics object to your paint() method. Graphics has methods for drawing shapes, text, and images on a Canvas. A typical Canvas implementation, then, looks something like this:

```
import javax.microedition.lcdui.*;

public class JonathanCanvas
    extends Canvas {
  public void paint(Graphics g) {
    // Draw stuff using g.
  }
}
```

What if you want to tell the Canvas to draw itself? You can't call paint()
directly, because you don't have a suitable Graphics to pass to paint(). Instead,
you need to tell the MIDP implementation that it's time to paint the Canvas. The
way you do this is by calling repaint(). The first version of this method simply tells
Canvas to paint everything.

```
public void repaint()
public void repaint(int x, int y, int width, int height)
```

The second version is a way of saying, "I only want you to paint this rectangular portion of the screen." If the drawing you're doing is very complicated, you
can save some time by only painting the portion of the Canvas that has changed.
This is implemented using a technique called clipping. A later section discusses
clipping in more detail.

How exactly does repaint() work? When you call repaint(), paint() won't be
called right away. The call to repaint() just signals to the MIDP implementation
that you want the screen to be painted. Some time later, the implementation
services the repaint request, which results in an actual call to the paint() method
of the Canvas. The MIDP implementation may even combine several repaint
requests, particularly if their repaint regions overlap.

TIP Canvas *does not automatically clear itself when you call* repaint().
*If you want to change what's on the screen, rather than adding to it, you
should clear the screen in the* paint() *method. You'll see how to do this in
the* FontCanvas *example later in this chapter.*

An application can force the implementation to service all the repaint
requests by calling serviceRepaints() on the Canvas object. This method does not
return until all pending repaint requests have been serviced. If you are going to
call serviceRepaints(), you should make sure that you aren't trying to acquire
object locks in the paint() method that won't be released until serviceRepaints()
returns. In general, you won't need to call serviceRepaints(); you can usually use
Display's callSerially() method instead. (See the "Multithreading and Animation" section of this chapter for a discussion of callSerially().)

Drawing Shapes, Text, and Images

The Graphics class contains methods for drawing shapes, text, and images on a Canvas. It also maintains some state, like the current pen color and line style. MIDP's Graphics class is similar to the Graphics and Graphics2D classes in J2SE but much smaller.

Coordinate Space

All drawing on a Canvas takes place in a coordinate space based on the pixels of the device. By default, the origin of this coordinate space is located in the upper-left corner of the Canvas. X coordinates increase in the right-hand direction, while Y coordinates increase in the downward direction, as shown in Figure 10-1.

You can adjust the origin of this coordinate space by calling the translate() method of the Graphics class. This sets the origin to the given coordinates in the current coordinate system. To find out the location of the translated origin relative to the default origin, call getTranslateX() and getTranslateY().

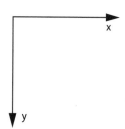

Figure 10-1. Canvas coordinate axes

Drawing and Filling Shapes

Graphics contains a collection of methods that draw and fill simple shapes. These are detailed in Table 10-1. MIDP 2.0 includes a new method, fillTriangle().

Table 10-1. Drawing and Filling Shapes with Graphics

SHAPE OUTLINE	FILLED SHAPE
drawLine(int x1, int y1, int x2, int y2)	–
–	fillTriangle(int x1, int y1, int x2, int y2, int x3, int y3)
drawRect(int x, int y, int width, int height)	fillRect(int x, int y, int width, int height)
drawRoundRect(int x, int y, int width, int height, int arcWidth, int arcHeight)	fillRoundRect(int x, int y, int width, int height, int arcWidth, int arcHeight)
drawArc(int x, int y, int width, int height, int startAngle, int arcAngle)	fillArc(int x, int y, int width, int height, int startAngle, int arcAngle)

These methods do basically what you'd expect. The following example demonstrates some simple drawing using Graphics. It consists of two pieces. First, PacerCanvas demonstrates some simple drawing and filling:

```
import javax.microedition.lcdui.*;

public class PacerCanvas
    extends Canvas {
  public void paint(Graphics g) {
    int w = getWidth();
    int h = getHeight();

    g.setColor(0xffffff);
    g.fillRect(0, 0, w, h);
    g.setColor(0x000000);

    for (int x = 0; x < w; x += 10)
      g.drawLine(0, w - x, x, 0);

    int z = 50;
    g.drawRect(z, z, 20, 20);
    z += 20;
    g.fillRoundRect(z, z, 20, 20, 5, 5);
    z += 20;
    g.drawArc(z, z, 20, 20, 0, 360);
  }
}
```

The next class is `Pacer`, a MIDlet that uses `PacerCanvas`.

```
import javax.microedition.lcdui.*;
import javax.microedition.midlet.*;

public class Pacer
    extends MIDlet{
  public void startApp() {
    Displayable d = new PacerCanvas();

    d.addCommand(new Command("Exit", Command.EXIT, 0));
    d.setCommandListener(new CommandListener() {
      public void commandAction(Command c, Displayable s) {
        notifyDestroyed();
      }
    } );

    Display.getDisplay(this).setCurrent(d);
  }

  public void pauseApp() { }

  public void destroyApp(boolean unconditional) { }
}
```

When you run Pacer in Sun's J2ME Wireless Toolkit emulator, it looks like Figure 10-2.

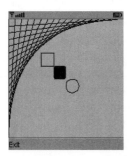

Figure 10-2. Playing around with Graphics

Working with Color

The Graphics class maintains a current drawing color that is used for drawing shape outlines, filling shapes, and drawing text. Colors are represented as combinations of red, green, and blue, with eight bits for each color component. You can set the current drawing color using the following method:

```
public void setColor(int RGB)
```

This method expects the red, green, and blue values in a packed integer, as shown in Figure 10-3.

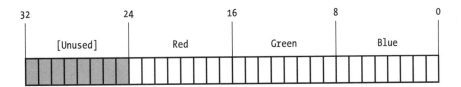

Figure 10-3. Packing a color into an integer

An alternate convenience method accepts red, green, and blue values as integers in the range from 0 to 255 inclusive:

```
public void setColor(int red, int green, int blue)
```

You can retrieve the current drawing color (as a packed integer) with getColor(). Alternately, you can retrieve each component separately using getRedComponent(), getGreenComponent(), and getBlueComponent().

Of course, different devices will have different levels of color support, from black and white (affectionately known as "one-bit color") through full 24-bit color. As I mentioned in Chapter 5, the isColor() and numColors() methods in Display return useful information about the capabilities of the device.

For grayscale devices, Graphics provides setGrayScale() as a convenience method. You pass it a number from 0 (black) to 255 (white). You can find out the current grayscale value by calling getGrayScale(). If the current color of this Graphics is not a grayscale color (i.e., if the red, green, and blue values of the current color are not the same), then this method returns its best guess as to the brightness of the current color.

MIDP 2.0 adds a getDisplayColor() method to the Graphics class. This is a handy method that can tell you at runtime exactly how a requested color will be displayed on the device. You feed it a color int and it returns the color int that will actually be displayed on the device. For example, on the J2ME Wireless Toolkit's **DefaultGrayPhone** emulator, pure green (0x00ff00) maps to the gray level 0x959595.

Line Styles

Graphics also maintains a current line style, called a *stroke style*, which is used for drawing shape outlines and lines. There are two choices for line style, represented by constants in the Graphics class:

- SOLID is the default.

- DOTTED lines may also be drawn.

It's up to the implementation to decide exactly how dotted lines are implemented, so dotted lines on one device may look dashed on another. You can set or retrieve the current style using setStrokeStyle() and getStrokeStyle(). For example, the following code draws a square with a solid outline (the default) and another square with a dotted outline:

```
public void paint(Graphics g) {
  g.drawRect(20, 10, 35, 35);
  g.setStrokeStyle(Graphics.DOTTED);
  g.drawRect(20, 60, 35, 35);
}
```

Drawing Text

The Graphics class makes it easy to draw text anywhere on the screen. Text drawing is based around the idea of an anchor point. The anchor point determines exactly where the text will be drawn. Anchor points are described with a horizontal and vertical component. The Graphics class defines the horizontal and vertical anchor points as constants. Figure 10-4 illustrates the various anchor points for a string of text. Each anchor point is described as a combination of a horizontal and vertical anchor point.

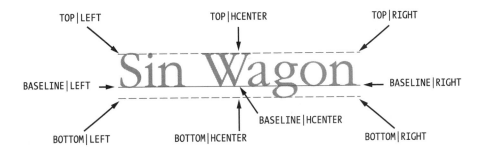

Figure 10-4. Text anchor points

To draw text, you just need to specify the text itself and the location and type of anchor point. You could, for example, place some text in the upper-left corner of the screen by using a TOP | LEFT anchor point located at 0, 0.

Text is specified as a String or an array of chars, which means you can draw text in many languages, provided that the fonts you're using have the corresponding glyphs.

Graphics provides four different methods for drawing text. You can draw characters or Strings, depending on what you have available:

```
public void drawChar(char character, int x, int y, int anchor)
public void drawChars(char[] data, int offset, int length,
    int x, int y, int anchor)
public void drawString(String str, int x, int y, int anchor)
public void drawSubstring(String str, int offset, int len,
    int x, int y, int anchor)
```

The following example shows how to place text at various places on a Canvas:

```
import javax.microedition.lcdui.*;

public class TextCanvas
    extends Canvas {
  public void paint(Graphics g) {
    int w = getWidth();
    int h = getHeight();

    g.setColor(0xffffff);
    g.fillRect(0, 0, w, h);
    g.setColor(0x000000);
```

```
    // First label the four corners.
    g.drawString("corner", 0, 0,
        Graphics.TOP | Graphics.LEFT);
    g.drawString("corner", w, 0,
        Graphics.TOP | Graphics.RIGHT);
    g.drawString("corner", 0, h,
        Graphics.BOTTOM | Graphics.LEFT);
    g.drawString("corner", w, h,
        Graphics.BOTTOM | Graphics.RIGHT);

// Now put something in the middle (more or less).
    g.drawString("Sin Wagon", w / 2, h / 2,
        Graphics.BASELINE | Graphics.HCENTER);
  }
}
```

To see this Canvas, you'll have to create a MIDlet that displays it. I suggest using Pacer; just edit the source file so it instantiates a TextCanvas instead of a PacerCanvas. The finished product is shown in Figure 10-5.

Figure 10-5. TextCanvas *in the flesh*

Note that Canvas denies us some real estate at the bottom of the screen. This is to allow space for Commands. Canvas, like any other Displayable, can display commands and have a command listener.

Selecting a Font

MIDP fonts are represented by a *font face, style,* and *size.* You won't find a big selection of fonts, but there are a few choices. Three faces are available, as shown in Figure 10-6. These are represented by constants in the Font class: FACE_SYSTEM, FACE_MONOSPACE, and FACE_PROPORTIONAL.

Figure 10-6. The three font faces in italics

Once you've chosen a font face, you can also specify a style and a size. The styles are what you'd expect, and they are represented by constants in the Font class: STYLE_PLAIN, STYLE_BOLD, STYLE_ITALIC, and STYLE_UNDERLINE. You can combine styles, like bold and italic, by ORing the constants together. The size is simply SIZE_SMALL, SIZE_MEDIUM, or SIZE_LARGE.

You could create a small, italic, proportional font with the following call:

```
Font f = Font.getFont(
    Font.FACE_PROPORTIONAL,
    Font.STYLE_ITALIC,
    Font.SIZE_SMALL);
```

To tell Graphics to use a new font for subsequent text, call setFont(). You can get a reference to the current font by calling getFont(). You can also find out information about a Font with the getFace(), getStyle(), and getSize() methods. For convenience, Font also includes isPlain(), isBold(), isItalic(), and isUnderlined() methods.

The MIDP implementation has a default font that you can retrieve from Font's static method getDefaultFont().

The following Canvas demonstrates the creation and use of fonts.

```
import javax.microedition.lcdui.*;

public class FontCanvas
    extends Canvas {
  private Font mSystemFont, mMonospaceFont, mProportionalFont;

  public FontCanvas() { this(Font.STYLE_PLAIN); }

  public FontCanvas(int style) { setStyle(style); }
```

```
public void setStyle(int style) {
    mSystemFont = Font.getFont(Font.FACE_SYSTEM,
        style, Font.SIZE_MEDIUM);
    mMonospaceFont = Font.getFont(Font.FACE_MONOSPACE,
        style, Font.SIZE_MEDIUM);
    mProportionalFont = Font.getFont(Font.FACE_PROPORTIONAL,
        style, Font.SIZE_MEDIUM);
}

public boolean isBold() {
    return mSystemFont.isBold();
}
public boolean isItalic() {
    return mSystemFont.isItalic();
}
public boolean isUnderline() {
    return mSystemFont.isUnderlined();
}

public void paint(Graphics g) {
    int w = getWidth();
    int h = getHeight();

    // Clear the Canvas.
    g.setGrayScale(255);
    g.fillRect(0, 0, w - 1, h - 1);
    g.setGrayScale(0);
    g.drawRect(0, 0, w - 1, h - 1);

    int x = w / 2;
    int y = 20;

    y += showFont(g, "System", x, y, mSystemFont);
    y += showFont(g, "Monospace", x, y, mMonospaceFont);
    y += showFont(g, "Proportional", x, y, mProportionalFont);
}

private int showFont(Graphics g, String s, int x, int y, Font f) {
    g.setFont(f);
    g.drawString(s, x, y, Graphics.TOP | Graphics.HCENTER);
    return f.getHeight();
}
}
```

To see this Canvas in action, you'll need a MIDlet that shows it. You could modify Pacer again, if you wish, or use the following code:

```
import javax.microedition.lcdui.*;
import javax.microedition.midlet.*;

public class FontMIDlet
    extends MIDlet
    implements CommandListener {
  private FontCanvas mFontCanvas;
  private Command mBoldCommand, mItalicCommand, mUnderlineCommand;

  public FontMIDlet() {
    mFontCanvas = new FontCanvas();

    mBoldCommand = new Command("Bold", Command.SCREEN, 0);
    mItalicCommand = new Command("Italic", Command.SCREEN, 0);
    mUnderlineCommand = new Command("Underline", Command.SCREEN, 0);
    Command exitCommand = new Command("Exit", Command.EXIT, 0);

    mFontCanvas.addCommand(mBoldCommand);
    mFontCanvas.addCommand(mItalicCommand);
    mFontCanvas.addCommand(mUnderlineCommand);
    mFontCanvas.addCommand(exitCommand);
    mFontCanvas.setCommandListener(this);
  }

  public void startApp() {
    Display.getDisplay(this).setCurrent(mFontCanvas);
  }

  public void pauseApp() {}

  public void destroyApp(boolean unconditional) {}

  public void commandAction(Command c, Displayable s) {
    if (c.getCommandType() == Command.EXIT) {
      notifyDestroyed();
      return;
    }
```

```
        boolean isBold = mFontCanvas.isBold() ^ (c == mBoldCommand);
        boolean isItalic = mFontCanvas.isItalic() ^ (c == mItalicCommand);
        boolean isUnderline = mFontCanvas.isUnderline() ^
            (c == mUnderlineCommand);

    int style =
        (isBold ? Font.STYLE_BOLD : 0) |
        (isItalic ? Font.STYLE_ITALIC : 0) |
        (isUnderline ? Font.STYLE_UNDERLINED : 0);

    mFontCanvas.setStyle(style);
    mFontCanvas.repaint();
  }
}
```

Measuring Text

The Font class can tell you useful information about the dimensions of text. If you read the previous example carefully, you'll notice we already used one of these methods, getHeight(). This method returns the height of an entire line of text and can be used to position multiple lines.

If you really need to know the location of the baseline, call getBaselinePosition(). This returns the distance from the top of a line of text to the baseline. However, given the flexibility offered by the anchor points in Graphics, you probably won't ever need to find the baseline yourself.

The rest of the methods in Font for measuring text measure the width of various pieces of text. The names and parameters of these methods are the same as text drawing methods in Graphics:

```
public int charWidth(char ch)
public int charsWidth(char ch, int offset, int length)
public int stringWidth(String str)
public int substringWidth(String str, int offset, int len)
```

You could draw a box around a string, for example:

```
import javax.microedition.lcdui.*;

public class BoxTextCanvas
    extends Canvas {
  private Font mFont;
```

```
public BoxTextCanvas() {
    mFont = Font.getFont(Font.FACE_PROPORTIONAL,
        Font.STYLE_PLAIN, Font.SIZE_LARGE);
}

public void paint(Graphics g) {
    int w = getWidth();
    int h = getHeight();

    g.setColor(0xffffff);
    g.fillRect(0, 0, w, h);
    g.setColor(0x000000);

    String s = "dolce";
    int stringWidth = mFont.stringWidth(s);
    int stringHeight = mFont.getHeight();
    int x = (w - stringWidth) / 2;
    int y = h / 2;

    g.setFont(mFont);
    g.drawString(s, x, y, Graphics.TOP | Graphics.LEFT);
    g.drawRect(x, y, stringWidth, stringHeight);
  }
}
```

Drawing Images

The Graphics class contains a single method for drawing an image:

```
public void drawImage(Image img, int x, int y, int anchor)
```

The drawImage() method uses an anchor point, just like the anchor point
in the text drawing methods. The available anchor points are slightly different.
BASELINE is no longer an option for the vertical anchor point of an image, as the
concept of baseline is specific to text. Instead, VCENTER is an additional option for
the vertical anchor point. Figure 10-7 shows the available combinations of anchor
points.

Figure 10-7. Image anchor points

MIDP 2.0 specifically requires support for rendering images with transparency.

Advanced Image Rendering

In MIDP 2.0, the Graphics class also includes a drawRegion() method for rendering a region of an image and possibly manipulating it at the same time. The method looks like this:

```
public void drawRegion(Image src,
    int x_src, int y_src, int width, int height,
    int transform, int x_dest, int y_dest, int anchor)
```

The x_src, y_src, width, and height parameters describe a rectangular region of the image that will be rendered on the drawing surface of the Graphics. The region is drawn at x_dest and y_dest subject to the anchor, just as in the drawImage() method.

The transform parameter opens up a whole new world of possibilities. It may be any of the transformations described by constants in the Sprite class, listed below. (Sprite is part of MIDP 2.0's Game API and is described in the next chapter.)

- TRANS_NONE

- TRANS_ROT90

- TRANS_ROT180

- TRANS_ROT270

- TRANS_MIRROR

- TRANS_MIRROR_ROT90

- TRANS_MIRROR_ROT180

- TRANS_MIRROR_ROT270

The ROT transformations rotate the source image region by 90, 180, or 270 degrees. The MIRROR_ROT transformations first mirror the region around its vertical center, then rotate the mirrored region.

The drawRegion() method allows easy manipulation and display of animation frames that are packed into a single image.

Images as Integer Arrays

You've already seen how a single color can be represented as an integer. By extension, an image can be represented as an array of integers, where each integer in the array contains the color for a single pixel in the image.

MIDP 2.0 supports rendering integer arrays as images with the following method:

```
public void drawRGB(int[] rgbData, int offset, int scanlength,
    int x, int y, int width, int height,
    boolean processAlpha)
```

The image data is contained in the rgbData array, starting at offset. Consecutive rows of data are contained at offsets measured by multiples of scanlength. The image will be rendered at x and y with a size defined by width and height.

The relationship between width and scanlength is a little confusing at first. The following example should clear things up.

Consider the following code.

```
int[] rgbData = {
    0x123456, 0x123456, 0x123456,
    0x000000, 0xffffff, 0xffffff, 0x000000, 0x654321, 0x654321,
    0x000000, 0x000000, 0xffffff, 0x000000, 0x654321, 0x654321,
    0x000000, 0xffffff, 0x000000, 0x000000, 0x654321, 0x654321,
    0x000000, 0xffffff, 0xffffff, 0x000000, 0x654321, 0x654321
};

g.drawRGB(rgbData, 3, 6, 10, 10, 4, 4, false);
```

This code produces the very small image shown at great magnification in Figure 10-8. The first three elements of the array are ignored by passing an offset of 3. Although the image width is 4 pixels, each row of data is separated by 6 positions in the integer array. The image will be rendered at 10, 10, with a size of 4 by 4 pixels.

Figure 10-8. A very small image

The final parameter in the drawRGB() method, processAlpha, indicates whether the integer array is considered to contain an alpha (opacity) component. If the parameter is false, every pixel of the image is considered fully opaque. If processAlpha is true, the opacity of each pixel is determined by the high-order byte of the integer value and the pixel's color will be blended with the drawing surface appropriately. An alpha value of 0 is fully transparent, while an alpha value of 255 is fully opaque.

Blitting in MIDP 2.0

Blitting, the copying of one region of the screen to another location, is a crucial operation for some types of games. The MIDP 2.0 Graphics class includes one method for blitting:

```
public void copyArea(int x_src, int y_src, int width, int height,
    int x_dest, int y_dest, int anchor)
```

This method is pretty self-explanatory. It copies a portion of the screen, described by x_src, y_src, width, and height, to a destination describe by x_dest, y_dest, and anchor. The anchor works the same as for the drawImage() method.

This method works only on a Graphics object that does not draw directly to the screen. A Graphics object that draws to an image is fine, as is a Graphics object that works on a double-buffered Canvas. A Graphics object from GameCanvas's getGraphics() method will also work. By contrast, a Graphics object for a non-double-buffered Canvas will throw an IllegalStateException if the copyArea() method is called. (See the upcoming section on double buffering for more information on the technique.)

Clipping

Graphics maintains a rectangular *clipping shape*. The clipping shape limits drawing, such that any drawing that takes place outside of the clipping shape will not be displayed. It's kind of like painting through a stencil, except you can only use a rectangular stencil. If you were writing a game that had some kind of border on the game board, you might set the clipping rectangle to be the inside of the game board, so that no drawing could overwrite the border.

You can find out the current clipping rectangle by calling getClipX(), getClipY(), getClipWidth(), and getClipHeight().

If you would like to modify the clipping rectangle, there are two methods that you can use. First, you can set the clipping rectangle directly by calling the following method:

```
public void setClip(int x, int y, int width, int height);
```

The other possibility is to limit the current clipping rectangle with another rectangle. The following method takes the intersection of the current clipping rectangle and the supplied rectangle and uses it to set the new clipping rectangle:

```
public void clipRect(int x, int y, int width, int height);
```

Key Events

Canvas handles events at a lower level than the other Displayable subclasses. Although you can add Commands and respond to them, Canvas also includes a set of methods that handle interaction with the individual keys of a device.

The following methods are called whenever the user presses and releases a key.

```
protected void keyPressed(int keyCode)
protected void keyReleased(int keyCode)
```

The key code that is passed to these methods will most likely be one of the constants defined in Graphics, from KEY_NUM0 through KEY_NUM9 and including KEY_STAR and KEY_POUND. Devices may have more keys than this, which will be returned as device-specific key codes. Assuming there's an obvious mapping between the key and some Unicode character, the rule of thumb is that a key should have a code equal to its Unicode character value. Keys that don't have a Unicode mapping should use negative values. This means that, given a positive key code, you can find out the corresponding Unicode character by casting the int key code to char.

Note that key presses and key releases are separate events, which allows you considerable flexibility in how you design your user interface. The time between the press and the release could determine how high a game character jumps or how powerful a laser blast will be.

Depending on the device and the MIDP implementation, a key that is held down may spit out repeated key events. You can find out if repeated keys are supported by calling hasRepeatEvents(). If repeated key events are supported, the keyRepeated() method will be called with these events.

Finally, you can find a text description of a given key code by calling getKeyName().

In MIDP 2.0, the Game API offers a mechanism to bypass the key event callback methods. You can poll the state of the device's keys directly using a method in GameCanvas. For more information, see the following chapter.

Game Actions

Key codes may be useful in certain situations, but they're fairly specific to a device. MIDP offers a simple abstraction called a *game action* that makes it easier to map user key events to events that will be useful for games and other applications with specialized user interfaces.

The concept is simple: Supply a key code to getGameAction(), and you'll receive a game action—one of the following values: UP, DOWN, LEFT, RIGHT, FIRE, GAME_A, GAME_B, GAME_C, or GAME_D. Basically game actions are a way to map the physical keys on a device to a set of video game buttons such as you might find on game platforms like Sega Genesis or Nintendo Game Boy.

To understand how this maps to a physical device, think about how you might map the UP, DOWN, LEFT, and RIGHT game actions to keys. On Sun's MIDP emulator, there are navigation keys that have an obvious relationship to these game actions. Think about a simpler phone, however, one that has only a numeric keypad. In this case, you might want to map UP to the 2 key, DOWN to the 8 key, LEFT to the 4 key, and RIGHT to the 6 key.

Using game actions saves you from having to make these decisions yourself; the MIDP implementation simply provides a reasonable mapping for the device. To find the game action for a key code, pass the key code to getGameAction(). You can also find the key code for a game action by calling getKeyCode().

The following example listens for key presses in the keyPressed() method. It converts the key code to a game action and displays the game action on the screen.

```
import javax.microedition.lcdui.*;

public class KeyCanvas
    extends Canvas {
  private Font mFont;
  private String mMessage = "[Press keys]";

  public KeyCanvas() {
    mFont = Font.getFont(Font.FACE_PROPORTIONAL,
        Font.STYLE_PLAIN, Font.SIZE_MEDIUM);
  }

  public void paint(Graphics g) {
    int w = getWidth();
    int h = getHeight();

    // Clear the Canvas.
    g.setGrayScale(255);
    g.fillRect(0, 0, w - 1, h - 1);
    g.setGrayScale(0);
    g.drawRect(0, 0, w - 1, h - 1);

    g.setFont(mFont);
```

```
    int x = w / 2;
    int y = h / 2;

    g.drawString(mMessage, x, y, Graphics.BASELINE | Graphics.HCENTER);
  }

  protected void keyPressed(int keyCode) {
    int gameAction = getGameAction(keyCode);
    switch(gameAction) {
      case UP:     mMessage = "UP";              break;
      case DOWN:   mMessage = "DOWN";            break;
      case LEFT:   mMessage = "LEFT";            break;
      case RIGHT:  mMessage = "RIGHT";           break;
      case FIRE:   mMessage = "FIRE";            break;
      case GAME_A: mMessage = "GAME_A";          break;
      case GAME_B: mMessage = "GAME_B";          break;
      case GAME_C: mMessage = "GAME_C";          break;
      case GAME_D: mMessage = "GAME_D";          break;
      default:     mMessage = ""; break;
    }
    repaint();
  }
}
```

To run this example, you'll need a corresponding MIDlet to display KeyCanvas. At this point, I think you can do this by yourself.

Pointer Events

Some devices, particularly PDAs, may support a pointer. The popular Palm platform, for example, is based around the use of a stylus and a touch-sensitive screen. You can find out at runtime if your device supports pointer events by calling hasPointerEvents() and hasPointerMotionEvents(). If the device supports pointer events, the following methods get called when the pointer is pressed and released:

```
protected void pointerPressed(int x, int y)
protected void pointerReleased(int x, int y)
```

If the device supports pointer motion events, the following method will be called as the user drags the stylus around the screen.

```
protected void pointerDragged(int x, int y)
```

Double Buffering

Double buffering is a well-known technique for reducing flicker in drawing and animations. Imagine you are implementing an animation that clears and redraws the entire screen for each frame of the animation. Without double buffering, the animation will flicker badly as the screen is cleared and redrawn. With double buffering, the new frame is drawn into an off-screen image (the buffer). When the off-screen drawing is complete, the image is drawn on the screen in one smooth, quick move. You pay a price in the memory that's needed for the off-screen image, but the improvement in the quality of the animation is dramatic.

The MIDP implementation may provide double buffering by default. You can find out whether a Canvas is double buffered by calling the isDoubleBuffered() method.

If the implementation does not give you double buffering, you'll have to do it yourself. Fortunately, it's not terribly difficult. The process looks like this:

1. Create an off-screen image by calling the static Image.createImage(int width, int height) method.

2. Obtain a Graphics that draws *into the image* by calling getGraphics() on the Image.

3. Draw stuff into the off-screen image using the Graphics object.

4. In the paint() method of the Canvas, use drawImage() to put the off-screen image on the Canvas.

Here's a Canvas subclass that creates a simple off-screen image and displays it:

```
import javax.microedition.lcdui.*;

public class OffscreenCanvas
    extends Canvas {
  private Image mImage;
```

```
public void paint(Graphics g) {
  if (mImage == null)
    initialize();
  g.drawImage(mImage, 0, 0, Graphics.TOP | Graphics.LEFT);
}

private void initialize() {
  int w = getWidth();
  int h = getHeight();

  mImage = Image.createImage(w, h);

  Graphics g = mImage.getGraphics();

  g.drawRect(0, 0, w - 1, h - 1);
  g.drawLine(0, 0, w - 1, h - 1);
  g.drawLine(w - 1, 0, 0, h - 1);
  }
}
```

Multithreading and Animation

As with any graphic-interface toolkit, threading with the MIDP user-interface classes is a little tricky. The user-interface implementation has its own thread that handles both user-interface methods and screen painting. For example, when the user presses a key on their device, the implementation calls keyPressed() in your Canvas subclass. The thread that calls this method belongs to the MIDP implementation. As such, it should be handled with some care. In MIDP implementations, the same thread that calls event methods also calls paint().

NOTE *All event-driven user-interface toolkits have this idea of a system-owned user-interface thread. In AWT and Swing, it's called the* event dispatch thread. *The same rule applies: If you're running inside a thread that doesn't belong to you, don't take all day about it.*

Methods that are called by a thread that doesn't belong to you are *callbacks.* The rule of thumb for callbacks is that you shouldn't do anything that takes a long time. Since the thread doesn't belong to you, you shouldn't hold it up a long time performing your work. Because this thread is responsible for operating the user interface, holding it up with lengthy computations will make your application look lobotomized. Suppose, for example, that you had to retrieve some data from the network. In response to a Command, you might do something like this:

```
public void commandAction(Command c, Displayable s) {
  if (c == mNetworkCommand) {
    // Create a progress screen, progressScreen.
    mDisplay.setCurrent(progressForm);
    // Now do the network stuff.
    // Oops! Users never see progressScreen.
  }
  // ...
}
```

The problem is that the progress screen won't be shown. The commandAction() method is called from the user-interface thread, the same thread that's responsible for painting the screen. If you tie up this thread with some lengthy processing of your own, the user-interface thread never has a chance to update the screen. If you need to do something that takes a long time, create a separate thread for it. In the Jargoneer example in Chapter 2, for example, network access was performed in a separate thread.

In certain situations, you will need to ask the user-interface thread to execute code on your behalf. If you are showing an animation, for example, you'll want to make sure that the frames of the animation are properly synchronized with the repainting cycle. Otherwise, you're likely to end up showing frames that are partially drawn.

Display has a mechanism for executing your code in the user-interface thread. It has a method, callSerially(), that accepts a Runnable. When the user-interface thread is ready, meaning when it has finished servicing all repaint requests, it will execute the run() method of the Runnable from the user-interface thread. A typical animation, then, looks like this:

```
public class AnimationCanvas
    extends Canvas
    implements Runnable {
  public start() {
    run();
  }

public void paint(Graphics g) {
    // Paint a frame of the animation.
  }
```

```
public void run() {
  // Update our state.
  // Now request a paint of the new frame.
  repaint();
  Display.callSerially(this);
  }
}
```

You'd kick off the animation by calling start(), which in turn would simply call run(). Inside run(), we update our state and call repaint() to request the painting of a new frame. Then we use callSerially() to request that we get called again when the painting is done.

This technique results in an animation that runs as fast as the device allows. Many applications, however, need to provide a consistent experience across different devices. In these cases, it makes much more sense to use a separate animation thread with a consistent frame delay. The following example demonstrates this technique. It consists of two classes, Sweep and SweepCanvas. Sweep is a MIDlet that displays the class that actually implements the animation, SweepCanvas. The running SweepCanvas is shown in Figure 10-9.

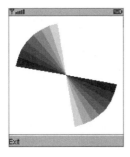

Figure 10-9. SweepCanvas *animation running on a grayscale emulator*

First, here's the source code for Sweep:

```
import javax.microedition.lcdui.*;
import javax.microedition.midlet.*;

public class Sweep
    extends MIDlet {
  public void startApp() {
    final SweepCanvas sweeper = new SweepCanvas();
    sweeper.start();
```

```
    sweeper.addCommand(new Command("Exit", Command.EXIT, 0));
    sweeper.setCommandListener(new CommandListener() {
      public void commandAction(Command c, Displayable s) {
        sweeper.stop();
        notifyDestroyed();
      }
    });

    Display.getDisplay(this).setCurrent(sweeper);
  }

  public void pauseApp() {}

  public void destroyApp(boolean unconditional) {}
}
```

And here's the code for SweepCanvas:

```
import javax.microedition.lcdui.*;

public class SweepCanvas
    extends Canvas
    implements Runnable {
  private boolean mTrucking;
  private int mTheta;
  private int mBorder;
  private int mDelay;

  public SweepCanvas() {
    mTheta = 0;
    mBorder = 10;
    mDelay = 50;
  }

  public void start() {
    mTrucking = true;
    Thread t = new Thread(this);
    t.start();
  }

  public void stop() {
    mTrucking = false;
  }
```

```
public void paint(Graphics g) {
  int width = getWidth();
  int height = getHeight();

  // Clear the Canvas.
  g.setGrayScale(255);
  g.fillRect(0, 0, width - 1, height - 1);

  int x = mBorder;
  int y = mBorder;
  int w = width - mBorder * 2;
  int h = height - mBorder * 2;
  for (int i = 0; i < 8; i++) {
    g.setGrayScale((8 - i) * 32 - 16);
    g.fillArc(x, y, w, h, mTheta + i * 10, 10);
    g.fillArc(x, y, w, h, (mTheta + 180) % 360 + i * 10, 10);
  }
}

public void run() {
  while (mTrucking) {
    mTheta = (mTheta + 1) % 360;
    repaint();
    try { Thread.sleep(mDelay); }
    catch (InterruptedException ie) {}
  }
}
}
```

The Game API in MIDP 2.0 offers another option for running an animation. In the next chapter, you'll see how Sweep's simple animation can be implemented using GameCanvas.

Summary

We've covered a lot of ground in this chapter. The Canvas class provides a low-level interface for games or other demanding applications. You can draw shapes, text, and images on a Canvas using the Graphics class. Furthermore, you can receive detailed input information about key and pointer events. Game actions are a simple generalized input method based on key events. Finally, you should understand the multithreading issues with repainting and event callbacks. Lengthy processing should be placed in a separate thread so that it doesn't bring the system-owned user-interface thread to a grinding halt. Animations can use Display's callSerially() method to synchronize with the user-interface thread, although more commonly they will be implemented using a separate animation thread. The next chapter details MIDP 2.0's new Game API.

CHAPTER 11

The Game API

MANY OF THE new features in MIDP 2.0 are aimed at making MIDP an attractive platform for games, which are the leading edge of consumer J2ME software. You've already read about some of the new goodies: RGB images and blitting in Canvas are two good examples. In the next chapter, you'll read about MIDP 2.0's support for multimedia. This chapter describes the new Game API, which simplifies writing 2D games.

Overview

The Game API builds on the Canvas and Graphics classes you read about in Chapter 10. The entire API is composed of five classes in the javax.microedition.lcdui.game package. One class, GameCanvas, provides methods for animation and key polling. The other four classes deal with *layers*, which can be used to compose scenes from several different elements.

GameCanvas offers two main advantages over Canvas. First, your application has control over exactly *when* the display is updated, instead of having to wait for the system software to call paint(). Second, you can control what region of the screen is updated. GameCanvas gives your application very specific control of display updates.

Driving Animation with GameCanvas

GameCanvas extends javax.microedition.lcdui.Canvas with methods for animation and key state polling. GameCanvas is used differently than Canvas:

- To use Canvas, you subclass it and define the paint() method. Inside paint(), you use a Graphics to render graphics on the screen. When you change something and want to update the screen, you call repaint() and the system calls paint() again for you.

- To use GameCanvas, you subclass it. To draw on the screen, you use the Graphics returned from getGraphics(). When you want updates to appear on the screen, call flushGraphics(), which does not return until the screen

is updated. For more specific updates, use the method
`flushGraphics(int x, int y, int width, int height)`, which
only updates a region of the screen.

```
public void flushGraphics(int x, int y, int width, int height)
```

GameCanvas's model of use makes it easy to use it inside a game loop like this:

```
Graphics g = getGraphics();
while(true) {
  // Check for user input.
  // Update game state.
  // Draw stuff using g.
  flushGraphics();
}
```

To subclass GameCanvas, you need to call its protected constructor from your
subclass's constructor. This constructor accepts a single boolean argument, which
indicates whether the normal key event mechanism should be suppressed for the
GameCanvas instance. The normal key event mechanism refers to the callback
mechanism of keyPressed(), keyReleased(), and keyRepeated(). Suppressing
the normal mechanism may result in better performance. GameCanvas provides
an alternate method for responding to key events, which is detailed in the next
section.

To show how GameCanvas works for drawing, I'll rewrite the SweepCanvas
example from Chapter 10 using GameCanvas. Note that the subclass no longer
overrides paint(). All the action happens in run(), which is executed in a separate
thread that drives the animation. The run() method calls render(), which does the
actual drawing (and is identical to the old paint()).

Listing 11-1. Using GameCanvas for Animation

```
import javax.microedition.lcdui.*;
import javax.microedition.lcdui.game.*;

public class SweepGameCanvas
    extends GameCanvas
    implements Runnable {
  private boolean mTrucking;
  private int mTheta;
  private int mBorder;
  private int mDelay;
```

```
  public SweepGameCanvas() {
    super(true);
    mTheta = 0;
    mBorder = 10;
    mDelay = 50;
  }

  public void start() {
    mTrucking = true;
    Thread t = new Thread(this);
    t.start();
  }

  public void stop() {
    mTrucking = false;
  }

  public void render(Graphics g) {
    int width = getWidth();
    int height = getHeight();

    // Clear the Canvas.
    g.setGrayScale(255);
    g.fillRect(0, 0, width - 1, height - 1);

    int x = mBorder;
    int y = mBorder;
    int w = width - mBorder * 2;
    int h = height - mBorder * 2;
    for (int i = 0; i < 8; i++) {
      g.setGrayScale((8 - i) * 32 - 16);
      g.fillArc(x, y, w, h, mTheta + i * 10, 10);
      g.fillArc(x, y, w, h, (mTheta + 180) % 360 + i * 10, 10);
    }
  }

  public void run() {
    Graphics g = getGraphics();
    while (mTrucking) {
      mTheta = (mTheta + 1) % 360;
      render(g);
      flushGraphics();
      try { Thread.sleep(mDelay); }
      catch (InterruptedException ie) {}
    }
  }
}
```

I'll assume you can write your own MIDlet to display SweepGameCanvas. If you've downloaded the online examples, SweepGame is a MIDlet that displays SweepGameCanvas.

Polling for Key States

GameCanvas offers an alternate method for responding to key presses, which are expected to be the way for the user to control the game. Instead of passively waiting for the key event callbacks defined in Canvas, GameCanvas offers a method that returns the current state of the keys:

```
public int getKeyStates()
```

This is attractive for games because it gives your application more control. Instead of waiting for the system to invoke the key callback methods in Canvas, you can immediately find out the state of the device keys.

The returned integer uses one bit to represent each of the nine game actions. A one bit indicates a key press, while a zero bit indicates no key press. Each of the bits is represented by a constant in the GameCanvas class as shown in Table 11-1.

Table 11-1. Game Action Bit Constants in GameCanvas

GAMECANVAS BIT CONSTANTS	CORRESPONDING CANVAS GAME ACTION CONSTANT
UP_PRESSED	UP
DOWN_PRESSED	DOWN
LEFT_PRESSED	LEFT
RIGHT_PRESSED	RIGHT
FIRE_PRESSED	FIRE
GAME_A_PRESSED	GAME_A
GAME_B_PRESSED	GAME_B
GAME_C_PRESSED	GAME_C
GAME_D_PRESSED	GAME_D

By grabbing the current state of the keys (a technique called *polling*), you can respond to user actions within the game loop instead of relying on the event callback methods, which run in a different thread. You could expand the example GameCanvas loop presented above as follows to respond to key presses:

```
Graphics g = getGraphics();
```

```
while(true) {
  // Check for user input.
  int ks = getKeyStates();
  if ((ks & UP_PRESSED) != 0)
    moveUp();
  else if ((ks & DOWN_PRESSED) != 0)
    moveDown();
  // ...

  // Update game state.
  // Draw stuff using g.
  flushGraphics();
}
```

If you're still paying attention, you're probably wondering what happens when the user presses and release a key between the times when your application calls getKeyStates(). The key states are *latched*, which means that a key press sets the corresponding bit and makes it stick until the next call to getKeyStates(). Every time you call getKeyStates(), the latched values are all cleared.

Understanding Layers

The rest of the Game API is devoted to *layers*. Layers are graphic elements that can be combined to create a complete scene. You might, for example, have a background of mountains, another background of city buildings, and several smaller items in the foreground: people, spaceships, cars, whatever.

The technique of combining layers resembles traditional hand-drawn animations. Background and foreground images are drawn on transparent cels, which are placed one on top of another and photographed to create the final scene.

In the Game API, an instance of the javax.microedition.lcdui.game.Layer class represents a layer. Layer is abstract, with two concrete subclasses. Layer itself is pretty straightforward. It has a location, a size, and can be visible or invisible. The location and size are accessed and modified with the following methods, which are self-explanatory:

```
public final int getX()
public final int getY()
public final int getWidth()
public final int getHeight()
public void setPosition(int x, int y)
```

Layer also offers a handy method for moving relative to the current position. Pass pixel offsets to the following method to adjust the position of the layer:

```
public void move(int dx, int dy)
```

The layer's visibility is accessed using getVisible() and setVisible().

The last method in Layer is paint(), which is declared abstract. Subclasses override this method to define their appearance.

Managing Layers

Before I tell you about Layer's concrete children, I'll explain how layers are put together to form a complete scene. You could do it yourself, maintaining a list of layers and drawing each of them using their paint() methods. Fortunately, the Game API includes LayerManager, a class that handles most of the details for you. To create a LayerManager, just call its no-argument constructor.

Most of LayerManager's job is keeping an ordered list of layers. Layers have an index, which indicates their position front to back. A position of 0 is on top, closest to the user, while larger indices are farther away, towards the bottom. (The order of layers is sometimes called the *z order*.)

Layers may be added to the bottom of the list using this method:

```
public void append(Layer l)
```

You can add a layer at a specific location using insert():

```
public void insert(Layer l, int index)
```

For example, you could add a layer to the top of the list by inserting a layer at index 0.

You can find the number of layers in the LayerManager by calling getSize(). If you'd like to retrieve the layer at a certain position, pass the index to the getLayerAt() method.

Finally, you can remove a layer by passing the Layer object to the remove() method.

LayerManager includes the concept of a *view window*, which is the rectangular portion of the scene that will be drawn. The assumption is that the overall scene is larger than the screen of the device, so only a portion will be drawn at any time. By default, the view window has its origin at 0, 0 and is as large as it can be

(Integer.MAX_VALUE for both width and height). You can set the view window using the following method, where the x and y coordinates are relative to the origin of the LayerManager.

```
public void setViewWindow(int x, int y, int width, int height)
```

To actually draw the scene represented by the LayerManager's layers, call the paint() method:

```
public void paint(Graphics g, int x, int y)
```

The view window of the scene will be drawn using the given Graphics at the specified location, which is specified in the coordinate system of the Graphics.

If you're still fuzzy on the relationship between a layer manager, its layers, and its view window, see the API documentation for LayerManager, which contains two very helpful figures.

Using Tiled Layers

A tiled layer is made from a palette of tiles, just as you might assemble decorative tiles to create a pretty design next to your bathtub. The tiles come from a single image that is divided into equal-sized pieces.

A TiledLayer is drawn on a Graphics object using the paint() method inherited from Layer. Like any other Layer, a tiled layer renders itself at its current location in the coordinate system of the Graphics. Furthermore, like any other Layer, a tiled layer can be part of a LayerManager and can be rendered automatically when the LayerManager is rendered using *its* paint() method.

For example, Figure 11-1 is 240 pixels wide and 96 pixels high.

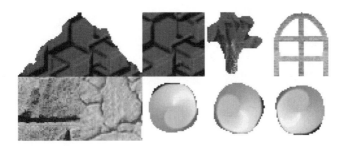

Figure 11-1. A source image for a tiled layer

The image can be divided into 10 square tiles, each with a width and height of 48 pixels. Tiles are numbered as shown in Figure 11-2.

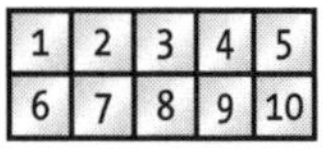

1	2	3	4	5
6	7	8	9	10

Figure 11-2. Tile numbering

The image could have been laid out several different ways to achieve the same result. Two of the other possibilities are shown in Figure 11-3.

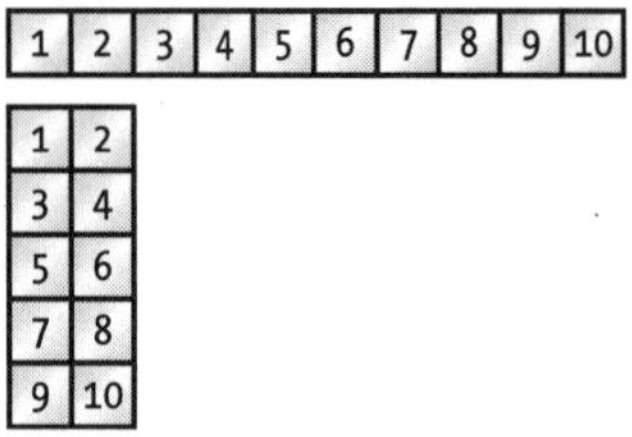

1	2	3	4	5	6	7	8	9	10

1	2
3	4
5	6
7	8
9	10

Figure 11-3. Other tile image layouts

Note that tile indices are numbered starting at one, while row and column numbers start at zero.

The tiled layer itself is a grid of *cells*, where each cell is occupied by one tile. You specify the number of rows and columns in the tiled layer at construction. The exact size of a tiled layer is as follows:

```
width = [number of columns] x [tile width]
height = [number of rows] x [tile height]
```

Creating and Initializing a TiledLayer

To create a TiledLayer, supply the number of columns and rows, the source image, and the tile dimensions to the constructor:

```
public TiledLayer(int columns, int rows,
    Image image, int tileWidth, int tileHeight)
```

The image and tile dimensions describe a *static tile set.* You can change the static tile set on an existing TiledLayer with the following method:

```
public void setStaticTileSet(Image image, int tileWidth, int tileHeight)
```

The number of columns and rows in a TiledLayer can be retrieved with getColumns() and getRows(). To retrieve the tile dimensions, use getCellWidth() and getCellHeight(). (Although the method naming isn't quite consistent, this works because the pixel size of each cell is the same as the pixel size of the tiles.)

A TiledLayer is empty when you first create it. To assign a tile to a cell, use this method:

```
public void setCell(int col, int row, int tileIndex)
```

All the cells in the TiledLayer are initially filled with tile index 0, which indicates a blank tile. You can retrieve the tile index of a particular cell by passing its column and row number to getCell(). If you would like to assign the same tile to a range of cells, use the fillCells() method:

```
public void fillCells(int col, int row, int numCols, int numRows,
    int tileIndex)
```

The col, row, numCols, and numRows parameters describe a rectangular region of cells that will be filled with the specified tile. For example, fillCells(2, 0, 1, 2, 6) would assign tile 6 to the cells in the first and second rows of the third column of the tiled layer.

The following excerpt (adapted from *QuatschCanvas.java* in the source code download for this book, available from http://www.apress.com/) demonstrates one way to create and initialize a TiledLayer.

```
Image backgroundImage = Image.createImage("/background_tiles.png");
TiledLayer background = new TiledLayer(8, 4, backgroundImage, 48, 48);
background.setPosition(12, 0);
int[] map = {
  1, 2, 0, 0, 0, 0, 0, 0,
  3, 3, 2, 0, 0, 0, 5, 0,
  3, 3, 3, 2, 4, 1, 3, 2,
  6, 6, 6, 6, 6, 6, 6, 6
};
for (int i = 0; i < map.length; i++) {
  int column = i % 8;
  int row = (i - column) / 8;
  background.setCell(column, row, map[i]);
}
```

Using the source image of Figure 11-1, this code produces the tiled layer shown in Figure 11-4.

Figure 11-4. A tiled layer

You now know almost everything there is to know about TiledLayer; it serves as a simple map between a palette of tiles and a fully assembled layer.

Using Animated Tiles

There is one additional wrinkle, *animated* tiles. An animated tile is a virtual tile whose mapping can be changed at runtime. Although you could accomplish the same thing by calling setCell() on all the cells you wanted to change, using an animated tile allows you to make a single call that changes all the affected cells.

To use an animated tile, you create one by calling this method:

```
public int createAnimatedTile(int staticTileIndex)
```

You pass a regular tile index to the method, which is the initial tile that should be used for the animated tile. The method returns a special animated tile index. (There's no magic here; it's just a negative number.)

To assign an animated tile to a cell, pass the return value from createAnimatedTile() to setCell(). When you want to change the contents of an animated tile, use the following method:

```
public void setAnimatedTile(int animatedTileIndex, int staticTileIndex)
```

This assigns the supplied tile index to the animated tile. All cells that have the supplied animated tile will now display the given tile.

If you need to retrieve the current tile associated with an animated tile, just pass the animated tile index to getAnimatedTile().

Using Sprites

While a TiledLayer uses a palette of tiles to fill a large area, a Sprite uses a palette of tiles to animate a layer that is the same size as a single tile. Usually a sprite represents one of the protagonists in a game. In Sprite parlance, tiles are called *frames* instead. As with a TiledLayer, a Sprite is created from a source image that is divided into equally sized frames.

```
public Sprite(Image image, int frameWidth, int frameHeight)
```

There's also a special case if the image contains just one frame, in which case it will not be animated:

```
public Sprite(Image image)
```

Interestingly, a Sprite cannot be created from separate frame images; the frames must be packed into a single source image.

If you want to change the source image after the Sprite is created, use setImage():

```
public void setImage(Image img, int frameWidth, int frameHeight)
```

The total number of frames contained in the Sprite is returned from getRawFrameCount().

Like any other Layer, Sprites are rendered when the paint() method is called. Usually the Sprite will belong to a LayerManager, in which case it is rendered automatically when the LayerManager is rendered.

Animating Sprites

Sprite animation is all about *frame sequences*. When a Sprite is created, it has a default frame sequence that includes every frame in the source image. For example, consider the source image for a fictional character named Dr. Quatsch, shown in Figure 11-5.

Figure 11-5. A sprite source image

This image is 192 × 48 pixels. If it is created with a 48 × 48-pixel frame size, there are four frames. The default frame sequence is { 0, 1, 2, 3 }. Note that frame indices are numbered starting at zero, while tile indices (in the TiledLayer class) were numbered starting at one.

In the image above, the first three frames represent Dr. Quatsch running, while the fourth is a frame that shows him standing still. The following method changes the current frame sequence:

```
public void setFrameSequence(int[] sequence)
```

For example, the following code shows how you could create a new Sprite and set its frame sequence to only include the running frames:

```
int[] runningSequence = { 0, 1, 2 };
Image quatschImage = Image.createImage("/quatsch.png");
Sprite quatsch = new Sprite(quatschImage, 48, 48);
quatsch.setFrameSequence(runningSequence);
```

Sprite provides several methods for navigating through the frame sequence. The animation doesn't happen automatically; your application needs to tell the Sprite when it's time to move to the next frame in the sequence. Usually this is accomplished in a separate thread, most likely as part of the animation thread. To move forward and backward in the sequence, use nextFrame() and prevFrame(). These methods do what you'd expect at the ends of the sequence, wrapping around to the next value. For example, using the frame sequence of { 0, 1, 2 }, if the Sprite's current frame is 2 and you call nextFrame(), the current frame will be set to 0.

You can jump directly to a particular frame using this method:

```
public void setFrame(int sequenceIndex)
```

Note that this method accepts a sequence index. If the Sprite's frame sequence was { 2, 3, 1, 9 }, then calling setFrame(1) would result in the Sprite's current frame being set to 3.

Nothing happens visually when you adjust the Sprite's current frame. Changes will only be visible the next time the Sprite is rendered using its paint() method. Typically, this will be at the end of your animation loop if you are using GameCanvas.

To find out the current frame sequence index, call getFrame(). Don't get confused here; the method does not return a frame index, but the current index in the current frame sequence. Interestingly, there is no getFrameSequence() method, so if you haven't saved the current frame sequence, there's no way to find out the current frame index. You can, however, retrieve the number of elements in the current frame sequence using getFrameSequenceLength().

Transforming Sprites

You may have noticed that the frames shown in Figure 11-5 only show Dr. Quatsch facing left. What if he's going to run to the right? Sprite includes support for *transformations* so that you can use the API to generate additional frames that are simple transformations of existing frames. The following method applies a transformation to a Sprite:

```
public void setTransform(int transform)
```

The transform argument can be any of the constant values defined in the Sprite class:

```
TRANS_NONE
TRANS_ROT90
TRANS_ROT180
TRANS_ROT270
TRANS_MIRROR
TRANS_MIRROR_ROT90
TRANS_MIRROR_ROT180
TRANS_MIRROR_ROT270
```

To make Dr. Quatsch face right instead of left, you would apply a TRANS_MIRROR transformation. To understand all the transformations, see the Sprite API documentation, which contains a set of fighter plane images that are very helpful.

The only tricky part about transformations is the *reference pixel*. All Sprites have a reference pixel, which is expressed in the Sprite's own coordinate space; by default, the reference pixel is located at 0, 0, the upper-left corner of the Sprite. When the Sprite is transformed, the reference pixel is also transformed.

When a transformation is applied, the Sprite's position is changed so that the current location of the reference pixel does not change, even after it is transformed. For example, Figure 11-6 shows how the position of the Sprite changes when a simple TRANS_MIRROR transformation is applied.

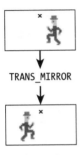

TRANS_MIRROR

Figure 11-6. The reference pixel doesn't move.

Suppose, for example, that the original position of the Sprite was 100, 100 (in the coordinate system of the container), and the reference pixel position was 0, 0 (in the coordinate system of the Sprite). After applying a TRANS_MIRROR rotation, the Sprite's position is adjusted so that the transformed reference pixel is in the same location as the original reference pixel. Because the frame width is 48 pixels, the Sprite's position (its upper-left corner) changes from 100, 100 to 52, 100.

To adjust the location of the reference point in the Sprite's untransformed coordinate system, use this method:

```
public void defineReferencePixel(int x, int y)
```

In the case of Dr. Quatsch, I want to apply a mirror transformation without having the Sprite move, so I set the reference pixel to be at the center of the 48 × 48 frame:

```
// Sprite quatsch is defined as before.
quatsch.defineReferencePixel(24, 24);
```

To find the current location of the Sprite's reference pixel in its containing coordinate system, use getRefPixelX() and getRefPixelY(). Don't get confused: defineReferencePixel() accepts coordinates relative to the Sprite's origin, while getRefPixelX() and getRefPixelY() return values relative to the Sprite's container.

It's also possible to set the position of the Sprite based on its reference point. You already know you can set the position of the Sprite's upper-left corner using the setPosition() method that is inherited from Layer, but the following method sets the current position of the Sprite's reference point:

```
public void setRefPointPosition(int x, int y)
```

This is more convenient than it might appear at first, as it allows you to place the reference point at a specific position, regardless of the current transformation.

Handling Collisions

Sprite provides methods to answer critical questions that come up in games—did the bullet hit the spaceship? Is Dr. Quatsch standing in front of the door?
The Game API supports two techniques for collision detection.

1. The implementation can compare rectangles representing a sprite and another sprite. A collision has occurred if the rectangles intersect. This is a quick way to test for collisions, but it may produce inaccurate results for non-rectangular shapes.

2. The implementation can compare each pixel of the sprite and another sprite. If an opaque pixel in the sprite overlaps an opaque pixel in the other sprite, a collision has occurred. This technique involves more computation but produces a more accurate result.

A Sprite has a *collision rectangle* that is used for collision detection. It is defined in the coordinate system of the Sprite itself, like the reference pixel. By default, the collision rectangle is located at 0, 0 and is the same width and height as the Sprite. You can change the collision rectangle using this method:

```
public void defineCollisionRectangle(int x, int y, int width, int height);
```

The collision rectangle serves two purposes. If pixel-level collision detection is not used, the collision rectangle is used to determine collisions. If pixel-level collision detection is used, then only pixels inside the collision rectangle are examined.
Sprite is capable of detecting collisions with other Sprites, TiledLayers, and Images.

```
public final boolean collidesWith(Sprite s, boolean pixelLevel)
public final boolean collidesWith(TiledLayer t, boolean pixelLevel)
public final boolean collidesWith(Image image,
    int x, int y, boolean pixelLevel)
```

The semantics of each method are subtly different, as described in Table 11-1.

Table 11-1. Collision Detection with Sprite

TARGET	INTERSECTING RECTANGLE	PIXEL LEVEL
Sprite	Compares collision rectangles	Compares pixels inside the collision rectangles
TiledLayer	Compares the Sprite's collision rectangle and tiles in the TiledLayer	Compares pixels inside the Sprite's collision rectangle with pixels in the TiledLayer
Image	Compares the Sprite's collision rectangle and the Image's bounds	Compares pixels inside the Sprite's collision rectangle with pixels in the Image

Copying Sprites

Sprite includes a copy constructor:

```
public Sprite(Sprite s)
```

This is more powerful than you might think. It creates a new Sprite with all of the attributes of the original, including

- Source image frames

- Frame sequence

- Current frame

- Current transformation

- Reference pixel

- Collision rectangle

Putting It All Together

QuatschCanvas, shown in Listing 11-2, is an example that showcases many of the features of the Game API. Although it looks long, it's broken into manageable methods and demonstrates quite a few features of the Game API:

- Using an animation loop in GameCanvas

- Polling for key state using GameCanvas

- Using a LayerManager to maintain multiple layers

- Creating a Sprite and TiledLayers

- Animating a Sprite, including changing frame sequences and transformations

- Using an animated tile in a TiledLayer

A corresponding MIDlet, QuatschMIDlet, is available in the code download but not presented here. It creates and displays a QuatschCanvas and provides commands for showing and hiding the layers.

Figure 11-7 shows QuatschMIDlet running in the emulator.

Figure 11-7. The whole iguana: sprites and tiled layers

Listing 11-2 contains the source code for QuatschCanvas.

Listing 11-2. QuatschCanvas, *a Game API Example*

```
import java.io.IOException;

import javax.microedition.lcdui.*;
import javax.microedition.lcdui.game.*;

public class QuatschCanvas
    extends GameCanvas
    implements Runnable {
  private boolean mTrucking;

  private LayerManager mLayerManager;

  private TiledLayer mAtmosphere;
  private TiledLayer mBackground;
  private int mAnimatedIndex;

  private Sprite mQuatsch;
  private int mState, mDirection;

  private static final int kStanding = 1;
  private static final int kRunning = 2;

  private static final int kLeft = 1;
  private static final int kRight = 2;

  private static final int[] kRunningSequence = { 0, 1, 2 };
  private static final int[] kStandingSequence = { 3 };

  public QuatschCanvas(String quatschImageName,
      String atmosphereImageName, String backgroundImageName)
      throws IOException {
    super(true);

    // Create a LayerManager.
    mLayerManager = new LayerManager();
    int w = getWidth();
    int h = getHeight();
    mLayerManager.setViewWindow(96, 0, w, h);
```

```
        createBackground(backgroundImageName);
        createAtmosphere(atmosphereImageName);
        createQuatsch(quatschImageName);
    }

    private void createBackground(String backgroundImageName)
        throws IOException {
      // Create the tiled layer.
      Image backgroundImage = Image.createImage(backgroundImageName);
      int[] map = {
        1, 2, 0, 0, 0, 0, 0, 0,
        3, 3, 2, 0, 0, 0, 5, 0,
        3, 3, 3, 2, 4, 1, 3, 2,
        6, 6, 6, 6, 6, 6, 6, 6
      };
      mBackground = new TiledLayer(8, 4, backgroundImage, 48, 48);
      mBackground.setPosition(12, 0);
      for (int i = 0; i < map.length; i++) {
        int column = i % 8;
        int row = (i - column) / 8;
        mBackground.setCell(column, row, map[i]);
      }
      mAnimatedIndex = mBackground.createAnimatedTile(8);
      mBackground.setCell(3, 0, mAnimatedIndex);
      mBackground.setCell(5, 0, mAnimatedIndex);
      mLayerManager.append(mBackground);
    }

    private void createAtmosphere(String atmosphereImageName)
        throws IOException {
      // Create the atmosphere layer
      Image atmosphereImage = Image.createImage(atmosphereImageName);
      mAtmosphere = new TiledLayer(8, 1, atmosphereImage,
          atmosphereImage.getWidth(), atmosphereImage.getHeight());
      mAtmosphere.fillCells(0, 0, 8, 1, 1);
      mAtmosphere.setPosition(0, 96);
      mLayerManager.insert(mAtmosphere, 0);
    }

    private void createQuatsch(String quatschImageName)
        throws IOException {
```

```
  // Create the sprite.
  Image quatschImage = Image.createImage(quatschImageName);
  mQuatsch = new Sprite(quatschImage, 48, 48);
  mQuatsch.setPosition(96 + (getWidth() - 48) / 2, 96);
  mQuatsch.defineReferencePixel(24, 24);
  setDirection(kLeft);
  setState(kStanding);
  mLayerManager.insert(mQuatsch, 1);
}

public void start() {
  mTrucking = true;
  Thread t = new Thread(this);
  t.start();
}

public void run() {
  int w = getWidth();
  int h = getHeight();
  Graphics g = getGraphics();
  int frameCount = 0;
  int factor = 2;
  int animatedDelta = 0;

  while (mTrucking) {
    if (isShown()) {
      int keyStates = getKeyStates();
      if ((keyStates & LEFT_PRESSED) != 0) {
        setDirection(kLeft);
        setState(kRunning);
        mBackground.move(3, 0);
        mAtmosphere.move(3, 0);
        mQuatsch.nextFrame();
      }
      else if ((keyStates & RIGHT_PRESSED) != 0) {
        setDirection(kRight);
        setState(kRunning);
        mBackground.move(-3, 0);
        mAtmosphere.move(-3, 0);
        mQuatsch.nextFrame();
      }
      else {
        setState(kStanding);
      }
```

```
        frameCount++;
        if (frameCount % factor == 0) {
          int delta = 1;
          if (frameCount / factor < 10) delta = -1;
          mAtmosphere.move(delta, 0);
          if (frameCount / factor == 20) frameCount = 0;

          mBackground.setAnimatedTile(mAnimatedIndex,
              8 + animatedDelta++);
          if (animatedDelta == 3) animatedDelta = 0;
        }

        g.setColor(0x5b1793);
        g.fillRect(0, 0, w, h);

        mLayerManager.paint(g, 0, 0);

        flushGraphics();
      }

      try { Thread.sleep(80); }
      catch (InterruptedException ie) {}
    }
  }

  public void stop() {
    mTrucking = false;
  }

  public void setVisible(int layerIndex, boolean show) {
    Layer layer = mLayerManager.getLayerAt(layerIndex);
    layer.setVisible(show);
  }

  public boolean isVisible(int layerIndex) {
    Layer layer = mLayerManager.getLayerAt(layerIndex);
    return layer.isVisible();
  }
```

```
  private void setDirection(int newDirection) {
    if (newDirection == mDirection) return;
    if (mDirection == kLeft)
      mQuatsch.setTransform(Sprite.TRANS_MIRROR);
    else if (mDirection == kRight)
      mQuatsch.setTransform(Sprite.TRANS_NONE);
    mDirection = newDirection;
  }

  private void setState(int newState) {
    if (newState == mState) return;
    switch (newState) {
      case kStanding:
        mQuatsch.setFrameSequence(kStandingSequence);
        mQuatsch.setFrame(0);
        break;
      case kRunning:
        mQuatsch.setFrameSequence(kRunningSequence);
        break;
      default:
        break;
    }
    mState = newState;
  }
}
```

Special Effects

Although they are not strictly contained in the Game API, two other methods in
the Display class are closely related:

```
public boolean flashBacklight(int duration)
public boolean vibrate(int duration)
```

Both methods accept a duration in milliseconds that specifies how long
the backlight should be turned on or how long the device should vibrate. Both
methods return true to indicate success or false if the device does not support a
backlight or vibration (or if your application is not running in the foreground).

Summary

This chapter described MIDP 2.0's Game API, a set of classes that simplify developing two-dimensional games. The GameCanvas class provides a drawing surface that can easily be rendered in a game thread. GameCanvas also provides key state polling, also useful for detecting user input in a game thread. The remainder of the Game API is based on layers, which are elements that can be combined to create complex scenes. LayerManager makes it easy to maintain multiple layers. The Sprite class supports animation and collision detection. Large scenes or backgrounds can be constructed efficiently using TiledLayer. Finally, MIDP 2.0's Display includes methods for controlling the backlight and vibration of a device. Game developers have a lot to be happy about. Read on to the next chapter for more good news about MIDP 2.0's sound capabilities.

CHAPTER 12

Sound and Music

MIDP 2.0 INCLUDES basic audio capabilities. The media APIs in MIDP 2.0 are a strict subset of the Mobile Media API (MMAPI), a more general API for multimedia rendering. For full details on MMAPI, see the specification here:

```
http://jcp.org/jsr/detail/135.jsp
```

The MMAPI itself is kind of a pint-sized version of the Java Media Framework (JMF), which is an optional package for J2SE. More information on the JMF is available here:

```
http://java.sun.com/products/java-media/jmf/
```

The subset of the MMAPI that is included in MIDP 2.0 is called the Audio Building Block (ABB). It includes the capability to play simple tones and sampled audio. The ABB is implemented in the javax.microedition.media and javax.microedition.media.control packages. This chapter begins with a rush of runnable code, and then backs off to explain some of the concepts and dig into the APIs more carefully.

Quick Start

You can play tones by calling this method in javax.microedition.media.Manager:

```
public static void playTone(int note, int duration, int volume)
```

In this method, note is specified just like a MIDI note, where each integer corresponds to a single key on a piano keyboard. Middle C is 60, and the A above middle C (a 440 Hz tone) is 69. The duration is in milliseconds, and volume can range from 0, silent, to 100, loudest.

Like most other methods in the ABB, playTone() may throw a MediaException. Although support for simple tones is required by the specification, the device may be temporarily unable to play tones. (For example, a mobile phone might be using the tone generation hardware to ring the phone.)

Figure 12-1 shows PianoCanvas, an example that displays a simple piano keyboard and allows the user to navigate through the keys to play different tones.
PianoCanvas is presented in Listing 12-1. The code for playing the tones is very
compact, consisting solely of a call to playTone() in the keyPressed() method.
The rest of the code is devoted to the user interface.

Figure 12-1. An itty bitty piano

Listing 12-1. PianoCanvas *Source Code*

```
import javax.microedition.lcdui.*;
import javax.microedition.media.*;

public class PianoCanvas
    extends Canvas {
  private static final int[] kNoteX = {
    0, 11, 16, 29, 32, 48, 59, 64, 76, 80, 93, 96
  };

  private static final int[] kNoteWidth = {
    16,  8, 16,  8, 16, 16,  8, 16,  8, 16,  8, 16
  };

  private static final int[] kNoteHeight = {
    96, 64, 96, 64, 96, 96, 64, 96, 64, 96, 64, 96
  };

  private static final boolean[] kBlack = {
    false, true, false, true, false,
        false, true, false, true, false, true, false
  };

  private int mMiddleCX, mMiddleCY;
```

```
  private int mCurrentNote;

  public PianoCanvas() {
    int w = getWidth();
    int h = getHeight();

    int fullWidth = kNoteWidth[0] * 8;
    mMiddleCX = (w - fullWidth) / 2;
    mMiddleCY = (h - kNoteHeight[0]) / 2;

    mCurrentNote = 60;
  }

  public void paint(Graphics g) {
    int w = getWidth();
    int h = getHeight();

    g.setColor(0xffffff);
    g.fillRect(0, 0, w, h);
    g.setColor(0x000000);

    for (int i = 60; i <= 72; i++)
      drawNote(g, i);

    drawSelection(g, mCurrentNote);
  }

  private void drawNote(Graphics g, int note) {
    int n = note % 12;
    int octaveOffset = ((note - n) / 12 - 5) * 7 * kNoteWidth[0];
    int x = mMiddleCX + octaveOffset + kNoteX[n];
    int y = mMiddleCY;
    int w = kNoteWidth[n];
    int h = kNoteHeight[n];

    if (isBlack(n))
      g.fillRect(x, y, w, h);
    else
      g.drawRect(x, y, w, h);
  }

  private void drawSelection(Graphics g, int note) {
    int n = note % 12;
    int octaveOffset = ((note - n) / 12 - 5) * 7 * kNoteWidth[0];
```

```
      int x = mMiddleCX + octaveOffset + kNoteX[n];
      int y = mMiddleCY;
      int w = kNoteWidth[n];
      int h = kNoteHeight[n];

      int sw = 6;
      int sx = x + (w - sw) / 2;
      int sy = y + h - 8;
      g.setColor(0xffffff);
      g.fillRect(sx, sy, sw, sw);
      g.setColor(0x000000);
      g.drawRect(sx, sy, sw, sw);
      g.drawLine(sx, sy, sx + sw, sy + sw);
      g.drawLine(sx, sy + sw, sx + sw, sy);
    }

    private boolean isBlack(int note) {
      return kBlack[note];
    }

    public void keyPressed(int keyCode) {
      int action = getGameAction(keyCode);
      switch (action) {
        case LEFT:
          mCurrentNote--;
          if (mCurrentNote < 60)
            mCurrentNote = 60;
          repaint();
          break;
        case RIGHT:
          mCurrentNote++;
          if (mCurrentNote > 72)
            mCurrentNote = 72;
          repaint();
          break;
        case FIRE:
          try { Manager.playTone(mCurrentNote, 1000, 100); }
          catch (MediaException me) {}
          break;
        default:
          break;
      }
    }
  }
```

The ABB also offers support for playing sampled audio files, although the specification does not require support for this feature. To play sampled audio, you just need to get a Player for the data you wish to hear, then start the Player running. You can get a Player by asking Manager for one. In its simplest form, playing sampled audio data looks like this:

```
URL url = "http://65.215.221.148:8080/wj2/res/relax.wav";
Player p = Manager.createPlayer(url);
p.start();
```

In this approach, the web server provides the content type of the data. Another approach is to obtain an InputStream to the audio data, then create a Player by telling Manager the content type of the data. This is handy for reading audio files that are stored as resources in the MIDlet suite JAR. For example:

```
InputStream in = getClass().getResourceAsStream("/relax.wav");
Player player = Manager.createPlayer(in, "audio/x-wav");
player.start();
```

Listing 12-2 is a simple MIDlet that demonstrates both techniques.

Listing 12-2. Playing Audio Files

```
import java.io.*;

import javax.microedition.io.*;
import javax.microedition.lcdui.*;
import javax.microedition.midlet.*;
import javax.microedition.media.*;

public class AudioMIDlet
    extends MIDlet
    implements CommandListener, Runnable {
  private Display mDisplay;
  private List mMainScreen;

  public void startApp() {
    mDisplay = Display.getDisplay(this);

    if (mMainScreen == null) {
      mMainScreen = new List("AudioMIDlet", List.IMPLICIT);
```

```
      mMainScreen.append("Via HTTP", null);
      mMainScreen.append("From resource", null);
      mMainScreen.addCommand(new Command("Exit", Command.EXIT, 0));
      mMainScreen.addCommand(new Command("Play", Command.SCREEN, 0));
      mMainScreen.setCommandListener(this);
    }

    mDisplay.setCurrent(mMainScreen);
  }

  public void pauseApp() {}

  public void destroyApp(boolean unconditional) {}

  public void commandAction(Command c, Displayable s) {
    if (c.getCommandType() == Command.EXIT) notifyDestroyed();
    else {
      Form waitForm = new Form("Loading...");
      mDisplay.setCurrent(waitForm);
      Thread t = new Thread(this);
      t.start();
    }
  }

  public void run() {
    String selection = mMainScreen.getString(
        mMainScreen.getSelectedIndex());
    boolean viaHttp = selection.equals("Via HTTP");

    if (viaHttp)
      playViaHttp();
    else
      playFromResource();
  }

  private void playViaHttp() {
    try {
      String url = getAppProperty("AudioMIDlet-URL");
      Player player = Manager.createPlayer(url);
      player.start();
    }
    catch (Exception e) {
      showException(e);
      return;
```

```
      }
      mDisplay.setCurrent(mMainScreen);
    }

    private void playFromResource() {
      try {
        InputStream in = getClass().getResourceAsStream("/relax.wav");
        Player player = Manager.createPlayer(in, "audio/x-wav");
        player.start();
      }
      catch (Exception e) {
        showException(e);
        return;
      }
      mDisplay.setCurrent(mMainScreen);
    }

    private void showException(Exception e) {
      Alert a = new Alert("Exception", e.toString(), null, null);
      a.setTimeout(Alert.FOREVER);
      mDisplay.setCurrent(a, mMainScreen);
    }
}
```

MIDP 2.0 Media Concepts

Audio data comes in a variety of *content types*. A content type is really just a file format, a specification that tells how each bit in the data contributes to the resulting sound. Common audio content types are MP3, AIFF, and WAV. In the MIDP 2.0 ABB, content types are specified using MIME types, which use a string to specify a primary and secondary type. For example, the MIME type for WAV audio is "audio/x-wav".

The content type tells how to translate bits into sound, but that's only half the battle. A *protocol* specifies how to get the data from its original location to the place where it will be rendered. You could use HTTP, for example, to transfer audio data from a server to a MIDP device.

In the ABB, a Player knows how to render audio data with a particular content type, while an associated *data source* handles transporting the data to the Player. In the Mobile Media API, the abstract DataSource class represents data sources. In the MIDP 2.0 ABB, data sources are not explicitly available, but implicitly associated with a Player. The path of the audio information is illustrated in Figure 12-2.

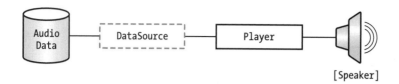

Figure 12-2. Audio data path

Manager doles out Players for content types and protocols requested via its createPlayer() methods. One or more *controls* may be associated with a Player to specify playback parameters like volume. In the ABB, javax.microedition.media.Control is an interface representing a control, while the javax.microedition.media.control package contains more specific subinterfaces. The relationship between the classes is shown in Figure 12-3.

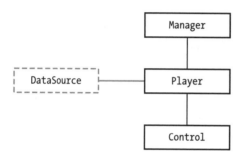

Figure 12-3. Class relationships

Supported Content Types and Protocols

One of the least understood aspects of the ABB is its supported content types. MIDP 2.0 is very flexible about the content types and protocols an implementation may support. All the specification says is that if sampled audio is supported at all, then 8-bit PCM WAV must be supported. Beyond that, the sky's the limit.

If you do ask Manager for data or a protocol that it can't handle, a MediaException will be thrown.

You can find out, at runtime, what content types and protocols are supported using two methods in the Manager class:

```
public static String getSupportedContentTypes(String protocol)
public static String getSupportedProtocols(String content_type)
```

You can find out the content types for a given protocol, or the protocols for a given content. If you supply null to either of these methods, you'll get a complete list of supported content types or protocols.

The MIDlet in Listing 12-3 finds all supported content types and prints out the corresponding protocols for each.

Listing 12-3. Examining Content Types and Protocols at Runtime

```java
import javax.microedition.lcdui.*;
import javax.microedition.midlet.*;
import javax.microedition.media.*;

public class MediaInformationMIDlet
    extends MIDlet
    implements CommandListener {
  private Form mInformationForm;

  public void startApp() {
    if (mInformationForm == null) {
      mInformationForm =
          new Form("Content types and protocols");
      String[] contentTypes =
          Manager.getSupportedContentTypes(null);
      for (int i = 0; i < contentTypes.length; i++) {
        String[] protocols =
            Manager.getSupportedProtocols(contentTypes[i]);
        for (int j = 0; j < protocols.length; j++) {
          StringItem si = new StringItem(contentTypes[i] + ": ",
              protocols[j]);
          si.setLayout(Item.LAYOUT_NEWLINE_AFTER);
          mInformationForm.append(si);
        }
      }
      Command exitCommand = new Command("Exit", Command.EXIT, 0);
      mInformationForm.addCommand(exitCommand);
      mInformationForm.setCommandListener(this);
    }
```

```
        Display.getDisplay(this).setCurrent(mInformationForm);
    }

    public void pauseApp() {}

    public void destroyApp(boolean unconditional) {}

    public void commandAction(Command c, Displayable s) {
        notifyDestroyed();
    }
}
```

Figure 12-4 shows the results if you run `MediaInformationMIDlet` on the J2ME Wireless Toolkit emulator (in the 2.0 beta 2 release). There are three things to understand about this list:

1. HTTP is a file transfer protocol, not a streaming media protocol. If you specify a media file with HTTP, the whole file will be downloaded before playback begins. By contrast, some devices may support real streaming protocols like RTP (see `http://www.ietf.org/rfc/rfc1889.txt`).

2. The "audio/x-tone-seq" content type is not really sampled audio; it's a special case for tone sequences, which I'll describe soon.

3. The list includes some features and content types (video, MIDI, audio capture) from the wireless toolkit's MMAPI implementation. If you want to see a bare-bones list of supported content types and protocols, turn off the MMAPI support as described near the end of this chapter.

Figure 12-4. `MediaInformationMIDlet` *running on the toolkit's 2.0 beta2 emulator*

To find out the content type of an existing `Player`, just call `getContentType()`.

Player Life Cycle

Because playing audio may use scarce resources on a MIDP device, and because sampled audio files are relatively large, Player has a detailed life cycle that allows its behavior to be closely controlled. The life cycle is described in terms of *states*, represented by constants in the Player interface. The usual order of states in the Player's life cycle is as follows:

A Player begins its life as UNREALIZED. This means that a Player implementation has been created, but it hasn't tried to find the audio data it's supposed to render, and it hasn't tried to acquire resources like the audio hardware.

A Player becomes REALIZED after it locates the media data, for example by initiating a network connection and sending headers.

The next state, PREFETCHED, means the Player has done everything else it needed to do to get ready to start rendering audio. This might include obtaining control of the audio hardware, filling up buffers, or other operations.

When the Player has begun rendering audio data, it is in the STARTED state.

One final state, CLOSED, indicates that the Player has released all resources, shut down all network connections, and cannot be used again.

Player contains a corresponding set of methods that move from state to state:

```
public void prefetch()
public void realize()
public void start()
```

These methods work as you'd expect, for the most part. If you skip a step, the intervening states are implied. In the example above, I call start() on a freshly created Player, which implies calls to prefetch() and realize().

If anything goes wrong with locating the media data or acquiring system resources, these methods throw a MediaException.

Several other methods allow for backward state transitions, although their names are not as intuitive. The stop() method takes a STARTED Player back to PREFETCHED. The deallocate() method moves a PREFETCHED or STARTED Player back to the REALIZED state by releasing resources. The deallocate() method has one additional wrinkle; it will take an UNREALIZED Player that is stuck trying to locate its media (in the middle of realize()) back to the UNREALIZED state.

Finally, the close() method moves a Player in any state to CLOSED. All resources are released, all network connections are closed, and the Player cannot be used again.

You may retrieve the Player's current state by calling getState().

Now that you understand Player's life cycle, you can probably imagine ways to improve on the simple AudioMIDlet presented above. You might, for example, call prefetch() on the newly created Player to ensure that playback could begin as soon as possible after the user selects the **Play** command. You might not have noticed much of delay, but a real device will perform much slower:

- Your desktop computer running the emulator has a lot more processing power and memory than a MIDP device.

- The emulator on your desktop probably has a much faster network connection than a real MIDP device.

- The file *relax.wav* that is used by AudioMIDlet is very small (1530 bytes). A larger media file would produce more noticeable delays.

As with network and persistent storage operations, any time-consuming operations with a Player should be performed in a thread that is separate from the user interface thread. Although the start() method does not block, both realize() and prefetch() will not return until they have finished their potentially slow work.

Controlling Players

A Player's *media time* is its current position in the audio playback. For example, a Player that is halfway through a 4-second audio clip would have a media time of 2,000,000 microseconds. If you want to jump to a particular point in an audio clip, call setMediaTime(). You can find out the current media time using getMediaTime(). The total time represented by the audio clip is returned from getDuration(). For some types of streaming media, the duration cannot be determined, in which case the special value TIME_UNKNOWN will be returned.

Players can also loop, which means the audio clip is played over and over again. You can control this behavior by calling setLoopCount() before the Player is started. Pass a value of –1 to loop indefinitely.

Beyond the Player interface is a whole world of Controls. You can obtain a list of Controls for a Player by calling getControls() (a method Player inherits from the Controllable interface). This method returns an array of Controls that are appropriate for the Player. The ABB only defines a VolumeControl and a ToneControl, but implementations are free to provide other controls appropriate for the content types and protocols they support.

To obtain just one control, pass its name to Player's getControl() method (again inherited from Controllable). The name is the name of an interface in the javax.microedition.media.control package.

The Player must be in at least a REALIZED state to return its controls.

To use a VolumeControl to set playback volume to half its maximum, for example, you would do something like this:

```
// Player player = Manager.createPlayer(...);
player.prefetch();
VolumeControl vc = (VolumeControl)player.getControl("VolumeControl");
vc.setLevel(50);
```

Listening for Player Events

Player includes methods for adding and removing listeners that will be notified about various milestones in the Player's life:

```
public void addPlayerListener(PlayerListener playerListener)
public void removePlayerListener(PlayerListener playerListener)
```

PlayerListener defines a single method that is called with a variety of informational messages:

```
public void playerUpdate(Player player, String event, Object eventData)
```

The player parameter, of course, is the Player generating the event. The event is described by a string, event, and may include additional information, eventData. Constants in the PlayerListener interface describe common events: STARTED, END_OF_MEDIA, and VOLUME_CHANGED are a few. See the API documentation for the full list.

Tones and Tone Sequences

You've already seen how easy it is to play single tones using Manager. There's a somewhat more sophisticated tone sequence player lurking in the MIDP 2.0 media APIs. It's implemented within the Player and Control architecture, which is kind of a kluge, considering that tone sequences have little in common with sampled audio.

To obtain the tone sequence Player, just pass a special value (Manager's TONE_DEVICE_LOCATOR) to createPlayer(). If you examine TONE_DEVICE_LOCATOR, you'll see it is the value "device://tone", which kind of means a "device" protocol and an "audio/x-tone-seq" content type. You may remember seeing this in the output of MediaInformationMIDlet. As I said, it's kind of a kluge.

Once you've obtained the tone sequence Player, you can give it a tone sequence using its associated ToneControl object. To get this control, call getControl("ToneControl"). (Remember, the Player needs to be REALIZED first.)

ToneControl encapsulates a byte array whose syntax and construction is obtusely described in the API documentation. Master it and you'll be able to make any song into a monophonic masterpiece, Bobby McFerrin style. I'll describe the byte array format and present several examples.

The tones themselves are defined with note number and duration pairs. Note numbers are the same as for Manager's playTone() method, where 60 is middle C and 69 is the 440-Hz A above middle C. Duration is specified as multiples of the *resolution*. By default, the resolution of a tone sequence is 1/64 of one measure of 4/4 time (four beats). Therefore, a duration of 64 corresponds to a whole note (four beats), 16 corresponds to a quarter note (one beat), 8 is an eighth note, and so on.

All tone sequences must begin with a version. This is not the version of your data, but rather the version of the tone sequence format you're using. Currently the only accepted version is 1. A simple tone sequence looks like this:

```
byte[] sequence = new byte[] {
  ToneControl.VERSION, 1,
  67, 16, // The
  69, 16, // hills
  67,  8, // are
  65,  8, // a -
  64, 48, // live
  62,  8, // with
  60,  8, // the
  59, 16, // sound
  57, 16, // of
  59, 32, // mu -
  59, 32  // sic
};
```

This tone sequence relies on several default values. The default tempo is 120 beats per minute (bpm) and the default resolution is 1/64. The default volume is 100 (the loudest).

There are other features available in tone sequences. A reasonable amount of control is possible:

- Set the tempo by using the TEMPO constant and passing the tempo, in beats per minute, divided by four. For example, ToneControl.TEMPO, 15 sets the tempo to 60 bpm, or one beat per second. This may be done only once at the beginning of a sequence (following the VERSION).

- The resolution can be changed from its default of 1/64 using the RESOLUTION constant. The argument that is passed is the denominator, for example, using ToneControl.RESOLUTION, 64 will restore the default resolution of 1/64. This may be done only once at the beginning of a sequence (following the TEMPO).

- Reusable *blocks* of tones can be defined. To begin a block definition, use ToneControl.BLOCK_START and supply a block number. Then supply the notes and durations that go into the block. To end a block definition, use ToneControl.BLOCK_END and supply the same block number. To actually play a block, use ToneControl.PLAY_BLOCK and supply the number of the block you wish to play. Blocks must be defined following the VERSION, TEMPO, and RESOLUTION in a sequence.

- The volume can be set at any time during a sequence for dramatic dynamic effects. For example, ToneControl.SET_VOLUME, 25 sets the volume to one quarter of its maximum value.

- To indicate a rest of a certain duration, use the special note value ToneControl.SILENCE.

- You can repeat a single note multiple times. For example, ToneControl.REPEAT, 7, 60, 16 plays middle C (60) 7 times with a duration of 16.

The MIDlet in Listing 12-4 contains several examples that will help you write your own tone sequences.

Listing 12-4. Old Classics in Monophonic Glory

```java
import java.io.*;

import javax.microedition.io.*;
import javax.microedition.lcdui.*;
import javax.microedition.midlet.*;
import javax.microedition.media.*;
import javax.microedition.media.control.*;

public class ToneMIDlet
    extends MIDlet
    implements CommandListener {
  private final static String kSoundOfMusic = "Sound of Music";
  private final static String kQuandoMenVo = "Quando men vo";
  private final static String kTwinkle = "Twinkle number VII";

  private Display mDisplay;
  private List mMainScreen;

  public void startApp() {
    mDisplay = Display.getDisplay(this);

    if (mMainScreen == null) {
      mMainScreen = new List("AudioMIDlet", List.IMPLICIT);

      mMainScreen.append(kSoundOfMusic, null);
      mMainScreen.append(kQuandoMenVo, null);
      mMainScreen.append(kTwinkle, null);
      mMainScreen.addCommand(new Command("Exit", Command.EXIT, 0));
      mMainScreen.addCommand(new Command("Play", Command.SCREEN, 0));
      mMainScreen.setCommandListener(this);
    }

    mDisplay.setCurrent(mMainScreen);
  }

  public void pauseApp() {}

  public void destroyApp(boolean unconditional) {}
```

```java
public void commandAction(Command c, Displayable s) {
  if (c.getCommandType() == Command.EXIT) notifyDestroyed();
  else run();
}


public void run() {
  String selection = mMainScreen.getString(
      mMainScreen.getSelectedIndex());

  byte[] sequence = null;
  if (selection.equals(kSoundOfMusic)) {
    sequence = new byte[] {
      ToneControl.VERSION, 1,
      67, 16, // The
      69, 16, // hills
      67,  8, // are
      65,  8, // a -
      64, 48, // live
      62,  8, // with
      60,  8, // the
      59, 16, // sound
      57, 16, // of
      59, 32, // mu -
      59, 32  // sic
    };
  }
  else if (selection.equals(kQuandoMenVo)) {
    sequence = new byte[] {
      ToneControl.VERSION, 1,
      ToneControl.TEMPO, 22,
      ToneControl.RESOLUTION, 96,
      64, 48, ToneControl.SILENCE, 8, 52, 4, 56, 4, 59, 4, 64, 4,
      63, 48, ToneControl.SILENCE, 8, 52, 4, 56, 4, 59, 4, 63, 4,
      61, 72,
      ToneControl.SILENCE, 12, 61, 12,
          63, 12, 66, 2, 64, 10, 63, 12, 61, 12,
      64, 12, 57, 12, 57, 48,
      ToneControl.SILENCE, 12, 59, 12,
          61, 12, 64, 2, 63, 10, 61, 12, 59, 12,
      63, 12, 56, 12, 56, 48,
    };
  }
```

```
            else if (selection.equals(kTwinkle)) {
              sequence = new byte[] {
                ToneControl.VERSION, 1,
                ToneControl.TEMPO, 22,
                ToneControl.BLOCK_START, 0,
                60, 8,         62, 4, 64, 4, 65, 4, 67, 4, 69, 4, 71, 4,
                72, 4, 74, 4, 76, 4, 77, 4, 79, 4, 81, 4, 83, 4, 84, 4,
                83, 4, 81, 4, 80, 4, 81, 4, 86, 4, 84, 4, 83, 4, 81, 4,
                81, 4, 79, 4, 78, 4, 79, 4, 60, 4, 79, 4, 88, 4, 79, 4,
                57, 4, 77, 4, 88, 4, 77, 4, 59, 4, 77, 4, 86, 4, 77, 4,
                56, 4, 76, 4, 86, 4, 76, 4, 57, 4, 76, 4, 84, 4, 76, 4,
                53, 4, 74, 4, 84, 4, 74, 4, 55, 4, 74, 4, 83, 4, 74, 4,
                84, 16, ToneControl.SILENCE, 16,
                ToneControl.BLOCK_END, 0,
                ToneControl.BLOCK_START, 1,
                79, 4, 84, 4, 88, 4, 86, 4, 84, 4, 83, 4, 81, 4, 79, 4,
                77, 4, 76, 4, 74, 4, 72, 4, 71, 4, 69, 4, 67, 4, 65, 4,
                64, 8,         76, 8,        77, 8,        78, 8,
                79, 12,                 76, 4, 74, 8, ToneControl.SILENCE, 8,
                ToneControl.BLOCK_END, 1,

                ToneControl.SET_VOLUME, 100, ToneControl.PLAY_BLOCK, 0,
                ToneControl.SET_VOLUME,  50, ToneControl.PLAY_BLOCK, 0,
                ToneControl.SET_VOLUME, 100, ToneControl.PLAY_BLOCK, 1,
                ToneControl.SET_VOLUME,  50, ToneControl.PLAY_BLOCK, 1,
                ToneControl.SET_VOLUME, 100, ToneControl.PLAY_BLOCK, 0,
              };
            }
            try {
              Player player = Manager.createPlayer(Manager.TONE_DEVICE_LOCATOR);
              player.realize();
              ToneControl tc = (ToneControl)player.getControl("ToneControl");
              tc.setSequence(sequence);
              player.start();
            }
            catch (Exception e) {
              Alert a = new Alert("Exception", e.toString(), null, null);
              a.setTimeout(Alert.FOREVER);
              mDisplay.setCurrent(a, mMainScreen);
            }
          }
        }
      }
```

Remember, Player's start() method does not block. If you want, you can start all three songs running simultaneously in the emulator. This works because the toolkit emulator is using a polyphonic device to play the tone sequences. On a real device, playing multiple sequences simultaneously is probably not possible. But you can set one sequence running, and assuming it doesn't suck up too much processor time, your MIDlet can go and do other tasks, like drawing a game display or connecting to a network.

The Mobile Media API

MIDP 2.0's audio support is a subset of the full power of the Mobile Media API. If you're using the J2ME Wireless Toolkit, its emulators support the full MMAPI by default. This means that you have other APIs available and several additional content types supported by the implementation.

If you'd like to remove MMAPI support, leaving only MIDP 2.0 audio, choose **Edit ➤ Preferences** from the KToolbar menu, then click on the **API Availability** tab. You can uncheck the **Mobile Media API** if you do not wish to use it.

If you are using the toolkit's MMAPI implementation, you can customize the supported content types and media features in the **MMedia** tab of the preferences window.

For more information on the MMAPI, see http://wireless.java.sun.com/apis/articles/mmapi_overview/.

Summary

In this chapter you learned about playing tones and sampled audio in MIDP 2.0. A subset of the Mobile Media API, the Audio Building Block, is included in MIDP 2.0. It is based on Players that know how to render audio data and implicit protocol objects that understand how to transport audio data to the Player. Aside from optional and flexible support for sampled audio, the ABB also includes tone sequence player. Your MIDlets can now benefit from the excitement of music and sampled audio.

CHAPTER 13

Performance Tuning

MIDP IS A small platform. The processor on a MIDP device will probably be much slower than a typical desktop computer processor, and the available memory will be much smaller also. Making your application run fast and lean is important. You'll need to use memory sparingly, make your application run fast enough to be easily usable, and structure it so that the code itself is as small as it can be.

This chapter describes simple methods for benchmarking your existing code. It then goes on to describe various optimizations that can make your code run faster or use less memory. Common sense will take you a long way, but this chapter is devoted to giving you the basic techniques for optimizing your application.

The important rule of thumb is this: only optimize where it's needed. Said another way: if it ain't broke, don't fix it. I suggest that your first pass at coding your application should concentrate on cleanliness and maintainability. If there are performance problems, identify them and begin optimizing. You shouldn't be optimizing code as you write it—that's just likely to result in hard-to-read, hard-to-maintain code. Write first, then test, then optimize.

Benchmarking

In the J2SE world, there are many tools for examining the performance of code, the location of bottlenecks, and memory usage. Unfortunately, little of this is available in the J2ME world. For the most part, you'll have to perform benchmarking the old-fashioned way. For this, there are several methods in the MIDP API that will be useful. To test memory use, you can use the following methods in `java.lang.Runtime`:

```
public long freeMemory()
public long totalMemory()
```

The first method tells how much memory, in bytes, is currently available. The second method gives the total number of bytes in the current runtime environment, whether they are used for objects or not. Interestingly, this number can change because the host environment (device operating system) can give more memory to the Java runtime environment.

To find out how much memory an object uses, you can do something like this:

```
Runtime runtime = Runtime.getRuntime();
long before, after;
System.gc();
before = runtime.freeMemory();
Object newObject = new String();
after = runtime.freeMemory();
long size = before - after;
```

Aside from examining memory usage, you may also be concerned with the speed of your application. Again, you can test this the old-fashioned way—look at the clock before you start doing something, then look at it again when you're finished. The relevant method comes from the java.lang.System class:

```
public static long currentTimeMillis()
```

You might calculate the execution time for a method like this:

```
long start, finish;
start = System.currentTimeMillis();
someMethod();
finish = System.currentTimeMillis();
long duration = finish - start;
```

For accurate timing, you should measure the duration multiple times and calculate an average.

Diagnostic Tools in the J2ME Wireless Toolkit

Starting with version 1.0.4, the J2ME Wireless Toolkit contains three tools you can use to understand your application's performance.

The first tool is a memory monitor. You can see a graph of memory usage in your application over time or a detailed breakdown of every object in your application. Turn on the memory monitor by choosing **Edit ➤ Preferences** from the KToolbar menu. Click the **Monitoring** tab and check off **Enable Memory Monitor**. Next time you run the emulator, an additional window will pop up. You can examine the total memory used, which is useful when you're trying to make an application fit on a device with a limited heap size. (You can even set the heap size of the emulator in the **Storage** tab of the preferences window.) Figure 13-1 shows the memory monitor graph.

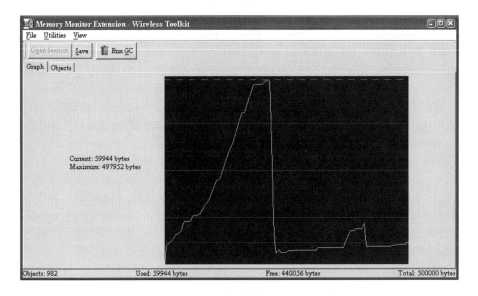

Figure 13-1. Graph of memory use over time

If you click the **Objects** tab in the memory monitor window, you'll see a detailed listing of the objects in your application. Figure 13-2 shows this view.

Name	Live	Total	Total Size	Average Size
java.util.TaskQueue	2	2	40	20
java.util.TimerTask[ ]	2	2	64	32
java.util.TimerThread	2	2	64	32
javax.microedition.lcdui.ImmutableImage	10	10	240	24
javax.microedition.lcdui.ImageItem	0	1	0	0
javax.microedition.lcdui.Display$DisplayManagerImpl	1	1	40	40
javax.microedition.lcdui.Display	3	4	144	48
javax.microedition.lcdui.Display$DisplayAccessor	3	4	72	24
com.sun.midp.lcdui.DisplayDeviceAccess	1	1	16	16
com.sun.midp.lcdui.EmulEventHandler	1	1	84	84
com.sun.midp.lcdui.DefaultEventHandler$QueuedEvent…	1	1	16	16
com.sun.midp.lcdui.DefaultEventHandler$EventQueue	1	1	68	68
com.sun.midp.lcdui.DefaultEventHandler$VMEventHan…	1	1	20	20
javax.microedition.lcdui.Graphics	1	1	92	92
short[ ]	2	2	48	24
java.lang.NullPointerException	0	1	0	0
com.sun.midp.dev.PersistentSelector	1	1	48	48
javax.microedition.midlet.MIDletStateMapImpl	1	1	12	12

Figure 13-2. Objects and their memory

You can click on any column in the table to sort by that column. You can even search for specific items using **View ➤ Find**. Examining the memory monitor window will help you identify the places where memory is consumed most in your application.

Aside from the memory monitor, the toolkit also includes a *code profiler*—a tool that shows how much time is spent in every method in your application. To turn on the profiler, choose **Edit ➤ Preferences** from the KToolbar menu. Choose the **Monitoring** tab and check off **Enable Profiling**.

You won't see the profiler until you exit the emulator. When you do, the profiler window pops up, summarizing time spent in every method in your application during the last emulator run. Note that what you do in the emulator will affect the output in the profiler; if you want to test the performance of your application as a whole, you'll have to exercise all of its options. Figure 13-3 shows the emulator after running the QuatschMIDlet example from Chapter 11.

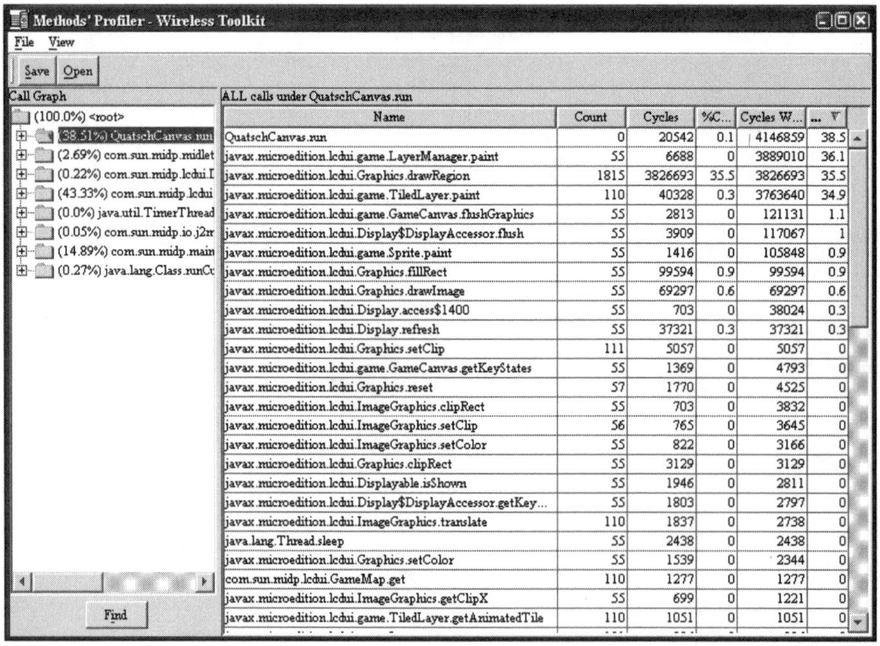

Figure 13-3. The profiler times everything.

Finally, the J2ME Wireless Toolkit also includes a network monitor. Although it's probably more useful for debugging network protocols than for optimization, it deserves mention here. To turn on the network monitor, choose **Edit ➤ Preferences** from the KToolbar menu. Choose the **Monitoring** tab and check off **Enable Network Monitoring**. Next time you run the emulator, a new window will pop up that tracks network usage. Figure 13-4 shows a few network interactions from the PeekAndPick application (http://wireless.java.sun.com/applications/peekandpick/2.0/).

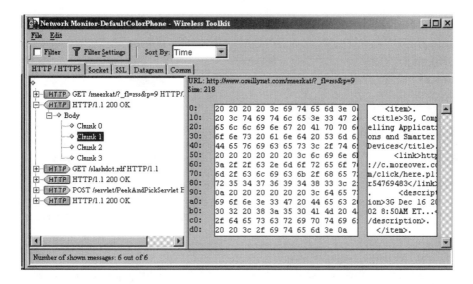

Figure 13-4. Network activity from the PeekAndPick application

Optimizing Memory Use

It's easy for J2SE programmers to be blasé about memory usage. After all, having a garbage collector means that you don't have to worry about explicitly freeing memory—objects that are no longer in use will be magically harvested by the garbage collector, running in a low-priority thread. In the J2ME universe, however, memory is scarce and should be treated with respect. Furthermore, both the allocation of memory and the work of the garbage collector can drag down the speed of your application. In this section, we'll look at techniques for efficient object use, particularly with Strings and StringBuffers. Finally, I'll talk about gracefully handling the situation where there really isn't any memory left.

Creating and Discarding Objects

If you're creating a new object inside a loop, it should be setting off alarm bells in your head. Every time you create an object (using new), memory is allocated. Allocating memory takes time. Worse, objects created at the beginning of a loop are likely to fall out of scope by the end of the loop, which means that each iteration through the loop pushes the runtime system closer to running the garbage collector. Here's an example:

```
// Set up the inputs and results arrays.
Object[] inputs = new Object[1000];
int[] results = new int[1000];
// Process each input to calculate a result.
int length = inputs.length;
for (int i = 0; i < length; i++) {
  Processor p = new Processor(inputs[i]);
  results[i] = p.calculateResult();
}
```

Creating objects in a loop imposes a double penalty in terms of performance. A new Processor is created every time through the loop; if these objects are large enough, then garbage collection may be forced one or more times before the loop is finished. You pay a price up front when the object is first created, then later when the object is garbage collected.

You can almost always restructure your code to avoid this problem. For example, instead of creating a new Processor for each input, you could do something like this:

```
// Set up the inputs and results arrays.
Object[] inputs = new Object[1000];
int[] results = new int[1000];
// Process each input to calculate a result.
int length = inputs.length;
Processor p = new Processor();
for (int i = 0; i < length; i++) {
  p.setInput(inputs[i]);
  results[i] = p.calculateResult();
}
```

Strings and StringBuffers

Strings have a special status in Java. They are the only objects for which the plus operator (+) is overloaded. Each time you concatenate strings using the plus operator, be wary—behind the scenes, new String and StringBuffer objects are probably being created for you.

String and StringBuffer share a curious relationship. When you can create and modify a StringBuffer, the actual work is performed on an internal character array. When you create a String from the StringBuffer, the String points to the same character array. Everything is fine so far, right? But if you further modify the StringBuffer, it cleverly creates a new character array, a copy of the old one. Thus, while StringBuffer is generally an efficient way to create Strings, it is not always obvious exactly when new objects are created.

The moral of the story is that every place you see string concatenation, there may be new objects being created. If you're assembling strings inside a loop, you should think about a different approach, possibly involving StringBuffer. Another possible optimization is to forego String and StringBuffer entirely and just use character arrays. While this may be a fast and efficient solution in your own code, keep in mind that many APIs require Strings as parameters and return Strings from methods, so you may end up doing a lot of conversion between character arrays and Strings.

Failing Gracefully

Given the paucity of memory in a typical MIDP device, your application should be prepared for disappointment each time it asks for memory. Each time objects are created, your code should catch java.lang.OutOfMemoryError. It is far better for you to catch OutOfMemoryErrors than for your host environment to catch them. You, at least, have a chance to do something reasonable—free up some memory and try again, or fail gracefully with a politely worded message to the user. The host environment is not likely to be so kind, and user perception of your application will be much worse. Bear in mind that you will probably need to free up memory by discarding large data structures before you will have enough space to create an Alert for your message to the user.

Coding for Speed

Small devices have small, relatively slow processors. Part of your task as a developer is ensuring that your application runs fast enough that users won't reject it.

Optimize Loops

One simple optimization has to do with looping. A typical loop through a Vector v might look like this:

```
for (int i = 0; i < v.size(); i++) {
  Object o = v.elementAt(i);
  // Process the Object o.
}
```

Each time through the loop, v's size() method is called. An optimized version would store the size of the vector first, like this:

```
int size = v.size();
for (int i = 0; i < size; i++) {
  Object o = v.elementAt(i);
  // Process the Object o.
}
```

This is a simple example, but it illustrates that loop conditions are one place you can look for speed optimizations.

Use Arrays Instead of Objects

Arrays are usually faster and leaner than collection classes. We touched on this theme earlier in our discussion of Strings and StringBuffers; if it's not too clumsy, using character arrays directly will probably be more efficient than dealing with String and StringBuffer objects. The same rule applies to the MIDP collection classes Vector and Hashtable. Although Vector and Hashtable are simple and convenient, they do impose some overhead that can be trimmed. Vector is basically just a wrapper for an array, so if you can work with an array directly, you'll save yourself some memory and processing time. Similarly, if you have a simple mapping of key objects to value objects, it might make sense to use object arrays instead of Hashtable.

If you do decide to use Hashtable or Vector, try to size them correctly when you create them. Both Vector and Hashtable grow larger as needed, but it is relatively expensive. Vector creates a new internal array and copies elements from the old array to the new array. Hashtable allocates new arrays and performs a computationally expensive operation called *rehashing*. Both Vector and Hashtable have constructors that allow you to specify the initial size of the collection. You should specify the initial size of these collections as accurately as possible.

If you are using the persistent storage APIs, you may be tempted to wrap stream classes around the record data. For example, you might read a record, then wrap a ByteArrayInputStream around the record's data, and then wrap a DataInputStream around the ByteArrayInputStream to read primitive types from the record. This is likely too heavy to be practical. If at all possible, work directly with the record's byte array.

Use Buffered I/O

Don't read bytes one at a time from a stream, and don't write them out one at a time. Although the stream classes provide methods that read and write a single byte, you should avoid them if at all possible. It will almost always be more efficient to read or write a whole array full of data.

J2SE provides BufferedReader and BufferedWriter classes that provide buffering functionality "for free." There is no such luxury in the MIDP universe, so if you want to use buffering, you'll have to do it yourself.

Be Clean

One simple piece of advice is to clean up after yourself. Releasing resources as soon as you are done with them can improve the performance of your application. If you have internal arrays or data structures, you should free them when you're not using them. One way to do this is to set your array reference to null so that the array can be garbage collected. You could even call the garbage collector explicitly with System.gc() if you're anxious to release memory back to the runtime system.

Network connections should also be released as soon as you're done with them. One good way to do this is to use a finally clause. Consider the following code, which does not use a finally clause:

```
HttpConnection hc = null;
InputStream in = null;
try {
  hc = (HttpConnection)Connector.open(url);
  in = hc.openInputStream();
  // Read data from in.
  in.close();
  hc.close();
}
catch (IOException ioe) {
  // Handle the exception.
}
```

The problem occurs if an exception is thrown while you're trying to read data from the connection's input stream. In this case, execution jumps down to the exception handler, and the input stream and connection are never closed. In a J2SE environment, with memory to burn, this is probably not a big deal. But on a MIDP device, a hanging connection could be a disaster. When you absolutely, positively want to be sure to run some code, you should put it in a `finally` block like this:

```
HttpConnection hc = null;
InputStream in = null;
try {
  hc = (HttpConnection)Connector.open(url);
  in = hc.openInputStream();
  // Read data from in.
}
catch (IOException ioe) {
  // Handle the exception.
}
finally {
  try {
    if (in != null) in.close();
    if (hc != null) hc.close();
  }
  catch (IOException ioe) { }
}
```

This is starting to look a little ugly, particularly the try and catch inside our finally block. A cleaner solution would be to enclose this code in a method and declare that the method throws IOException. This cleans up the code considerably:

```
private void doNetworkStuff(String url) throws IOException {
  HttpConnection hc = null;
  InputStream in = null;
  try {
    hc = (HttpConnection)Connector.open(url);
    in = hc.openInputStream();
    // Read data from in.
  }
  finally {
    if (in != null) in.close();
    if (hc != null) hc.close();
  }
}
```

The deal with `finally` is that its code gets executed no matter how control leaves the `try` block. If an exception is thrown, or if somebody calls `return`, or even if control leaves the `try` block normally, our `finally` block still gets executed. Note that there is still a small amount of room for trouble here: if an exception is thrown when we try to close `in`, then `hc` will never be closed. You could enclose each `close()` call in its own `try` and `catch` block to handle this problem.

Being clean applies to any type of stream, records stores, and record enumerations. Anything that can be closed should be, preferably in a `finally` block.

Optimize the User Interface

It's important to remember that you are trying to optimize the *perceived* speed of your application, not the actual speed of the application. Users get fidgety if the application freezes up for a few seconds; adding some sort of progress indicator can go a long way toward making users happier. There's really nothing you can do to make the network run faster, but if you display a spinning clock or a moving progress bar, your application will at least look like it's still alive while it's waiting for the network.

Keep in mind that users of mobile phones and other small "consumer" devices will be much more demanding than typical desktop computer users. Through years of experience, bitter desktop computer users have fairly low expectations of their applications. They realize that most desktop applications have a learning curve and are frequently cantankerous. Consumer devices, on the other hand, are much more likely to work right the first time, requiring neither manuals nor advanced degrees to operate.

With this in mind, be sure that your MIDlet user interface is uncomplicated, fast, responsive, and informative.

Optimizing Application Deployment

One last area of optimization has to do with the actual deployment of your application. As you may remember from Chapter 3, MIDlets are packaged in MIDlet suites, which are really just fancy JAR files. One way to optimize your application is partition your classes so that only the ones you need are loaded into the runtime environment. If you are careful, you can reduce the size or your MIDlet suite JAR by eliminating classes you don't need. Finally, a code obfuscator may be used to further reduce the size or the MIDlet suite JAR.

Partition Your Application

The MIDP runtime environment loads classes as they are needed. You can use this to your advantage to optimize the runtime footprint of your application. For example, suppose you write a datebook application that has the capability to send you reminder e-mails, or *ticklers*. You would probably realize that many people will not take advantage of the tickler feature. Why should tickler code take up space in a MIDP device if the user is not using ticklers? If you partition your code correctly, all of the tickler functionality can be encapsulated in a single class. If the rest of the application never calls the tickler code, the class will not be loaded, resulting in a slimmer runtime footprint.

Only Include Classes You Need

You may be using third-party packages in your MIDlet suite, like an XML parser (see Chapter 14) or a cryptography package (see Chapter 15). For development, you might have simply dumped the whole package into your MIDlet suite. But come deployment time, you should prune out the excess packages to reduce the size or your MIDlet suite JAR. In some cases this will be fairly easy, like dumping out WAP support classes if you're simply parsing XML. Other times it will not be so obvious which classes you need and which ones you can get rid of. However, if you really want to reduce your MIDlet suite JAR size, this is a crucial step. You don't need to do this by hand; an *obfuscator* will do the work for you.

Use an Obfuscator

Finally, a *bytecode obfuscator* can reduce the size of your class files. A bytecode obfuscator is a tool that is supposed to make it difficult to decompile class files. Decompilation is a process by which someone can recreate the source code that was used to make a particular class file. People who are worried about competitors stealing their code use obfuscators to make decompilation more difficult. However, obfuscation has the side effect of reducing class file size, mainly because the descriptive method and variable names you created are replaced with small machine-generated names. If you're very serious about reducing the size of your MIDlet suite JAR, try obfuscating your code. I suggest running the obfuscator before preverifying the class files, but it's conceivable it would work the other way around, too. Here are two obfuscators to get you started:

```
http://proguard.sourceforge.net/
http://www.retrologic.com/retroguard-main.html
```

Summary

MIDP applications are targeted to run on a small platform, which means that using memory and processing power efficiently is important. Creating and destroying objects is expensive, so one way to optimize your code is to reduce the number of objects you create. One common source of new objects is code that creates `Strings`. Consider optimizing `String` manipulation using `StringBuffer` or character arrays. Similarly, you may be able to streamline code by using object arrays in place of `Vectors` or `Hashtables`. Remember that performance is as much about perception as anything else; provide a responsive, active user interface and handle failures gracefully. You can also optimize the delivery of your application in several ways. First, partitioning the functionality of your application intelligently can reduce the runtime footprint of your application. Next, trimming out excess classes can reduce the size of your MIDlet suite JAR. Finally, a bytecode obfuscator can further reduce the size of your MIDlet suite JAR.

CHAPTER 14

Parsing XML

ON THE DESKTOP and in the enterprise, Java and XML are a winning combination. In brief, Java is portable code and XML is portable data. Developing in Java gives you the ability to deploy code on many different platforms, while XML supplies a highly portable data format for exchanging data between application components and applications themselves.

XML's popularity reaches into the J2ME world. This chapter describes XML parsers that are available for MIDP environments. This is fun stuff, right at the raw edge of J2ME development. Standards are on the way, but they haven't arrived yet. See http://jcp.org/en/jsr/detail?id=172 for details on an XML parsing and web services JSR.

XML Overview

XML is the Extensible Markup Language. An XML file is some collection of data that is demarcated by tags. XML files are structured and highly portable.

Let's consider the Jargoneer application from Chapter 2 again. In that application, the MIDP device talks to an intermediate server. This server retrieves an HTML page from the Jargon File server, performs the parsing, and sends a distilled version of the data down to the MIDP device. Figure 14-1 shows this architecture.

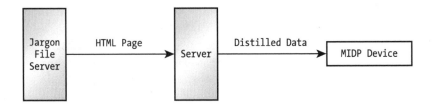

Figure 14-1. A simple architecture for Jargoneer

What, exactly, could get sent from the intermediate server to the MIDP device? The Jargoneer example application actually sends flat text, but there are many other possibilities. The next simplest technique for exchanging data between a server and a device would be to use a properties file, like this:

```
word: grok
pronunciation: /grok/
type: vt.
meaning: [from the novel "Stranger in ...
```

This works fine and is probably all you would need for simple applications. You'd have to write a class that could parse this input (MIDP doesn't include `java.util.Properties`), but that wouldn't be too bad.

However, chances are excellent that some parts of your application are already speaking XML, and it would likely simplify your life considerably if your MIDlet could parse XML instead of having its own specific data format. Furthermore, using XML validation during the development cycle may be a big help in flushing out bugs.

As an XML file, then, the same information would probably look like this:

```
<?xml version="1.0" encoding="ISO-8859-1"?>
<jargon-definition>
  <word>grok</word>
  <pronunciation>/grok/</pronunciation>
  <type>vt.</type>
  <meaning>[from the novel "Stranger in ...</meaning>
</jargon-definition>
```

This simple XML document illustrates some important points. First, tags mark off every piece of data (element) in the document. In essence, every element has a name. Matching start and end tags are used to clearly separate elements. For example, the start tag `<word>` and the end tag `</word>` surround the word itself. Also note that elements may be nested. The `jargon-definition` element is simply a collection of other elements. Any of the other elements could contain further nested elements.

Element tags may also contain attributes. An alternate way of writing the previous XML file looks like this:

```
<?xml version="1.0" encoding="ISO-8859-1"?>
<jargon-definition word="grok" pronunciation="/grok/" type="vt.">
  [from the novel "Stranger in ...
</jargon-definition>
```

It's up to you exactly how you structure your XML data. Usually it depends on the structure of your application and the systems with which you will be exchanging data.

....

XML and HTML

XML looks a lot like HTML, but there are some important differences. First, HTML has a fixed set of tags, like <TITLE>, <BODY>, <H1>, <P>, and so forth. In XML, you can define whatever tags you want.

HTML is also pretty lax about requiring closing tags. For example, HTML documents typically have <P> tags at the beginning of each paragraph, but it's unusual to have matching </P> close tags. As a matter of fact, the HTML world is pretty loose about document formatting in general. You can throw all sorts of strange documents at a browser and it will do its best to display them.

It is possible to write HTML so that it complies with XML; this is XHTML. For more information on XHTML, see http://www.w3.org/TR/xhtml1/.

....

Understanding SAX

SAX is the Simple API for XML, a standard API for Java applications that want to parse XML data. The API is documented online at http://www.megginson.com/SAX/, but SAX-compliant parsers usually include the SAX API as part of their software. The current version of SAX is 2.0, but the small parsers covered in this chapter are only at the 1.0 level if they implement SAX at all.

SAX 1.0 revolves around the org.xml.sax.Parser interface. Parser has a method, parse(), that parses through an entire XML document, spitting out events to listening objects. Typically, your application will implement a DocumentHandler that receives notification about start tags, end tags, element data, and other important events. A SAX 1.0 application looks something like this:

```
try {
  Parser p = new SAXParser(); // Create a specific parser implementation.
  // Create some DocumentHandler named handler.
  p.setDocumentHandler(handler);
  p.parse();
}
catch (Exception e) {  // Handle exceptions. }
```

The call to parse() proceeds until the document has been fully parsed. During the parse, callback methods in the registered DocumentHandler are invoked. In these methods, you'll process the data from the XML document.

SAX 1.0 is not MIDP-compliant straight out of the box. The Parser interface includes a setLocale() method that references the java.util.Locale class, a class that is missing in the MIDP platform.

Another standard API, the Document Object Model (DOM), takes a different approach to XML parsing. With DOM, the parser creates an internal model of a document as it is parsed. After parsing is complete, an application can examine the entire document. DOM is further described here at http://www.w3.org/TR/DOM-Level-2-Core/. Although none of the parsers described in this chapter implement DOM directly, some of them do follow the DOM paradigm of creating an internal representation of a parsed document.

A more recent XML parser API standard is XmlPull, which is documented at http://www.xmlpull.org/. XmlPull is implemented by kXML 2, which is presented later.

Validation and Development Cycle

XML documents may also make reference to a Document Type Definition (DTD) or an XML Schema; these are files that describe the contents of a particular kind of XML document. We could, for example, write a DTD that specified the contents of a jargon-definition document. This is part of the power of XML, and it's the reason XML is sometimes called *self-describing data*.

Given a document, you can determine if it conforms to its DTD, which is a great way to determine if part of your system is producing data that's unreadable by the rest of your system. In XML terms, a document that follows the rules of its DTD or schema is *valid*. In the J2SE and J2EE worlds, parsers may be validating or non-validating. The J2ME world is too small to support XML document validation, so all of the parsers we'll discuss in this chapter are non-validating.

Even though you won't be able to perform validation on a MIDP device, you may well want to use validating parsers during your development and test cycle. For example, you might write code that emulates the MIDP client, having it request data from your server and validate the results. This helps flush out bugs in the server code before you make the switch over to the MIDP client software.

Design Tips

Common sense, as always, takes you a long way. As you contemplate the use of XML in your MIDP application, keep three things in mind:

- Keep the documents small. If you're sending some 100KB document down to the MIDP deviceand only using a few elements, it's time to rethink your server-side strategy. You can probably transform the document at the server and just send what you need to the device. Keep in mind that network connectivity is likely to be slow and there's not much memory on the device.

- Don't use comments in the XML that you send to the MIDP device, except perhaps as a debugging aid during the development cycle. Comments will only make the document longer, which implies a slower download and more memory usage on the device.

- Choose a parser that fits your needs. Some of the parsers we'll examine build an entire model of a document in memory as the document is parsed. This is like writing a blank check to the supplier of the XML document. If the server sends you a 1MB file, these types of parsers will attempt to read through the whole thing, right up until they run out of memory. On the other hand, if you know the size of the files you'll be parsing, and they are small enough, you might choose a model-building parser, as it is slightly easier to use than the other types of parsers.

- Consider using a compact representation of the XML document. Representing XML documents in ASCII or Unicode is not efficient, and there are various schemes for more compact representations. The WAP forum, in fact, has defined a standard for binary coded XML called WBXML. A parser called SWX can handle WBXML and is appropriate for small platforms like MIDP: `http://www.trantor.de/wbxml/`. For another approach to this problem, see the JXME project at `http://jxme.jxta.org/`.

Finally, you may be concerned about the performance of a small XML parser. This is a valid concern, especially on a small device that has a relatively slow processor. For a fascinating comparison of XML parser performance, see `http://www.extreme.indiana.edu/~aslom/exxp/`. With small documents, the small parsers can hold their own or outperform larger parsers.

As with other potentially time-consuming operations, parsing should be done in its own thread so the user interface doesn't freeze.

MIDP XML Parser Roundup

Table 14-1 lists small, open-source XML parsers that can be used with the MIDP platform. Each of these parsers is released under some type of open-source software license as listed in the License column. The Size column shows the approximate size of the compressed class files for the parser. The Type column describes the parsing paradigm using one of the following:

- "Pull" indicates that the programmer repeatedly calls a method on the parser to propel it through a document.

- "Push" means that the parser runs through the entire document by itself, invoking callback methods in your code when important events happen. SAX parsers implement the push paradigm.

- "Model" indicates that the parser builds some internal representation (in memory) of the document. After parsing is finished, your code can examine this model and pull out element data.

The MIDP column indicates whether or not the parser source code compiles without modification on the MIDP platform.

Table 14-1. Small XML Parsers

NAME	VERSION	URL	LICENSE	SIZE	MIDP	TYPE
kXML	1.21	http://kxml.enhydra.org/	EPL	21KB	Yes	Pull
kXML	2.1.6	http://kxml.org/	CPL	9KB	Yes	Pull
MinML	1.7	http://www.wilson.co.uk/xml/minml.htm	BSD	14KB	No	Push
NanoXML	2.2.2 lite	http://web.wanadoo.be/cyberelf/nanoxml/	zlib/libpng	6KB	No	Model
TAM	-	http://simonstl.com/projects/tam/	MPL	17KB	Yes	Push
TinyXML	0.7	http://www.gibaradunn.srac.org/tiny/	GPL	6KB	No	Model
XmlReader	-	http://kobjects.org/utils4me/	LGPL	5KB	Yes	Pull
XMLtp	1.7	http://mitglied.lycos.de/xmltp/	BSD	21KB	No	Model
Xparse-J	1.1	http://www.webreference.com/xml/tools/xparse-j.html	GPL	7KB	Yes	Model

Table 14-2 provides more information about each type of license, listing both the license name and a URL that provides more information.

Table 14-2. Software Licenses

NAME	URL
BSD	http://opensource.org/licenses/bsd-license.php
CPL	http://opensource.org/licenses/cpl.php
EPL	http://kxml.enhydra.org/software/license/
GPL	http://www.webreference.com/xml/tools/license.html
LGPL	http://opensource.org/licenses/lgpl-license.php
MPL	http://www.mozilla.org/MPL/MPL-1.1.html
zlib/libpng	http://opensource.org/licenses/zlib-license.php

In the following sections, I'll describe one of the more solid parsers, kXML 1.21. I'll also talk about techniques for porting the parsers that don't comply with MIDP.

Using kXML 1.21

Currently, kXML 1.21 is the most complete and well-supported parser. Originally developed at the Universität Dortmund in Germany, it is now part of the Enhydra web site. It is based on Common XML (http://simonstl.com/articles/cxmlspec.txt), which is a set of recommendations for using XML 1.0. Common XML specifies a core set of XML functionality and is really more of a state of mind than a specification.

kXML is specifically designed for KVM environments like CLDC and MIDP. Of all the parsers covered in this chapter, kXML is one of the few that compiles without modification in a MIDP environment. It is also relatively large; if you're concerned about memory, you might want to consider one of the other parsers, which are considerably smaller. On the other hand, using an obfuscator may significantly reduce the size of the code, especially if there are portions of the parser API you don't use in your application.

kXML implements a pull-based parser, based on the XmlPull standard, that is contained in the org.kxml.parser package. *Pull-based* means that you tell the parser to parse each element. A SAX parser, by contrast, parses the whole document in one shot and just lets you know when things happen.

Most of kXML's parser functionality is defined in the `AbstractXmlParser` class. In your code, you will use the concrete `XMLParser` subclass. The basic idea is to instantiate an `XMLParser`, passing in a `java.io.Reader` that represents the data to be parsed. Then call the `read()` method repeatedly, processing each element until the end of the document is reached. `read()` returns a `ParseEvent`, which could represent a start tag, an element text, or other parser events. In MIDlet code, it looks something like this:

```
// InputStream rawIn = ...
Reader in = new InputStreamReader(rawIn);
AbstractXmlParser p = new XmlParser(in);
ParseEvent pe = null;
while ((pe = p.read()) != null) {
  ; // Process the event.
  if (pe.getType() == org.kxml.Xml.END_DOCUMENT)
    break;
}
```

`ParseEvent` has a type property (returned by `getType()`) that will be one of the constants defined in the `org.kxml.Xml` class. `ParseEvent` also has various subclasses that represent some of the event types. However, downcasting will rarely be necessary because `ParseEvent` already contains most of the methods you need for accessing data.

In the previous sample code, I've explicitly tested for an `END_DOCUMENT` event type that signals that the parser is finished.

For a practical example of XML parsing from a MIDlet, see the PeekAndPick application at `http://wireless.java.sun.com/applications/peekandpick/2.0/`. This application parses RSS files (XML documents) that represent news feeds and displays the results on the MIDP device.

Porting Techniques

If you do decide to port one of the parsers that doesn't build in MIDP out of the box, there are several techniques you may wish to consider:

Dump features you don't need. If the parser code is modularized well, you may be able to remove entire subdirectories of the source code, assuming you don't need those features in your application. You might, for example, be able to drop off a package that puts a SAX interface on top of the parser or a WAP support package.

Parsers often won't compile because they use classes from J2SE that aren't present in MIDP. One way to fix this is to supply the missing J2SE classes. There are two challenges with this approach. First, there are legal restrictions on the use of J2SE source code. See the source license for the full details. You can work around this by supplying your own implementation. The second problem is that MIDP implementations won't load classes defined in the java.* and javax.* namespaces. You can work around this problem using an obfuscator that renames the classes into different packages. (Chapter 15 has some more details on this.)

A cleaner option is to use classes in the same package or inner classes to replace the missing pieces of J2SE.

Using Parsers in the J2ME Wireless Toolkit

Incorporating a parser into your MIDlet suite is surprisingly easy. If a compiled JAR or ZIP file of classes is available, you can drop it into the *lib* directory of your project. For example, if the J2ME Wireless Toolkit is installed in */WTK20*, your project is called *ParseProject*, and you're using kXML 1.21, then you would install the *kxml-min.zip* archive into */WTK20/apps/ParseProject/lib*.

On the other hand, if the source code of the parser is available, you can simply drop it into the *src* directory of your project.

You will probably want to use an obfuscator to reduce the size of your MIDlet suite JAR. It's a good idea to use an obfuscator whenever you add a third-party library to your application. A good obfuscator will remove methods and classes that you are not using in your code, which can result in significant size savings.

Summary

The world of XML on small devices is wild and untamed. Bold developers can parse XML in a MIDP environment using one of the parsers described in this chapter. As a means of transmitting data from server to client, XML is a great choice. Just remember to keep those documents small and simple.

Protecting Network Data

MIDLETS ARE UNDENIABLY cool—Java code that runs on a small device, and HTTP network connectivity, as well. But once you start thinking about the possibilities, you realize that a lot of applications just aren't possible without some form of data security. What if you were going to buy something? You shouldn't send credit card numbers over the Internet without some kind of protection, and you shouldn't be sending sensitive corporate information over the Internet to small devices. Many applications, then, need something else—something that keeps sensitive data from being stolen. The answer in the MIDP world is no different than the answer anywhere else: cryptography.

Cryptography Review

Cryptography is a branch of mathematics. It's based on the idea that certain kinds of mathematical problems are hard to solve. Using cryptography is a bit specu-lative; as research in mathematics continues, it's very possible that someone will discover a way to solve (or "break") most of the modern cryptographic algorithms. Nevertheless, for today at least, cryptography provides protection for sensitive data, and there aren't many acceptable alternatives in the everything-connects-to-everything modern world.

The Internet Is a Big Room

There are many aspects to the security of a system. We'll focus on the data your MIDlet sends and receives over the network. This data travels over some infra-structure we know nothing about (provided by your mobile carrier) and probably over the Internet, as well. The Internet is definitely not a secure network, and your carrier's mobile infrastructure probably isn't either. If you're passing sensitive data around, it's very possible that eavesdroppers at various points in the network can listen in on the data. They may even be able to change parts of it. If your MIDP application involves passing around credit card numbers or sensitive corporate data, you should be concerned.

Think of the Internet as a big room. You can talk to anyone else in the room, but everyone else can listen in on the conversation. Furthermore, you may be talking to someone on the other side of the room through intermediaries, like the children's game of "telephone." Any one of the intermediaries might be changing the conversation, and they can all hear what you're saying.

Data Security Needs and Cryptographic Solutions

Your applications will have some or all of the following data security needs:

- *Integrity.* At the simplest level, you'd like to be sure that the data you're sending is not getting changed or corrupted in any way. This is data integrity.

- *Authentication.* It's often important to verify the identity of the machine or person on the other end of your network connection. Authentication is the process of proving identity.

- *Confidentiality.* If you're sending sensitive data over the network, other people shouldn't be able to see that information. This is confidentiality.

Cryptography provides solutions for each of these needs:

- *Message digests.* A message digest smushes a large piece of data into a small piece of data. You might, for example, run an entire file through a message digest to end up with a 160-bit digest value. If you change even 1 bit of the file and run it through the message digest again, you'll get an entirely different digest value. A message digest value is sometimes called a *digital fingerprint.*

- *Digital signatures.* A digital signature is like a message digest except it is produced by a particular person, the *signer.* The signer must have a *private key* that is used to create the signature. A corresponding *public key* can be used by anyone to verify that the signature came from the signer. The private key and public key together are called a *key pair.* Keys are really just data—think of an array of bytes. *Certificates* are really just an extension of digital signatures. A certificate is a document, signed by some authority like the U.S. Postal Service, that proves your identity. It's like a driver's license, except it's based on digital signatures.

- *Ciphers.* Ciphers can either encrypt data or decrypt it. An encrypting cipher accepts your data, called *plaintext*, and produces an unreadable mess, called *ciphertext*. A decrypting cipher takes ciphertext and converts it back to plaintext. Ciphers use keys; if you encrypt the same plaintext with two different keys, you'll get two different sets of ciphertext. A *symmetric* cipher uses the same key for encryption and decryption. An *asymmetric* cipher operates with a key pair—one key is used for encrypting, while the matching key is used for decrypting.

Ciphers operate in different *modes* that determine how plaintext is encrypted into ciphertext. This, in turn, affects the use and security of the cipher.

 NOTE *For comprehensive coverage of cryptographic concepts and algorithms, see Bruce Schneier's* Applied Cryptography: Protocols, Algorithms, and Source Code in C *(John Wiley & Sons, 1995). To find out more about the JCA and JCE in J2SE, read my somewhat out-of-date* Java Cryptography *(O'Reilly, 1998). Sun's Wireless Developer web site also contains my four-part series on security and cryptography in MIDP, located at* http://wireless.java.sun.com/midp/articles/security1/.

HTTPS Is Almost Everything You Could Want

The Generic Connection Framework has always been flexible enough to allow MIDP implementations to include support for HTTPS, which is HTTP over a secure connection like TLS or SSL. Starting with MIDP 2.0, support for HTTPS is now built into the MIDP platform. (See Chapter 9 for the skinny on HTTPS and its supporting APIs.)

TLS provides server authentication and an encrypted data connection between client and server. The security provided by TLS is sufficient for most applications. There are only a handful of reasons you might want to implement cryptographic solutions beyond what's available from TLS, including the following:

Client authentication. TLS provides server authentication, usually via an RSA certificate. But although TLS will support client authentication, the APIs in MIDP 2.0 don't allow you to take advantage of this feature. A technique for using password or passphrase authentication is presented later in this chapter. If you're looking for something stronger, a scheme based on client certificates and signatures is described at http://wireless.java.sun.com/midp/articles/security3/.

Stronger encryption. TLS usually results in encryption using 128-bit keys that are valid for a particular session. (Although you can't control which cipher suites are accepted on the client, you will probably have control of the server and will be able to configure acceptable cipher suites there.) For many applications, 128-bit session keys provide plenty of data security. However, if your application deals with especially sensitive or valuable data, you might want something stronger.

Message-driven applications. HTTPS only provides encryption for channels. Some applications work by sending encrypted messages over insecure transport like HTTP or sockets. Here the MIDP APIs are insufficient and you'll need to do your own cryptography.

As I said, HTTPS support in MIDP 2.0 is all you need for many applications. Read on if you need something stronger, or if you're just curious.

More information about HTTPS and TLS in MIDP is at `http://wireless.java.sun.com/midp/articles/security2/`.

The Bouncy Castle Cryptography Package

In the J2SE world, Sun provides support for cryptography through the Java Cryptography Architecture (JCA) and the Java Cryptography Extension (JCE). The problem, of course, is that the JCA and JCE are too heavy for the MIDP platform. MIDP 2.0's HTTPS support is very useful, but it's definitely not a general-purpose cryptography toolkit.

If you're looking to move beyond HTTPS, your best bet is the Bouncy Castle cryptography package, an open-source effort based in Australia. It's a wonderful piece of work, featuring a clean API and a formidable toolbox of cryptographic algorithms. There are several other open source cryptography packages around the world, but Bouncy Castle specifically offers a lightweight J2ME distribution of their software. To download the package, go to `http://www.bouncycastle.org/`, follow the link for **latest releases**, and choose the **J2ME** release. As I write this, the current version is 1.17.

Download the zip file into the location of your choice and unpack it. If you're using the J2ME Wireless Toolkit, just drop the *midp_classes.zip* file into the *lib* directory of your project. You can go ahead and write MIDlets that use the Bouncy Castle packages.

Protecting Passwords with a Message Digest

Having installed the Bouncy Castle cryptography package, let's try a simple example involving authentication. Computer systems often use passwords instead of digital signatures (or certificates) because they're so much easier. A password is a *shared secret*, which means that you know it and the server knows it, but nobody else should know it.

What If Someone Steals Your Phone?

For convenience, an application will probably store your password in persistent storage. This is a conscious trade-off of security for usability. The user never enters a password, but the password is available in device storage, vulnerable to theft by other applications on the device. Furthermore, if someone steals the device itself, they'll be able to use the application without being challenged for a password.

JSR 177, Security and Trust Services for J2ME (`http://jcp.org/en/jsr/detail?id=177`) will address these concerns by providing an API to secure storage, among other things.

The Problem with Passwords

The problem with passwords is that you don't want to send them over an insecure network. Imagine, for example, that your MIDlet requires the user to sign on to a server using a user name and password. On the MIDP device, you key in your user name and password, then click the button to send the information up to the server. Unfortunately, your data is sent as plaintext in some HTTP request. Anybody snooping on the network can easily lift your password.

Using a Message Digest

Message digests provides a way to solve this problem. Instead of sending a password as plaintext, you create a message digest value from the password and send that instead. An attacker could just steal the digest value, of course, so you add some other stuff to the digest as well so that only the server, knowing the password, can re-create the same digest value. Figure 15-1 shows the process.

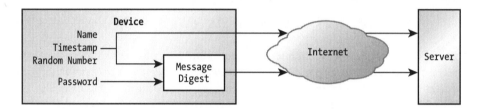

Figure 15-1. Protecting a password with a message digest

The MIDlet creates a timestamp and a random number, both of which are fed into the message digest along with the user name and the password. Then the MIDlet sends the user name, the timestamp, the random number, and the digest value up to the server. It does not send the password as cleartext, but the password is used to calculate the digest value.

The server takes the user name and looks up the corresponding password, which should be stored securely in a file or a database. Then it creates a digest value of the user name, password, timestamp, and random number. If the digest value created on the server matches the digest value sent by the client MIDlet, then the server knows that the user typed in the right password. The user has just logged in successfully.

The server needs some logic to prevent replay attacks. Specifically, the server should reject login attempts that use timestamps and random numbers that have been used before with that login. Although you could save the random numbers and timestamps of all user login attempts, it would be relatively expensive to compare each of these every time a user wanted to login. An easier way to implement this is to save the timestamp of each user's last login attempt. For each subsequent login attempt, the server looks up the saved timestamp. If the timestamp on the current attempt is later than the saved timestamp, the attempt is allowed. The current attempt's timestamp replaces the saved timestamp for this user.

Using the Bouncy Castle Cryptography Package

In the Bouncy Castle package, message digests are generically represented by the org.bouncycastle.crypto.Digest interface. You can add data into the message digest using one of two update() methods. To calculate the message digest value, call doFinal(). Specific implementations of the Digest interface are contained in the org.bouncycastle.crypto.digests package. We'll be using one called SHA1Digest, which implements the SHA-1 digest algorithm. The following line shows how to create a SHA-1 message digest object:

```
Digest digest = new SHA1Digest();
```

The cryptography code is pretty simple. Most of the effort, in fact, is devoted to converting the timestamp and random number to bytes that can be pushed into the message digest object. Then it's just a matter of calling the update() method with each array of bytes.

To calculate the digest, call Digest's doFinal() method. You'll need to pass in a byte array to hold the message digest value. To find out how long this array should be, call the getDigestSize() method.

```
byte[] digestValue = new byte[digest.getDigestSize()];
digest.doFinal(digestValue, 0);
```

Implementing a Protected Password Protocol

This section details an implementation of protected password login. On the client side, a MIDlet collects a user name and password, as shown in Figure 15-2.

Figure 15-2. A simple form collects a user name and password.

When the **Login** command is invoked, the MIDlet sends data to a servlet, which determines whether or not the client is authenticated. The servlet sends back a message, which is displayed on the screen of the device, as shown in Figure 15-3.

Figure 15-3. The server says whether you're logged in or not.

The MIDlet and servlet exchange various byte arrays, such as the timestamp, the random number, and the message digest value. To make this work smoothly in the context of HTTP headers, which are plain text, the byte arrays are exchanged as hexadecimal strings. A helper class, HexCodec, handles the translation between hexadecimal strings and byte arrays. This same class is used by the MIDlet and the servlet.

Let's look at the MIDlet first. Its main screen is a form where the user can enter a user name and a password. You might be tempted to use a PASSWORD TextField, but I chose not to. For one thing, it's hard to know exactly what text you're entering. For another thing, I'm assuming that the screen of a small device is reasonably private—probably no one will be peeking over your shoulder as you enter your password.

When the user invokes the **Login** command, the MIDlet calculates a message digest value as described above. It assembles various parameters into an HTTP request. It then reads the response from the server and displays the response in an Alert.

The meat of the protected password algorithm is in the login() method. We create a timestamp and a random number and convert these values to byte arrays using a helper method:

```
long timestamp = System.currentTimeMillis();
long randomNumber = mRandom.nextLong();
byte[] timestampBytes = getBytes(timestamp);
byte[] randomBytes = getBytes(randomNumber);
```

The user name and password strings, which come from the MIDlet's main form, are easily converted to byte arrays.

The entire source code for `PasswordMIDlet` is shown in Listing 15-1.

Listing 15-1. `PasswordMIDlet`, *A Protected Password Client*

```java
import java.io.*;
import java.util.Random;

import javax.microedition.io.*;
import javax.microedition.midlet.*;
import javax.microedition.lcdui.*;

import org.bouncycastle.crypto.Digest;
import org.bouncycastle.crypto.digests.SHA1Digest;

public class PasswordMIDlet
    extends MIDlet
    implements CommandListener, Runnable {
  private Display mDisplay;
  private Form mForm;
  private TextField mUserField, mPasswordField;
  private Random mRandom;

  public void startApp() {
    mDisplay = Display.getDisplay(this);
    mRandom = new Random(System.currentTimeMillis());

    if (mForm == null) {
      mForm = new Form("Login");
      mUserField = new TextField("Name", "jonathan", 32, 0);
      mPasswordField = new TextField("Password", "happy8", 32, 0);
      mForm.append(mUserField);
      mForm.append(mPasswordField);

      mForm.addCommand(new Command("Exit", Command.EXIT, 0));
      mForm.addCommand(new Command("Login", Command.SCREEN, 0));
      mForm.setCommandListener(this);
    }

    mDisplay.setCurrent(mForm);
  }
```

```
public void commandAction(Command c, Displayable s) {
  if (c.getCommandType() == Command.EXIT) notifyDestroyed();
  else {
    Form waitForm = new Form("Connecting...");
    mDisplay.setCurrent(waitForm);
    Thread t = new Thread(this);
    t.start();
  }
}

public void run() {
  // Gather the values we'll need.
  long timestamp = System.currentTimeMillis();
  long randomNumber = mRandom.nextLong();
  String user = mUserField.getString();
  byte[] userBytes = user.getBytes();
  byte[] timestampBytes = getBytes(timestamp);
  byte[] randomBytes = getBytes(randomNumber);
  String password = mPasswordField.getString();
  byte[] passwordBytes = password.getBytes();

  // Create the message digest.
  Digest digest = new SHA1Digest();
  // Calculate the digest value.
  digest.update(userBytes, 0, userBytes.length);
  digest.update(timestampBytes, 0, timestampBytes.length);
  digest.update(randomBytes, 0, randomBytes.length);
  digest.update(passwordBytes, 0, passwordBytes.length);
  byte[] digestValue = new byte[digest.getDigestSize()];
  digest.doFinal(digestValue, 0);

  // Create the GET URL. The hex encoded message digest value is
  //   included as a parameter.
  URLBuilder ub = new URLBuilder(getAppProperty("PasswordMIDlet-URL"));
  ub.addParameter("user", user);
  ub.addParameter("timestamp",
      new String(HexCodec.bytesToHex(timestampBytes)));
  ub.addParameter("random",
      new String(HexCodec.bytesToHex(randomBytes)));
  ub.addParameter("digest",
      new String(HexCodec.bytesToHex(digestValue)));
  String url = ub.toString();
```

```
      try {
        // Query the server and retrieve the response.
        HttpConnection hc = (HttpConnection)Connector.open(url);
        InputStream in = hc.openInputStream();

        int length = (int)hc.getLength();
        byte[] raw = new byte[length];
        in.read(raw);
        String response = new String(raw);
        Alert a = new Alert("Response", response, null, null);
        a.setTimeout(Alert.FOREVER);
        mDisplay.setCurrent(a, mForm);
        in.close();
        hc.close();
      }
      catch (IOException ioe) {
        Alert a = new Alert("Exception", ioe.toString(), null, null);
        a.setTimeout(Alert.FOREVER);
        mDisplay.setCurrent(a, mForm);
      }
    }

    private byte[] getBytes(long x) {
      byte[] bytes = new byte[8];
      for (int i = 0; i < 8; i++)
        bytes[i] = (byte)(x >> ((7 - i) * 8));
      return bytes;
    }

    public void pauseApp() { }

    public void destroyApp(boolean unconditional) { }
}
```

The HexCodec class contains a few static methods for converting between byte arrays and hex encoded strings. The complete class is shown in Listing 15-2.

Listing 15-2. The HexCodec *Helper Class*

```
public class HexCodec {
  private static final char[] kDigits = {
    '0', '1', '2', '3', '4', '5', '6', '7', '8', '9',
    'a', 'b', 'c', 'd', 'e', 'f'
  } ;

  public static char[] bytesToHex(byte[] raw) {
    int length = raw.length;
    char[] hex = new char[length * 2];
    for (int i = 0; i < length; i++) {
      int value = (raw[i] + 256) % 256;
      int highIndex = value >> 4;
      int lowIndex = value & 0x0f;
      hex[i * 2 + 0] = kDigits[highIndex];
      hex[i * 2 + 1] = kDigits[lowIndex];
    }
    return hex;
  }

  public static byte[] hexToBytes(char[] hex) {
    int length = hex.length / 2;
    byte[] raw = new byte[length];
    for (int i = 0; i < length; i++) {
      int high = Character.digit(hex[i * 2], 16);
      int low = Character.digit(hex[i * 2 + 1], 16);
      int value = (high << 4) | low;
      if (value > 127) value -= 256;
      raw[i] = (byte)value;
    }
    return raw;
  }

  public static byte[] hexToBytes(String hex) {
    return hexToBytes(hex.toCharArray());
  }
}
```

PasswordMIDlet also uses the URLBuilder class, which provides a simple interface for assembling GET URLs. The URLBuilder class is shown in Listing 15-3.

Listing 15-3. The URLBuilder *Helper Class*

```java
public class URLBuilder {
  private StringBuffer mBuffer;
  private boolean mHasParameters;

  public URLBuilder(String base) {
    mBuffer = new StringBuffer(base);
    mHasParameters = false;
  }

  public void addParameter(String name, String value) {
    // Append a separator.
    if (mHasParameters == false) {
      mBuffer.append('?');
      mHasParameters = true;
    }
    else
      mBuffer.append('&');
    // Now tack on the name and value pair. These should
    //   really be URL encoded (see java.net.URLEncoder in
    //   J2SE) but this class appends the name and value
    //   as is, for simplicity. Names or values with spaces
    //   or other special characters will not work correctly.
    mBuffer.append(name);
    mBuffer.append('=');
    mBuffer.append(value);
  }

  public String toString() {
    return mBuffer.toString();
  }
}
```

A simple implementation of a protected password servlet is shown in Listing 15-4.

Listing 15-4. The PasswordServlet *Class*

```
import javax.servlet.http.*;
import javax.servlet.*;
import java.io.*;
import java.util.*;

import org.bouncycastle.crypto.Digest;
import org.bouncycastle.crypto.digests.SHA1Digest;

public class PasswordServlet extends HttpServlet {
  public void doGet(HttpServletRequest request,
      HttpServletResponse response)
      throws ServletException, IOException {
    System.out.println("user = " + request.getParameter("user"));
    System.out.println("timestamp = " + request.getParameter("timestamp"));
    System.out.println("random = " + request.getParameter("random"));
    System.out.println("digest = " + request.getParameter("digest"));

    // Retrieve the user name.
    String user = request.getParameter("user");
    // Look up the password for this user.
    String password = lookupPassword(user);
    // Pull the timestamp and random number (hex encoded) out
    //    of the request.
    String timestamp = request.getParameter("timestamp");
    String randomNumber = request.getParameter("random");

    // Compare the timestamp with the last saved
    //    timestamp for this user. Accept only timestamps
    //    that are greater than the last saved timestamp for this user.
    // [not implemented]

    // Gather values for the message digest.
    byte[] userBytes = user.getBytes();
    byte[] timestampBytes = HexCodec.hexToBytes(timestamp);
    byte[] randomBytes = HexCodec.hexToBytes(randomNumber);
    byte[] passwordBytes = password.getBytes();
    // Create the message digest.
```

```
      Digest digest = new SHA1Digest();
      // Calculate the digest value.
      digest.update(userBytes, 0, userBytes.length);
      digest.update(timestampBytes, 0, timestampBytes.length);
      digest.update(randomBytes, 0, randomBytes.length);
      digest.update(passwordBytes, 0, passwordBytes.length);
      byte[] digestValue = new byte[digest.getDigestSize()];
      digest.doFinal(digestValue, 0);

      // Now compare the digest values.
      String message = "";
      String clientDigest = request.getParameter("digest");
      if (isEqual(digestValue, HexCodec.hexToBytes(clientDigest)))
        message = "User " + user + " logged in.";
      else
        message = "Login was unsuccessful.";

      // Send a response to the client.
      response.setContentType("text/plain");
      response.setContentLength(message.length());
      PrintWriter out = response.getWriter();
      out.println(message);
  }

  private String lookupPassword(String user) {
      // Here you could do a real lookup based on the user name.
      //    You might look in a text file or a database. Here, I
      //    just use a hardcoded value.
      return "happy8";
  }

  private boolean isEqual(byte[] one, byte[] two) {
      if (one.length != two.length) return false;
      for (int i = 0; i < one.length; i++)
        if (one[i] != two[i]) return false;
      return true;
  }
}
```

The basic procedure is to pull the parameters out of the request from the MIDlet, and then independently calculate the message digest value. The servlet looks up the user's password in the lookupPassword() method. In a more serious implementation, the servlet would probably look up the password in a database of some sort.

Once the servlet figures out the user's password, it pumps the user name, password, timestamp, and random number into a message digest. Then it calculates the message digest value and compares this result with the digest value that was sent from the MIDlet. If the digest values match, the MIDlet client is authenticated.

Suggested Enhancements

One obvious enhancement to this system is to actually retrieve passwords (on the server side) from a database or password repository of some sort.

Furthermore, the servlet needs to validate the timestamp it receives from the client. Every time a user tries to login, the servlet should make sure that the user's timestamp is greater than the timestamp from the user's previous login attempt.

One possible enhancement on the client side is to store the user's name and password in a record store so that they can be automatically sent with each login attempt. Normally this might seem like a bad idea. But small devices are generally kept physically secure by their owners—you try to keep your mobile phone in your possession at all times, or you lock it up somewhere. It's a trade-off between convenience and security. But just considering how difficult it is to enter text on a mobile phone keypad, you might want to give your users the convenience of using a stored name and password.

Note that the authentication performed in this scheme is *per request*. Each time the client sends an HTTP request to the server, it is an entirely separate conversation. Therefore, each time, the client needs to authenticate itself to the server to perform some work, it must go through the whole process again—creating a timestamp and random number, calculating a message digest, and sending the whole mess up to the server. In this system, then, you would probably add parameters to the HTTP request that specify an action or command that should be performed on behalf of the authenticated user.

Securing Network Data

Let's look at something a little more complicated. Suppose you wish to conceal the data you are sending over the network. The protected password example showed one way for a client to authenticate itself to the server, but we've still got the problem of eavesdroppers picking up credit card numbers or other sensitive information off the network.

This example consists of a matched MIDlet and servlet. The MIDlet, StealthMIDlet, has a simple user interface that allows you to enter a message. This message is encrypted using an RC4 stream cipher and sent to the servlet. On the server side, StealthServlet receives the encrypted message, decrypts it, and sends back its own encrypted message. Both messages pass over the insecure Internet as ciphertext, which is difficult for attackers to read without the proper keys.

RC4 is a symmetric encryption algorithm, which means that the same key is used to encrypt and decrypt data. StealthMIDlet and StealthServlet use two keys, one for each direction of data travel. One key is used to encrypt data in the MIDlet and decrypt it in the servlet; the other key encrypts data in the servlet and decrypts it in the MIDlet.

The servlet services multiple client MIDlets, each with their own encrypting and decrypting keys. Therefore, the servlet must keep track of two keys per client without getting them mixed up. It uses an HTTP session object to do this. Every time a client request is received, the servlet finds the corresponding ciphers in the session object. If the ciphers don't exist, they are created and initialized using client-specific keys.

This system provides both data confidentiality and authentication. The client and server are authenticated to each other because they must possess the correct keys to exchange data.

Figure 15-4 shows the main user interface of StealthMIDlet. It allows you to enter a message you want to encrypt and send to the server. When you're ready, hit the **Send** command to kick things off.

Figure 15-4. Enter your secret message in StealthMIDlet*'s main screen.*

The servlet decrypts your message and sends back an encrypted response, which is displayed by the MIDlet as shown in Figure 15-5.

Figure 15-5. The servlet sends back its own secret message.

Using Bouncy Castle Ciphers

In the Bouncy Castle cryptography package, stream ciphers are represented by the org.bouncycastle.crypto.StreamCipher interface. You just need to initialize the cipher, using init(), and then you can encrypt or decrypt data using processBytes().

The Bouncy Castle package only provides one direct stream cipher implementation, org.bouncycastle.crypto.engines.RC4. If you'd prefer to use a different algorithm, you can use a block cipher instead. You can treat block ciphers like stream ciphers using Cipher Feedback (CFB) mode. In the Bouncy Castle package, this is implemented in the org.bouncycastle.crypto.StreamBlockCipher class.

This technique gives you access to Bouncy Castle's considerable arsenal of block cipher implementations, from the wizened DES through AES, Blowfish, Rijndael, and more. For more information on cipher modes, see Chapter 7 of *Java Cryptography*.

Our simple implementation instantiates a pair of RC4 objects, something like this:

```
StreamCipher inCipher = new RC4Engine();
StreamCipher outCipher = new RC4Engine();
```

The ciphers need to be initialized before they can be used. The first parameter to init() should be true if the cipher will be encrypting data, false for decryption. The second parameter is essentially the key, wrapped up in a KeyParameter object.

```
// Assume we have retrieved inKey and outKey, both byte arrays.
inCipher.init(false, new KeyParameter(inKey));
outCipher.init(true, new KeyParameter(outKey));
```

To encrypt data, we just need to create an array to hold the ciphertext. Then call the stream cipher's processBytes() method to perform the encryption. The processBytes() method accepts the plaintext array, an index into the plaintext, the number of bytes that should be processed, the ciphertext array, and the index at which the ciphertext should be written.

```
// Assume we have a byte array called plaintext.
byte[] ciphertext = new byte[plaintext.length];
outCipher.processBytes(plaintext, 0, plaintext.length, ciphertext, 0);
```

Decryption is identical, except you would use a cipher that has been initialized for decryption.

Implementation

The source code for StealthMIDlet is shown in Listing 15-5. This MIDlet has a simple user interface, initialized in the startApp() method. The MIDlet's ciphers are also created and initialized in startApp().

Listing 15-5. StealthMIDlet, *a Data Encryption MIDlet*

```
import java.io.*;

import javax.microedition.io.*;
import javax.microedition.midlet.*;
import javax.microedition.lcdui.*;

import org.bouncycastle.crypto.StreamCipher;
import org.bouncycastle.crypto.engines.RC4Engine;
import org.bouncycastle.crypto.params.KeyParameter;

public class StealthMIDlet
    extends MIDlet
    implements CommandListener, Runnable {
  private Display mDisplay;
  private TextBox mTextBox;

  private String mSession;
  private StreamCipher mOutCipher, mInCipher;

  public StealthMIDlet() {
    mOutCipher = new RC4Engine();
    mInCipher = new RC4Engine();
  }

  public void startApp() {
    if (mSession == null) {
      // Load the keys from resource files.
      byte[] inKey = getInKey();
      byte[] outKey = getOutKey();

      // Initialize the ciphers.
      mOutCipher.init(true, new KeyParameter(outKey));
      mInCipher.init(false, new KeyParameter(inKey));
    }

    mDisplay = Display.getDisplay(this);

    if (mTextBox == null) {
      mTextBox = new TextBox("StealthMIDlet",
          "The eagle has landed", 256, 0);
```

```
      mTextBox.addCommand(new Command("Exit", Command.EXIT, 0));
      mTextBox.addCommand(new Command("Send", Command.SCREEN, 0));
      mTextBox.setCommandListener(this);
    }

    mDisplay.setCurrent(mTextBox);
  }

  public void commandAction(Command c, Displayable s) {
    if (c.getCommandType() == Command.EXIT) notifyDestroyed();
    else {
      Form waitForm = new Form("Connecting...");
      mDisplay.setCurrent(waitForm);
      Thread t = new Thread(this);
      t.start();
    }
  }

  public void run() {
    // Encrypt our message.
    byte[] plaintext = mTextBox.getString().getBytes();
    byte[] ciphertext = new byte[plaintext.length];
    mOutCipher.processBytes(plaintext, 0, plaintext.length, ciphertext, 0);
    char[] hexCiphertext = HexCodec.bytesToHex(ciphertext);

    // Create the GET URL. Our user name and the encrypted, hex
    //   encoded message are included as parameters. The user name
    //   and base URL are retrieved as application properties.
    String baseURL = getAppProperty("StealthMIDlet-URL");
    URLBuilder ub = new URLBuilder(baseURL);
    ub.addParameter("user", getAppProperty("StealthMIDlet.user"));
    ub.addParameter("message", new String(hexCiphertext));
    String url = ub.toString();

    try {
      // Query the server and retrieve the response.
      HttpConnection hc = (HttpConnection)Connector.open(url);
      if (mSession != null)
        hc.setRequestProperty("cookie", mSession);
      InputStream in = hc.openInputStream();

      String cookie = hc.getHeaderField("Set-cookie");
      if (cookie != null) {
        int semicolon = cookie.indexOf(';');
```

```java
      mSession = cookie.substring(0, semicolon);
    }

    int length = (int)hc.getLength();
    ciphertext = new byte[length];
    in.read(ciphertext);
    in.close();
    hc.close();
  }
  catch (IOException ioe) {
    Alert a = new Alert("Exception", ioe.toString(), null, null);
    a.setTimeout(Alert.FOREVER);
    mDisplay.setCurrent(a, mTextBox);
  }


  // Decrypt the server response.
  String hex = new String(ciphertext);
  byte[] dehexed = HexCodec.hexToBytes(hex.toCharArray());
  byte[] deciphered = new byte[dehexed.length];
  mInCipher.processBytes(dehexed, 0, dehexed.length, deciphered, 0);

  String decipheredString = new String(deciphered);
  Alert a = new Alert("Response", decipheredString, null, null);
  a.setTimeout(Alert.FOREVER);
  mDisplay.setCurrent(a, mTextBox);
}

// Normally you would probably read keys from resource files
//    in the MIDlet suite JAR, using the getResourceAsStream()
//    method in Class. Here I just use hardcoded values that match
//    the hardcoded values in StealthServlet.
private byte[] getInKey() {
  return "Incoming MIDlet key".getBytes();
}

private byte[] getOutKey() {
  return "Outgoing MIDlet key".getBytes();
}

public void pauseApp() { }

public void destroyApp(boolean unconditional) { }
}
```

When the user invokes the **Send** command, StealthMIDlet encrypts the user's message with its outgoing cipher. It then encodes the ciphertext as hexadecimal text in preparation for sending it to the servlet. The user's name and the ciphertext are packaged into a GET URL and sent to the server. Additionally, StealthMIDlet keeps track of a cookie that is used for session tracking. If the server sends back a session ID cookie, it is saved in StealthMIDlet's mSession member variable. The saved cookie is sent with each subsequent request. This allows the server to retrieve session information for this client. Without this session information, each HTTP request from client to server would need to reinitialize the ciphers so that they didn't get unsynchronized.

StealthMIDlet retrieves the response from the server as hexadecimal ciphertext. It converts the string to a byte array, and then decrypts the byte array using the MIDlet's incoming cipher. The decrypted message is displayed in an Alert.

StealthMIDlet makes use of the same HexCodec and URLBuilder classes that were presented earlier in this chapter.

On the server side, things are a little more complicated. StealthServlet should be capable of handling multiple clients, which means it should maintain a pair of ciphers for each user that connects. This is done using HTTP sessions, one session per user. When a client request comes in, StealthServlet attempts to find two ciphers in the user's session. If they don't exist, as will be the case the first time a user connects to the servlet, new ciphers are created. The ciphers are initialized using keys that are unique to each user. Exactly how these keys are located is left up to you. In this simple implementation, the getInKey() and getOutKey() methods are hard-coded.

You should notice that the keys on the servlet side appear to be reversed from the MIDlet. This is because the servlet's incoming cipher should decrypt using the same key as the MIDlet's outgoing cipher.

Once StealthServlet has located or created the ciphers that correspond to a particular user, it decrypts the incoming message and prints it out to the server console. Then it encrypts a response message (also hard-coded) and sends the response back to the MIDlet.

The entire StealthServlet class is shown in Listing 15-6.

Listing 15-6. The Source Code for StealthServlet

```java
import javax.servlet.http.*;
import javax.servlet.*;
import java.io.*;
import java.util.*;

import org.bouncycastle.crypto.StreamCipher;
import org.bouncycastle.crypto.engines.RC4Engine;
import org.bouncycastle.crypto.params.KeyParameter;

public class StealthServlet extends HttpServlet {
  public void doGet(HttpServletRequest request,
      HttpServletResponse response)
      throws ServletException, IOException {
    String user = request.getParameter("user");

    // Try to find the user's cipher pair.
    HttpSession session = request.getSession();
    StreamCipher inCipher = (StreamCipher)session.getAttribute("inCipher");
    StreamCipher outCipher = (StreamCipher)session.getAttribute("outCipher");

    // If the ciphers aren't found, create and initialize a new pair.
    if (inCipher == null && outCipher == null) {
      // Retrieve the client's keys.
      byte[] inKey = getInKey(user);
      byte[] outKey = getOutKey(user);
      // Create and initialize the ciphers.
      inCipher = new RC4Engine();
      outCipher = new RC4Engine();
      inCipher.init(true, new KeyParameter(inKey));
      outCipher.init(false, new KeyParameter(outKey));
      // Now put them in the session object.
      session.setAttribute("inCipher", inCipher);
      session.setAttribute("outCipher", outCipher);
    }

    // Retrieve the client's message.
    String clientHex = request.getParameter("message");
    byte[] clientCiphertext = HexCodec.hexToBytes(clientHex);
    byte[] clientDecrypted = new byte[clientCiphertext.length];
    inCipher.processBytes(clientCiphertext, 0, clientCiphertext.length,
        clientDecrypted, 0);
    System.out.println("message = " + new String(clientDecrypted));
```

```
    // Create the response message.
    String message = "Hello, this is StealthServlet.";

    // Encrypt the message.
    byte[] plaintext = message.getBytes();
    byte[] ciphertext = new byte[plaintext.length];
    outCipher.processBytes(plaintext, 0, plaintext.length, ciphertext, 0);
    char[] hexCiphertext = HexCodec.bytesToHex(ciphertext);

    response.setContentType("text/plain");
    response.setContentLength(hexCiphertext.length);
    PrintWriter out = response.getWriter();
    out.println(hexCiphertext);
  }

  private byte[] getInKey(String user) {
    return "Outgoing MIDlet key".getBytes();
  }

private byte[] getOutKey(String user) {
    return "Incoming MIDlet key".getBytes();
  }
}
```

Suggested Enhancements

A few relatively minor enhancements would make this a serious application. The first area to tackle is key handling. StealthMIDlet should load its keys from resource files in the MIDlet suite JAR rather than using hard-coded values. This is possible using the getResourceAsStream() method in Class. The keys would probably be placed there at deployment time, which means the MIDlet would need to be deployed carefully, probably using HTTPS.

Likewise, StealthServlet should locate and load keys from a database or some kind of file repository. Something as simple as a standard naming scheme based on user names might be sufficient.

The keys themselves should be larger than the hard-coded samples here—how large is up to you. As long ago as 1996, the U.S. government was fairly sanguine about allowing the export of 40-bit RC4 technology, so you can rest assured that 40 bits is way too short. As the key length increases, of course, you may start to have memory or performance problems, particularly in a constrained environment like MIDP. Try to find a good balance between performance and security.

Furthermore, you might want to consider using a different algorithm, like Blowfish or Rijndael. The Bouncy Castle cryptography package has plenty of options in the `org.bouncycastle.crypto.engines` package. As I mentioned, you can treat a block cipher like a stream cipher using CFB mode.

Finally, the communication between the servlet and the MIDlet could be improved. It would be nice, for example, if the servlet had some way to tell the MIDlet it couldn't find a session. It's possible that the MIDlet will send up a cookie for a session that has expired on the server side. In the current implementation, the servlet will create a new set of ciphers, ones that are not synchronized with the MIDlet's ciphers. One way to solve this problem would be to have the servlet pass a response code to the MIDlet. One response code might mean, "I lost your session. Please reinitialize your ciphers and try again."

Deployment Issues

Suppose you dressed up this example and incorporated it into a product. What are the issues with distribution? For each copy of your software, you need to generate a pair of keys. These keys are stored as resource files inside the MIDlet suite JAR, which means that for each copy of your software, you'll need to generate a unique MIDlet suite JAR. At the same time, you need to save the keys on the server side somewhere. When the client MIDlet makes a connection, you need to be able to find the corresponding keys. None of this is particularly difficult, and it can be automated.

The MIDlet suite JAR contains keys that should be secret. Therefore, it is a security risk to transmit the JAR to a customer over the Internet. You might transfer it via HTTPS to a customer's browser, and then rely on him or her to install the MIDlet suite on a mobile telephone or other small device via a serial cable.

Trimming Bouncy Castle Down to Size

With both of the examples in this chapter, I'm only using a small subset of the Bouncy Castle cryptography package. I use an obfuscator to trim out the pieces I don't need. A good obfuscator will find the methods, instance variables, and even entire classes that are not used in an application and simply remove them. This is important with third-party libraries, where you may only be using a fraction of the available functionality. Bouncy Castle includes all sorts of stuff that isn't used in `PasswordMIDlet` and `StealthMIDlet`.

There is another reason an obfuscator is necessary when using Bouncy Castle and some other third-party APIs. Bouncy Castle includes implementations of classes in the core java.* namespace, like java.math.BigInteger. MIDP implementations will fail to load classes from this namespace in an application. An obfuscator can be used to rename these classes out of the forbidden namespace.

The sample code from this chapter (available from the Downloads section of the Apress web site [http:// www.apress.com]) contains an Ant build file that invokes the ProGuard 1.4 obfuscator. ProGuard is an excellent piece of software. It is written entirely in Java and may be used freely. For more information, see http://proguard.sourceforge.net/.

The Ant target that runs ProGuard looks something like this:

```
<target name="obfuscate_proguard" depends="compile, copylib">
  <mkdir dir="build/proguard"/>
  <jar basedir="build/classes"
      jarfile="build/proguard/$wj2-crypto-input.jar"/>

  <java fork="yes" classname="proguard.ProGuard"
      classpath="${proguard}">
    <arg line="-libraryjars ${midp_lib}"/>
    <arg line="-injars build/proguard/${project}-input.jar"/>
    <arg line="-outjar build/proguard/${project}-output.jar"/>
    <arg line="-keep
        'public class * extends javax.microedition.midlet.MIDlet'"/>
    <arg line="-defaultpackage"/>
    <arg line="-dontusemixedcaseclassnames"/>
  </java>

  <mkdir dir="build/obfuscated"/>
  <unjar src="build/proguard/${project}-output.jar"
      dest="build/obfuscated"/>
</target>
```

ProGuard expects its input classes to be packaged in a JAR, so the first thing to do is create a JAR based on the package name, *wj2-crypto-input.jar*. Note that this JAR includes the Bouncy Castle classes.

Next, ProGuard is run by forking a Java process. The first argument, -libraryjars, tells ProGuard where to find the MIDP classes. The next argument, -injars, points ProGuard to the JAR of input files. The output file name is specified using -outjar. Next come three important options. It's important that the MIDlet classes themselves retain their names so that MIDlet management software on a device can load and run the classes. The –keep argument makes this happen for all subclasses of MIDlet. The package renaming (moving things out of java.*) is accomplished using the -defaultpackage argument. Finally, -dontusemixedcaseclassnames works around asinine behavior in Windows where obfuscated class files like *a.class* and *A.class* cannot exist in the same directory.

For more information on ProGuard and its options, consult the documentation, which is quite good. For another example of its use, see http://wireless.java.sun.com/midp/articles/security3/.

The results are impressive. Without the obfuscator, the MIDlet suite JAR containing both PasswordMIDlet and StealthMIDlet is 493KB. Furthermore, it won't run because it contains classes in the java.* namespace. After running ProGuard, the MIDlet suite JAR is 38KB and the offending java.* classes have been renamed to something innocuous.

Summary

Data security is crucial for some types of applications. Data security is feasible in the MIDP world using the Bouncy Castle cryptography package. The Bouncy Castle package provides sophisticated, accessible, industrial-strength cryptography for the MIDP platform. This example presented two possible applications— one using a message digest for secure password authentication, and the other using ciphers to encrypt data sent between a MIDlet and a servlet.

Keep in mind that adding cryptography to an application or system won't necessarily make it more secure. You need to take a comprehensive system-level approach to security. Cryptography is just one of the tools in your box.

MIDP API Reference

THIS APPENDIX IS a reference for the classes and interfaces of the MIDP API. This reference is designed to help you quickly find the signature of a method in the MIDP API. Exceptions and errors are not included.

For a full description of any class, interface, or method, consult the API documentation, either in HTML (usually distributed with a MIDP toolkit) or in the MIDP specification itself.

The API listings are alphabetical, grouped by package.

This reference covers MIDP 1.0, CLDC 1.0, MIDP 2.0, and CLDC 1.1. Methods that are new in MIDP 2.0 or CLDC 1.1 are marked with a "+". Methods that have been removed (or moved) in MIDP 2.0 or CLDC 1.1 are marked with a "–". Initial implementations of MIDP 2.0 will be paired with CLDC 1.0; keep this in mind as you browse the reference.

Package java.io

Class java.io.ByteArrayInputStream

```
public class ByteArrayInputStream
    extends java.io.InputStream {
  // Constructors
  public ByteArrayInputStream(byte[] buf);
  public ByteArrayInputStream(byte[] buf, int offset, int length);

  // Methods
  public synchronized int available();
  public synchronized void close();
  public void mark(int readAheadLimit);
  public boolean markSupported();
  public synchronized int read();
  public synchronized int read(byte[] b, int off, int len);
  public synchronized void reset();
  public synchronized long skip(long n);
}
```

Class java.io.ByteArrayOutputStream

```
public class ByteArrayOutputStream
    extends java.io.OutputStream {
  // Constructors
  public ByteArrayOutputStream();
  public ByteArrayOutputStream(int size);

  // Methods
  public synchronized void close();
  public synchronized void reset();
  public int size();
  public synchronized byte[] toByteArray();
  public String toString();
  public synchronized void write(int b);
  public synchronized void write(byte[] b, int off, int len);
}
```

Interface java.io.DataInput

```
  public interface DataInput {
    // Methods
    public boolean readBoolean();
    public byte readByte();
    public char readChar();
+   public double readDouble();
+   public float readFloat();
    public void readFully(byte[] b);
    public void readFully(byte[] b, int off, int len);
    public int readInt();
    public long readLong();
    public short readShort();
    public String readUTF();
    public int readUnsignedByte();
    public int readUnsignedShort();
    public int skipBytes(int n);
  }
```

Class `java.io.DataInputStream`

```
public class DataInputStream
    extends java.io.InputStream
    implements DataInput {
  // Static methods
  public static final String readUTF(DataInput in);

  // Constructors
  public DataInputStream(InputStream in);

  // Methods
  public int available();
  public void close();
  public synchronized void mark(int readlimit);
  public boolean markSupported();
  public int read();
  public final int read(byte[] b);
  public final int read(byte[] b, int off, int len);
  public final boolean readBoolean();
  public final byte readByte();
  public final char readChar();
+ public final double readDouble();
+ public final float readFloat();
  public final void readFully(byte[] b);
  public final void readFully(byte[] b, int off, int len);
  public final int readInt();
  public final long readLong();
  public final short readShort();
  public final String readUTF();
  public final int readUnsignedByte();
  public final int readUnsignedShort();
  public synchronized void reset();
  public long skip(long n);
  public final int skipBytes(int n);
}
```

Interface java.io.DataOutput

```
public interface DataOutput {
  // Methods
  public void write(int b);
  public void write(byte[] b);
  public void write(byte[] b, int off, int len);
  public void writeBoolean(boolean v);
  public void writeByte(int v);
  public void writeChar(int v);
  public void writeChars(String s);
+ public void writeDouble(double v);
+ public void writeFloat(float v);
  public void writeInt(int v);
  public void writeLong(long v);
  public void writeShort(int v);
  public void writeUTF(String str);
}
```

Class java.io.DataOutputStream

```
public class DataOutputStream
    extends java.io.OutputStream
    implements DataOutput {
  // Constructors
  public DataOutputStream(OutputStream out);

  // Methods
  public void close();
  public void flush();
  public void write(int b);
  public void write(byte[] b, int off, int len);
  public final void writeBoolean(boolean v);
  public final void writeByte(int v);
  public final void writeChar(int v);
  public final void writeChars(String s);
+ public final void writeDouble(double v);
+ public final void writeFloat(float v);
  public final void writeInt(int v);
  public final void writeLong(long v);
  public final void writeShort(int v);
  public final void writeUTF(String str);
}
```

Class *java.io.InputStream*

```
public abstract class InputStream
    extends java.lang.Object {
  // Constructors
  public InputStream();

  // Methods
  public int available();
  public void close();
  public synchronized void mark(int readlimit);
  public boolean markSupported();
  public abstract int read();
  public int read(byte[] b);
  public int read(byte[] b, int off, int len);
  public synchronized void reset();
  public long skip(long n);
}
```

Class *java.io.InputStreamReader*

```
public class InputStreamReader
    extends java.io.Reader {
  // Constructors
  public InputStreamReader(InputStream is);
  public InputStreamReader(InputStream is, String enc);

  // Methods
  public void close();
  public void mark(int readAheadLimit);
  public boolean markSupported();
  public int read();
  public int read(char[] cbuf, int off, int len);
  public boolean ready();
  public void reset();
  public long skip(long n);
}
```

Class java.io.OutputStream

```
public abstract class OutputStream
    extends java.lang.Object {
  // Constructors
  public OutputStream();

  // Methods
  public void close();
  public void flush();
  public abstract void write(int b);
  public void write(byte[] b);
  public void write(byte[] b, int off, int len);
}
```

Class java.io.OutputStreamWriter

```
public class OutputStreamWriter
    extends java.io.Writer {
  // Constructors
  public OutputStreamWriter(OutputStream os);
  public OutputStreamWriter(OutputStream os, String enc);

  // Methods
  public void close();
  public void flush();
  public void write(int c);
  public void write(char[] cbuf, int off, int len);
  public void write(String str, int off, int len);
}
```

Class java.io.PrintStream

```
public class PrintStream
    extends java.io.OutputStream {
  // Constructors
  public PrintStream(OutputStream out);

  // Methods
  public boolean checkError();
  public void close();
  public void flush();
```

```
      public void print(boolean b);
      public void print(char c);
      public void print(int i);
      public void print(long l);
+     public void print(float f);
+     public void print(double d);
      public void print(char[] s);
      public void print(String s);
      public void print(Object obj);
      public void println();
      public void println(boolean x);
      public void println(char x);
      public void println(int x);
      public void println(long x);
+     public void println(float x);
+     public void println(double x);
      public void println(char[] x);
      public void println(String x);
      public void println(Object x);
      protected void setError();
      public void write(int b);
      public void write(byte[] buf, int off, int len);
    }
```

Class *java.io.Reader*

```
  public abstract class Reader
      extends java.lang.Object {
    // Constructors
    protected Reader();
    protected Reader(Object lock);

    // Methods
    public abstract void close();
    public void mark(int readAheadLimit);
    public boolean markSupported();
    public int read();
    public int read(char[] cbuf);
    public abstract int read(char[] cbuf, int off, int len);
    public boolean ready();
    public void reset();
    public long skip(long n);
  }
```

Class java.io.Writer

```
public abstract class Writer
    extends java.lang.Object {
  // Constructors
  protected Writer();
  protected Writer(Object lock);

  // Methods
  public abstract void close();
  public abstract void flush();
  public void write(int c);
  public void write(char[] cbuf);
  public abstract void write(char[] cbuf, int off, int len);
  public void write(String str);
  public void write(String str, int off, int len);
}
```

Package java.lang

Class java.lang.Boolean

```
  public final class Boolean
      extends java.lang.Object {
    // Constants
+   public static final Boolean FALSE;
+   public static final Boolean TRUE;

    // Constructors
    public Boolean(boolean value);

    // Methods
    public boolean booleanValue();
    public boolean equals(Object obj);
    public int hashCode();
    public String toString();
  }
```

Class *java.lang.Byte*

```
public final class Byte
    extends java.lang.Object {
  // Constants
  public static final byte MAX_VALUE;
  public static final byte MIN_VALUE;

  // Static methods
  public static byte parseByte(String s);
  public static byte parseByte(String s, int radix);

  // Constructors
  public Byte(byte value);

  // Methods
  public byte byteValue();
  public boolean equals(Object obj);
  public int hashCode();
  public String toString();
}
```

Class *java.lang.Character*

```
public final class Character
    extends java.lang.Object {
  // Constants
  public static final int MAX_RADIX;
  public static final char MAX_VALUE;
  public static final int MIN_RADIX;
  public static final char MIN_VALUE;

  // Static methods
  public static int digit(char ch, int radix);
  public static boolean isDigit(char ch);
  public static boolean isLowerCase(char ch);
  public static boolean isUpperCase(char ch);
  public static char toLowerCase(char ch);
  public static char toUpperCase(char ch);

  // Constructors
  public Character(char value);
```

```
   // Methods
   public char charValue();
   public boolean equals(Object obj);
   public int hashCode();
   public String toString();
 }
```

Class java.lang.Class

```
  public final class Class
      extends java.lang.Object {
    // Static methods
    public static native Class forName(String className);

    // Methods
    public native String getName();
    public InputStream getResourceAsStream(String name);
    public native boolean isArray();
    public native boolean isAssignableFrom(Class cls);
    public native boolean isInstance(Object obj);
    public native boolean isInterface();
    public native Object newInstance();
    public String toString();
  }
```

Class java.lang.Double

```
+ public final class Double
      extends java.lang.Object {
    // Constants
+   public static final double MAX_VALUE;
+   public static final double MIN_VALUE;
+   public static final double NEGATIVE_INFINITY;
+   public static final double NaN;
+   public static final double POSITIVE_INFINITY;

    // Static methods
+   public static native long doubleToLongBits(double value);
+   public static boolean isInfinite(double v);
+   public static boolean isNaN(double v);
```

```
+    public static native double longBitsToDouble(long bits);
+    public static double parseDouble(String s);
+    public static String toString(double d);
+    public static Double valueOf(String s);

     // Constructors
+    public Double(double value);

     // Methods
+    public byte byteValue();
+    public double doubleValue();
+    public boolean equals(Object obj);
+    public float floatValue();
+    public int hashCode();
+    public int intValue();
+    public boolean isInfinite();
+    public boolean isNaN();
+    public long longValue();
+    public short shortValue();
+    public String toString();
  }
```

Class java.lang.Float

```
+ public final class Float
      extends java.lang.Object {
    // Constants
+    public static final float MAX_VALUE;
+    public static final float MIN_VALUE;
+    public static final float NEGATIVE_INFINITY;
+    public static final float NaN;
+    public static final float POSITIVE_INFINITY;

     // Static methods
+    public static native int floatToIntBits(float value);
+    public static native float intBitsToFloat(int bits);
+    public static boolean isInfinite(float v);
+    public static boolean isNaN(float v);
+    public static float parseFloat(String s);
+    public static String toString(float f);
+    public static Float valueOf(String s);
```

```
      // Constructors
+     public Float(float value);
+     public Float(double value);

      // Methods
+     public byte byteValue();
+     public double doubleValue();
+     public boolean equals(Object obj);
+     public float floatValue();
+     public int hashCode();
+     public int intValue();
+     public boolean isInfinite();
+     public boolean isNaN();
+     public long longValue();
+     public short shortValue();
+     public String toString();
   }
```

Class java.lang.Integer

```
   public final class Integer
       extends java.lang.Object {
   // Constants
   public static final int MAX_VALUE;
   public static final int MIN_VALUE;

   // Static methods
   public static int parseInt(String s, int radix);
   public static int parseInt(String s);
   public static String toBinaryString(int i);
   public static String toHexString(int i);
   public static String toOctalString(int i);
   public static String toString(int i, int radix);
   public static String toString(int i);
   public static Integer valueOf(String s, int radix);
   public static Integer valueOf(String s);

   // Constructors
   public Integer(int value);

   // Methods
   public byte byteValue();
+  public double doubleValue();
   public boolean equals(Object obj);
+  public float floatValue();
```

```
   public int hashCode();
   public int intValue();
   public long longValue();
   public short shortValue();
   public String toString();
 }
```

Class java.lang.Long

```
   public final class Long
       extends java.lang.Object {
     // Constants
     public static final long MAX_VALUE;
     public static final long MIN_VALUE;

     // Static methods
     public static long parseLong(String s, int radix);
     public static long parseLong(String s);
     public static String toString(long i, int radix);
     public static String toString(long i);

     // Constructors
     public Long(long value);

     // Methods
+    public double doubleValue();
     public boolean equals(Object obj);
+    public float floatValue();
     public int hashCode();
     public long longValue();
     public String toString();
 }
```

Class java.lang.Math

```
   public final class Math
       extends java.lang.Object {
     // Constants
+    public static final double E;
+    public static final double PI;
```

```
      // Static methods
      public static int abs(int a);
      public static long abs(long a);
+     public static float abs(float a);
+     public static double abs(double a);
+     public static native double ceil(double a);
+     public static native double cos(double a);
+     public static native double floor(double a);
      public static int max(int a, int b);
      public static long max(long a, long b);
+     public static float max(float a, float b);
+     public static double max(double a, double b);
      public static int min(int a, int b);
      public static long min(long a, long b);
+     public static float min(float a, float b);
+     public static double min(double a, double b);
+     public static native double sin(double a);
+     public static native double sqrt(double a);
+     public static native double tan(double a);
+     public static double toDegrees(double angrad);
+     public static double toRadians(double angdeg);
    }
```

Class *java.lang.Object*

```
  public class Object {
    // Constructors
    public Object();

    // Methods
    public boolean equals(Object obj);
    public final native Class getClass();
    public native int hashCode();
    public final native void notify();
    public final native void notifyAll();
    public String toString();
    public final native void wait(long timeout);
    public final void wait(long timeout, int nanos);
    public final void wait();
  }
```

Interface java.lang.Runnable

```
public interface Runnable {
  // Methods
  public void run();
}
```

Class java.lang.Runtime

```
public class Runtime
    extends java.lang.Object {
  // Static methods
  public static Runtime getRuntime();

  // Methods
  public void exit(int status);
  public native long freeMemory();
  public native void gc();
  public native long totalMemory();
}
```

Class java.lang.Short

```
public final class Short
    extends java.lang.Object {
  // Constants
  public static final short MAX_VALUE;
  public static final short MIN_VALUE;

  // Static methods
  public static short parseShort(String s);
  public static short parseShort(String s, int radix);

  // Constructors
  public Short(short value);

  // Methods
  public boolean equals(Object obj);
  public int hashCode();
  public short shortValue();
  public String toString();
}
```

Class java.lang.String

```
public final class String
    extends java.lang.Object {
// Static methods
public static String valueOf(Object obj);
public static String valueOf(char[] data);
public static String valueOf(char[] data, int offset, int count);
public static String valueOf(boolean b);
public static String valueOf(char c);
public static String valueOf(int i);
public static String valueOf(long l);
+    public static String valueOf(float f);
+    public static String valueOf(double d);

// Constructors
public String();
public String(String value);
public String(char[] value);
public String(char[] value, int offset, int count);
public String(byte[] bytes, int off, int len, String enc);
public String(byte[] bytes, String enc);
public String(byte[] bytes, int off, int len);
public String(byte[] bytes);
public String(StringBuffer buffer);

// Methods
public native char charAt(int index);
public int compareTo(String anotherString);
public String concat(String str);
public boolean endsWith(String suffix);
public native boolean equals(Object anObject);
+    public boolean equalsIgnoreCase(String anotherString);
public byte[] getBytes(String enc);
public byte[] getBytes();
public void getChars(int srcBegin, int srcEnd, char[] dst, int dstBegin);
public int hashCode();
public native int indexOf(int ch);
public native int indexOf(int ch, int fromIndex);
public int indexOf(String str);
public int indexOf(String str, int fromIndex);
+    public native String intern();
public int lastIndexOf(int ch);
```

```
    public int lastIndexOf(int ch, int fromIndex);
    public int length();
    public boolean regionMatches(boolean ignoreCase, int toffset,
        String other, int ooffset, int len);
    public String replace(char oldChar, char newChar);
    public boolean startsWith(String prefix, int toffset);
    public boolean startsWith(String prefix);
    public String substring(int beginIndex);
    public String substring(int beginIndex, int endIndex);
    public char[] toCharArray();
    public String toLowerCase();
    public String toString();
    public String toUpperCase();
    public String trim();
  }
```

Class java.lang.StringBuffer

```
  public final class StringBuffer
      extends java.lang.Object {
    // Constructors
    public StringBuffer();
    public StringBuffer(int length);
    public StringBuffer(String str);

    // Methods
    public synchronized StringBuffer append(Object obj);
    public native synchronized StringBuffer append(String str);
    public synchronized StringBuffer append(char[] str);
    public synchronized StringBuffer append(char[] str, int offset, int len);
    public StringBuffer append(boolean b);
    public synchronized StringBuffer append(char c);
    public native StringBuffer append(int i);
    public StringBuffer append(long l);
+   public StringBuffer append(float f);
+   public StringBuffer append(double d);
    public int capacity();
    public synchronized char charAt(int index);
    public synchronized StringBuffer delete(int start, int end);
    public synchronized StringBuffer deleteCharAt(int index);
    public synchronized void ensureCapacity(int minimumCapacity);
```

```
        public synchronized void getChars(int srcBegin, int srcEnd,
            char[] dst, int dstBegin);
        public synchronized StringBuffer insert(int offset, Object obj);
        public synchronized StringBuffer insert(int offset, String str);
        public synchronized StringBuffer insert(int offset, char[] str);
        public StringBuffer insert(int offset, boolean b);
        public synchronized StringBuffer insert(int offset, char c);
        public StringBuffer insert(int offset, int i);
        public StringBuffer insert(int offset, long l);
+       public StringBuffer insert(int offset, float f);
+       public StringBuffer insert(int offset, double d);
        public int length();
        public synchronized StringBuffer reverse();
        public synchronized void setCharAt(int index, char ch);
        public synchronized void setLength(int newLength);
        public native String toString();
    }
```

Class java.lang.System

```
    public final class System
        extends java.lang.Object {
    // Constants
    public static final PrintStream err;
    public static final PrintStream out;

    // Static methods
    public static native void arraycopy(Object src, int src_position,
        Object dst, int dst_position, int length);
    public static native long currentTimeMillis();
    public static void exit(int status);
    public static void gc();
    public static String getProperty(String key);
    public static native int identityHashCode(Object x);
    }
```

Class java.lang.Thread

```
    public class Thread
        extends java.lang.Object
        implements Runnable {
```

```
    // Constants
    public static final int MAX_PRIORITY;
    public static final int MIN_PRIORITY;
    public static final int NORM_PRIORITY;

    // Static methods
    public static native int activeCount();
    public static native Thread currentThread();
    public static native void sleep(long millis);
    public static native void yield();

    // Constructors
    public Thread();
+   public Thread(String name);
    public Thread(Runnable target);
+   public Thread(Runnable target, String name);

    // Methods
+   public final String getName();
    public final int getPriority();
+   public void interrupt();
    public final native boolean isAlive();
    public final void join();
    public void run();
    public final void setPriority(int newPriority);
    public native synchronized void start();
    public String toString();
  }
```

Class java.lang.Throwable

```
  public class Throwable
      extends java.lang.Object {
    // Constructors
    public Throwable();
    public Throwable(String message);

    // Methods
    public String getMessage();
    public void printStackTrace();
    public String toString();
  }
```

Package java.lang.ref

Class java.lang.ref.Reference

```
+ public abstract class Reference
      extends java.lang.Object {
    // Methods
+   public void clear();
+   public Object get();
  }
```

Class java.lang.ref.WeakReference

```
+ public class WeakReference
      extends java.lang.ref.Reference {
    // Constructors
+   public WeakReference(Object ref);
  }
```

Package java.util

Class java.util.Calendar

```
  public abstract class Calendar
      extends java.lang.Object {
    // Constants
    public static final int AM;
    public static final int AM_PM;
    public static final int APRIL;
    public static final int AUGUST;
    public static final int DATE;
    public static final int DAY_OF_MONTH;
    public static final int DAY_OF_WEEK;
    public static final int DECEMBER;
    public static final int FEBRUARY;
    public static final int FRIDAY;
    public static final int HOUR;
    public static final int HOUR_OF_DAY;
    public static final int JANUARY;
    public static final int JULY;
```

```
    public static final int JUNE;
    public static final int MARCH;
    public static final int MAY;
    public static final int MILLISECOND;
    public static final int MINUTE;
    public static final int MONDAY;
    public static final int MONTH;
    public static final int NOVEMBER;
    public static final int OCTOBER;
    public static final int PM;
    public static final int SATURDAY;
    public static final int SECOND;
    public static final int SEPTEMBER;
    public static final int SUNDAY;
    public static final int THURSDAY;
    public static final int TUESDAY;
    public static final int WEDNESDAY;
    public static final int YEAR;

    // Static methods
    public static synchronized Calendar getInstance();
    public static synchronized Calendar getInstance(TimeZone zone);

    // Constructors
    protected Calendar();

    // Methods
    public boolean after(Object when);
    public boolean before(Object when);
+   protected abstract void computeFields();
+   protected abstract void computeTime();
    public boolean equals(Object obj);
    public final int get(int field);
    public final Date getTime();
    protected long getTimeInMillis();
    public TimeZone getTimeZone();
    public final void set(int field, int value);
    public final void setTime(Date date);
    protected void setTimeInMillis(long millis);
    public void setTimeZone(TimeZone value);
}
```

Class java.util.Date

```
public class Date
    extends java.lang.Object {
  // Constructors
  public Date();
  public Date(long date);

  // Methods
  public boolean equals(Object obj);
  public long getTime();
  public int hashCode();
  public void setTime(long time);
}
```

Interface java.util.Enumeration

```
public interface Enumeration {
  // Methods
  public boolean hasMoreElements();
  public Object nextElement();
}
```

Class java.util.Hashtable

```
public class Hashtable
    extends java.lang.Object {
  // Constructors
  public Hashtable(int initialCapacity);
  public Hashtable();

  // Methods
  public synchronized void clear();
  public synchronized boolean contains(Object value);
  public synchronized boolean containsKey(Object key);
  public synchronized Enumeration elements();
  public synchronized Object get(Object key);
  public boolean isEmpty();
  public synchronized Enumeration keys();
  public synchronized Object put(Object key, Object value);
```

```
    protected void rehash();
    public synchronized Object remove(Object key);
    public int size();
    public synchronized String toString();
  }
```

Class java.util.Random

```
  public class Random
      extends java.lang.Object {
    // Constructors
    public Random();
    public Random(long seed);

    // Methods
    protected synchronized int next(int bits);
+   public double nextDouble();
+   public float nextFloat();
    public int nextInt();
+   public int nextInt(int n);
    public long nextLong();
    public synchronized void setSeed(long seed);
  }
```

Class java.util.Stack

```
  public class Stack
      extends java.util.Vector {
    // Constructors
    public Stack();

    // Methods
    public boolean empty();
    public synchronized Object peek();
    public synchronized Object pop();
    public Object push(Object item);
    public synchronized int search(Object o);
  }
```

Class java.util.Timer

```
public class Timer
    extends java.lang.Object {
  // Constructors
  public Timer();

  // Methods
  public void cancel();
  public void schedule(TimerTask task, long delay);
  public void schedule(TimerTask task, Date time);
  public void schedule(TimerTask task, long delay, long period);
  public void schedule(TimerTask task, Date firstTime, long period);
  public void scheduleAtFixedRate(TimerTask task, long delay, long period);
  public void scheduleAtFixedRate(TimerTask task, Date firstTime,
      long period);
}
```

Class java.util.TimerTask

```
public abstract class TimerTask
    extends java.lang.Object
    implements Runnable {
  // Constructors
  protected TimerTask();

  // Methods
  public boolean cancel();
  public abstract void run();
  public long scheduledExecutionTime();
}
```

Class java.util.TimeZone

```
public abstract class TimeZone
    extends java.lang.Object {
  // Static methods
  public static String getAvailableIDs();
  public static synchronized TimeZone getDefault();
  public static synchronized TimeZone getTimeZone(String ID);
```

```
    // Constructors
    public TimeZone();

    // Methods
    public String getID();
    public abstract int getOffset(int era, int year, int month,
        int day, int dayOfWeek, int millis);
    public abstract int getRawOffset();
    public abstract boolean useDaylightTime();
}
```

Class java.util.Vector

```
public class Vector
    extends java.lang.Object {
    // Constructors
    public Vector(int initialCapacity, int capacityIncrement);
    public Vector(int initialCapacity);
    public Vector();

    // Methods
    public synchronized void addElement(Object obj);
    public int capacity();
    public boolean contains(Object elem);
    public synchronized void copyInto(Object[] anArray);
    public synchronized Object elementAt(int index);
    public synchronized Enumeration elements();
    public synchronized void ensureCapacity(int minCapacity);
    public synchronized Object firstElement();
    public int indexOf(Object elem);
    public synchronized int indexOf(Object elem, int index);
    public synchronized void insertElementAt(Object obj, int index);
    public boolean isEmpty();
    public synchronized Object lastElement();
    public int lastIndexOf(Object elem);
    public synchronized int lastIndexOf(Object elem, int index);
    public synchronized void removeAllElements();
    public synchronized boolean removeElement(Object obj);
    public synchronized void removeElementAt(int index);
    public synchronized void setElementAt(Object obj, int index);
    public synchronized void setSize(int newSize);
    public int size();
    public synchronized String toString();
    public synchronized void trimToSize();
}
```

Package javax.microedition.io

Interface javax.microedition.io.CommConnection

```
+ public interface CommConnection
      implements StreamConnection {
    // Methods
+    public int getBaudRate();
+    public int setBaudRate(int baudrate);
  }
```

Class javax.microedition.io.Connector

```
  public class Connector
      extends java.lang.Object {
    // Constants
    public static final int READ;
    public static final int READ_WRITE;
    public static final int WRITE;

    // Static methods
    public static Connection open(String name);
    public static Connection open(String name, int mode);
    public static Connection open(String name, int mode, boolean timeouts);
    public static DataInputStream openDataInputStream(String name);
    public static DataOutputStream openDataOutputStream(String name);
    public static InputStream openInputStream(String name);
    public static OutputStream openOutputStream(String name);
  }
```

Interface javax.microedition.io.Connection

```
  public interface Connection {
    // Methods
    public void close();
  }
```

Interface javax.microedition.io.ContentConnection

```
public interface ContentConnection
    implements StreamConnection {
// Methods
public String getEncoding();
public long getLength();
public String getType();
}
```

Interface javax.microedition.io.Datagram

```
public interface Datagram
    implements DataInput, DataOutput {
// Methods
public String getAddress();
public byte[] getData();
public int getLength();
public int getOffset();
public void reset();
public void setAddress(String addr);
public void setAddress(Datagram reference);
public void setData(byte[] buffer, int offset, int len);
public void setLength(int len);
}
```

Interface javax.microedition.io.DatagramConnection

```
public interface DatagramConnection
    implements Connection {
// Methods
public int getMaximumLength();
public int getNominalLength();
public Datagram newDatagram(int size);
public Datagram newDatagram(int size, String addr);
public Datagram newDatagram(byte[] buf, int size);
public Datagram newDatagram(byte[] buf, int size, String addr);
public void receive(Datagram dgram);
public void send(Datagram dgram);
}
```

Interface javax.microedition.io.HttpConnection

```
public interface HttpConnection
    implements ContentConnection {
// Constants
public static final String GET;
public static final String HEAD;
public static final int HTTP_ACCEPTED;
public static final int HTTP_BAD_GATEWAY;
public static final int HTTP_BAD_METHOD;
public static final int HTTP_BAD_REQUEST;
public static final int HTTP_CLIENT_TIMEOUT;
public static final int HTTP_CONFLICT;
public static final int HTTP_CREATED;
public static final int HTTP_ENTITY_TOO_LARGE;
public static final int HTTP_EXPECT_FAILED;
public static final int HTTP_FORBIDDEN;
public static final int HTTP_GATEWAY_TIMEOUT;
public static final int HTTP_GONE;
public static final int HTTP_INTERNAL_ERROR;
public static final int HTTP_LENGTH_REQUIRED;
public static final int HTTP_MOVED_PERM;
public static final int HTTP_MOVED_TEMP;
public static final int HTTP_MULT_CHOICE;
public static final int HTTP_NOT_ACCEPTABLE;
public static final int HTTP_NOT_AUTHORITATIVE;
public static final int HTTP_NOT_FOUND;
public static final int HTTP_NOT_IMPLEMENTED;
public static final int HTTP_NOT_MODIFIED;
public static final int HTTP_NO_CONTENT;
public static final int HTTP_OK;
public static final int HTTP_PARTIAL;
public static final int HTTP_PAYMENT_REQUIRED;
public static final int HTTP_PRECON_FAILED;
public static final int HTTP_PROXY_AUTH;
public static final int HTTP_REQ_TOO_LONG;
public static final int HTTP_RESET;
public static final int HTTP_SEE_OTHER;
public static final int HTTP_TEMP_REDIRECT;
public static final int HTTP_UNAUTHORIZED;
public static final int HTTP_UNAVAILABLE;
public static final int HTTP_UNSUPPORTED_RANGE;
public static final int HTTP_UNSUPPORTED_TYPE;
```

```
    public static final int HTTP_USE_PROXY;
    public static final int HTTP_VERSION;
    public static final String POST;

    // Methods
    public long getDate();
    public long getExpiration();
    public String getFile();
    public String getHeaderField(String name);
    public String getHeaderField(int n);
    public long getHeaderFieldDate(String name, long def);
    public int getHeaderFieldInt(String name, int def);
    public String getHeaderFieldKey(int n);
    public String getHost();
    public long getLastModified();
    public int getPort();
    public String getProtocol();
    public String getQuery();
    public String getRef();
    public String getRequestMethod();
    public String getRequestProperty(String key);
    public int getResponseCode();
    public String getResponseMessage();
    public String getURL();
    public void setRequestMethod(String method);
    public void setRequestProperty(String key, String value);
  }
```

Interface *javax.microedition.io.HttpsConnection*

```
+ public interface HttpsConnection
      implements HttpConnection {
    // Methods
+   public int getPort();
+   public SecurityInfo getSecurityInfo();
  }
```

Interface *javax.microedition.io.InputConnection*

```
public interface InputConnection
    implements Connection {
  // Methods
  public DataInputStream openDataInputStream();
  public InputStream openInputStream();
}
```

Interface *javax.microedition.io.OutputConnection*

```
public interface OutputConnection
    implements Connection {
  // Methods
  public DataOutputStream openDataOutputStream();
  public OutputStream openOutputStream();
}
```

Class *javax.microedition.io.PushRegistry*

```
+ public class PushRegistry
    extends java.lang.Object {
  // Static methods
+   public static String getFilter(String connection);
+   public static String getMIDlet(String connection);
+   public static String listConnections(boolean available);
+   public static long registerAlarm(String midlet, long time);
+   public static void registerConnection(String connection,
        String midlet, String filter);
+   public static boolean unregisterConnection(String connection);
}
```

Interface *javax.microedition.io.SecureConnection*

```
+ public interface SecureConnection
    implements SocketConnection {
  // Methods
+   public SecurityInfo getSecurityInfo();
}
```

Interface javax.microedition.io.SecurityInfo

```
+ public interface SecurityInfo {
    // Methods
+    public String getCipherSuite();
+    public String getProtocolName();
+    public String getProtocolVersion();
+    public Certificate getServerCertificate();
  }
```

Interface javax.microedition.io.ServerSocketConnection

```
+ public interface ServerSocketConnection
      implements StreamConnectionNotifier {
    // Methods
+    public String getLocalAddress();
+    public int getLocalPort();
  }
```

Interface javax.microedition.io.SocketConnection

```
+ public interface SocketConnection
      implements StreamConnection {
    // Constants
+    public static final byte DELAY;
+    public static final byte KEEPALIVE;
+    public static final byte LINGER;
+    public static final byte RCVBUF;
+    public static final byte SNDBUF;

    // Methods
+    public String getAddress();
+    public String getLocalAddress();
+    public int getLocalPort();
+    public int getPort();
+    public int getSocketOption(byte option);
+    public void setSocketOption(byte option, int value);
  }
```

Interface *javax.microedition.io.StreamConnection*

```
public interface StreamConnection
    implements InputConnection, OutputConnection {
}
```

Interface *javax.microedition.io.StreamConnectionNotifier*

```
public interface StreamConnectionNotifier
    implements Connection {
  // Methods
  public StreamConnection acceptAndOpen();
}
```

Interface *javax.microedition.io.UDPDatagramConnection*

```
+ public interface UDPDatagramConnection
      implements DatagramConnection {
    // Methods
+   public String getLocalAddress();
+   public int getLocalPort();
  }
```

Package javax.microedition.lcdui

Class *javax.microedition.lcdui.Alert*

```
  public class Alert
      extends javax.microedition.lcdui.Screen {
    // Constants
+   public static final Command DISMISS_COMMAND;
    public static final int FOREVER;

    // Constructors
    public Alert(String title);
    public Alert(String title, String alertText, Image alertImage,
        AlertType alertType);
```

```
      // Methods
      public void addCommand(Command cmd);
      public int getDefaultTimeout();
      public Image getImage();
+     public Gauge getIndicator();
      public String getString();
      public int getTimeout();
      public AlertType getType();
+     public void removeCommand(Command cmd);
      public void setCommandListener(CommandListener l);
      public void setImage(Image img);
+     public void setIndicator(Gauge indicator);
      public void setString(String str);
      public void setTimeout(int time);
      public void setType(AlertType type);
   }
```

Class javax.microedition.lcdui.AlertType

```
   public class AlertType
      extends java.lang.Object {
   // Constants
   public static final AlertType ALARM;
   public static final AlertType CONFIRMATION;
   public static final AlertType ERROR;
   public static final AlertType INFO;
   public static final AlertType WARNING;

   // Constructors
   protected AlertType();

   // Methods
   public boolean playSound(Display display);
   }
```

Class javax.microedition.lcdui.Canvas

```
public abstract class Canvas
    extends javax.microedition.lcdui.Displayable {
// Constants
public static final int DOWN;
public static final int FIRE;
public static final int GAME_A;
public static final int GAME_B;
public static final int GAME_C;
public static final int GAME_D;
public static final int KEY_NUM0;
public static final int KEY_NUM1;
public static final int KEY_NUM2;
public static final int KEY_NUM3;
public static final int KEY_NUM4;
public static final int KEY_NUM5;
public static final int KEY_NUM6;
public static final int KEY_NUM7;
public static final int KEY_NUM8;
public static final int KEY_NUM9;
public static final int KEY_POUND;
public static final int KEY_STAR;
public static final int LEFT;
public static final int RIGHT;
public static final int UP;

// Constructors
protected Canvas();

// Methods
public int getGameAction(int keyCode);
-    public int getHeight();
public int getKeyCode(int gameAction);
public String getKeyName(int keyCode);
-    public int getWidth();
public boolean hasPointerEvents();
public boolean hasPointerMotionEvents();
public boolean hasRepeatEvents();
protected void hideNotify();
public boolean isDoubleBuffered();
protected void keyPressed(int keyCode);
protected void keyReleased(int keyCode);
```

```
      protected void keyRepeated(int keyCode);
      protected abstract void paint(Graphics g);
      protected void pointerDragged(int x, int y);
      protected void pointerPressed(int x, int y);
      protected void pointerReleased(int x, int y);
      public final void repaint(int x, int y, int width, int height);
      public final void repaint();
      public final void serviceRepaints();
+     public void setFullScreenMode(boolean mode);
      protected void showNotify();
+     protected void sizeChanged(int w, int h);
    }
```

Interface *javax.microedition.lcdui.Choice*

```
    public interface Choice {
      // Constants
      public static final int EXCLUSIVE;
      public static final int IMPLICIT;
      public static final int MULTIPLE;
+     public static final int POPUP;
+     public static final int TEXT_WRAP_DEFAULT;
+     public static final int TEXT_WRAP_OFF;
+     public static final int TEXT_WRAP_ON;

      // Methods
      public int append(String stringPart, Image imagePart);
      public void delete(int elementNum);
+     public void deleteAll();
+     public int getFitPolicy();
+     public Font getFont(int elementNum);
      public Image getImage(int elementNum);
      public int getSelectedFlags(boolean[] selectedArray_return);
      public int getSelectedIndex();
      public String getString(int elementNum);
      public void insert(int elementNum, String stringPart, Image imagePart);
      public boolean isSelected(int elementNum);
      public void set(int elementNum, String stringPart, Image imagePart);
+     public void setFitPolicy(int fitPolicy);
+     public void setFont(int elementNum, Font font);
      public void setSelectedFlags(boolean[] selectedArray);
      public void setSelectedIndex(int elementNum, boolean selected);
      public int size();
    }
```

Class javax.microedition.lcdui.ChoiceGroup

```
public class ChoiceGroup
    extends javax.microedition.lcdui.Item
    implements Choice {
    // Constructors
    public ChoiceGroup(String label, int choiceType);
    public ChoiceGroup(String label, int choiceType,
        String[] stringElements, Image[] imageElements);

    // Methods
    public int append(String stringPart, Image imagePart);
    public void delete(int elementNum);
+   public void deleteAll();
+   public int getFitPolicy();
+   public Font getFont(int elementNum);
    public Image getImage(int elementNum);
    public int getSelectedFlags(boolean[] selectedArray_return);
    public int getSelectedIndex();
    public String getString(int elementNum);
    public void insert(int elementNum, String stringPart, Image imagePart);
    public boolean isSelected(int elementNum);
    public void set(int elementNum, String stringPart, Image imagePart);
-   public void setLabel(String label);
+   public void setFitPolicy(int fitPolicy);
+   public void setFont(int elementNum, Font font);
    public void setSelectedFlags(boolean[] selectedArray);
    public void setSelectedIndex(int elementNum, boolean selected);
    public int size();
}
```

Class javax.microedition.lcdui.Command

```
public class Command
    extends java.lang.Object {
    // Constants
    public static final int BACK;
    public static final int CANCEL;
    public static final int EXIT;
    public static final int HELP;
    public static final int ITEM;
    public static final int OK;
    public static final int SCREEN;
    public static final int STOP;
```

```
    // Constructors
    public Command(String label, int commandType, int priority);
+   public Command(String shortLabel, String longLabel,
        int commandType, int priority);


    // Methods
    public int getCommandType();
    public String getLabel();
+   public String getLongLabel();
    public int getPriority();
  }
```

Interface javax.microedition.lcdui.CommandListener

```
  public interface CommandListener {
    // Methods
    public void commandAction(Command c, Displayable d);
  }
```

Class javax.microedition.lcdui.CustomItem

```
+ public abstract class CustomItem
      extends javax.microedition.lcdui.Item {
    // Constants
+   protected static final int KEY_PRESS;
+   protected static final int KEY_RELEASE;
+   protected static final int KEY_REPEAT;
+   protected static final int NONE;
+   protected static final int POINTER_DRAG;
+   protected static final int POINTER_PRESS;
+   protected static final int POINTER_RELEASE;
+   protected static final int TRAVERSE_HORIZONTAL;
+   protected static final int TRAVERSE_VERTICAL;


    // Constructors
+   protected CustomItem(String label);


    // Methods
+   public int getGameAction(int keyCode);
+   protected final int getInteractionModes();
+   protected abstract int getMinContentHeight();
+   protected abstract int getMinContentWidth();
```

```
+    protected abstract int getPrefContentHeight(int width);
+    protected abstract int getPrefContentWidth(int height);
+    protected void hideNotify();
+    protected final void invalidate();
+    protected void keyPressed(int keyCode);
+    protected void keyReleased(int keyCode);
+    protected void keyRepeated(int keyCode);
+    protected abstract void paint(Graphics g, int w, int h);
+    protected void pointerDragged(int x, int y);
+    protected void pointerPressed(int x, int y);
+    protected void pointerReleased(int x, int y);
+    protected final void repaint();
+    protected final void repaint(int x, int y, int w, int h);
+    protected void showNotify();
+    protected void sizeChanged(int w, int h);
+    protected boolean traverse(int dir, int viewportWidth, int viewportHeight,
         int[] visRect_inout);
+    protected void traverseOut();
   }
```

Class *javax.microedition.lcdui.DateField*

```
   public class DateField
       extends javax.microedition.lcdui.Item {
     // Constants
     public static final int DATE;
     public static final int DATE_TIME;
     public static final int TIME;

     // Constructors
     public DateField(String label, int mode);
     public DateField(String label, int mode, TimeZone timeZone);

     // Methods
     public Date getDate();
     public int getInputMode();
     public void setDate(Date date);
     public void setInputMode(int mode);
-    public void setLabel(String label);
   }
```

Class javax.microedition.lcdui.Display

```
public class Display
    extends java.lang.Object {
  // Constants
+ public static final int ALERT;
+ public static final int CHOICE_GROUP_ELEMENT;
+ public static final int COLOR_BACKGROUND;
+ public static final int COLOR_BORDER;
+ public static final int COLOR_FOREGROUND;
+ public static final int COLOR_HIGHLIGHTED_BACKGROUND;
+ public static final int COLOR_HIGHLIGHTED_BORDER;
+ public static final int COLOR_HIGHLIGHTED_FOREGROUND;
+ public static final int LIST_ELEMENT;

  // Static methods
  public static Display getDisplay(MIDlet m);

  // Methods
  public void callSerially(Runnable r);
+ public boolean flashBacklight(int duration);
+ public int getBestImageHeight(int imageType);
+ public int getBestImageWidth(int imageType);
+ public int getBorderStyle(boolean highlighted);
+ public int getColor(int colorSpecifier);
  public Displayable getCurrent();
  public boolean isColor();
+ public int numAlphaLevels();
  public int numColors();
  public void setCurrent(Displayable nextDisplayable);
  public void setCurrent(Alert alert, Displayable nextDisplayable);
+ public void setCurrentItem(Item item);
+ public boolean vibrate(int duration);
}
```

Class javax.microedition.lcdui.Displayable

```
public abstract class Displayable
    extends java.lang.Object {
  // Methods
  public void addCommand(Command cmd);
+ public int getHeight();
+ public Ticker getTicker();
+ public String getTitle();
```

```
+   public int getWidth();
    public boolean isShown();
    public void removeCommand(Command cmd);
    public void setCommandListener(CommandListener l);
+   public void setTicker(Ticker ticker);
+   public void setTitle(String s);
+   protected void sizeChanged(int w, int h);
  }
```

Class javax.microedition.lcdui.Font

```
public final class Font
    extends java.lang.Object {
    // Constants
    public static final int FACE_MONOSPACE;
    public static final int FACE_PROPORTIONAL;
    public static final int FACE_SYSTEM;
+   public static final int FONT_INPUT_TEXT;
+   public static final int FONT_STATIC_TEXT;
    public static final int SIZE_LARGE;
    public static final int SIZE_MEDIUM;
    public static final int SIZE_SMALL;
    public static final int STYLE_BOLD;
    public static final int STYLE_ITALIC;
    public static final int STYLE_PLAIN;
    public static final int STYLE_UNDERLINED;

    // Static methods
    public static Font getDefaultFont();
+   public static Font getFont(int fontSpecifier);
    public static Font getFont(int face, int style, int size);

    // Methods
    public native int charWidth(char ch);
    public native int charsWidth(char[] ch, int offset, int length);
    public int getBaselinePosition();
    public int getFace();
    public int getHeight();
    public int getSize();
    public int getStyle();
    public boolean isBold();
    public boolean isItalic();
    public boolean isPlain();
    public boolean isUnderlined();
```

```
    public native int stringWidth(String str);
    public native int substringWidth(String str, int offset, int len);
  }
```

Class *javax.microedition.lcdui.Form*

```
  public class Form
      extends javax.microedition.lcdui.Screen {
    // Constructors
    public Form(String title);
    public Form(String title, Item[] items);

    // Methods
    public int append(Item item);
    public int append(String str);
    public int append(Image img);
    public void delete(int itemNum);
+   public void deleteAll();
    public Item get(int itemNum);
+   public int getHeight();
+   public int getWidth();
    public void insert(int itemNum, Item item);
    public void set(int itemNum, Item item);
    public void setItemStateListener(ItemStateListener iListener);
    public int size();
  }
```

Class *javax.microedition.lcdui.Gauge*

```
  public class Gauge
      extends javax.microedition.lcdui.Item {
    // Constants
+   public static final int CONTINUOUS_IDLE;
+   public static final int CONTINUOUS_RUNNING;
+   public static final int INCREMENTAL_IDLE;
+   public static final int INCREMENTAL_UPDATING;
+   public static final int INDEFINITE;

    // Constructors
    public Gauge(String label, boolean interactive, int maxValue,
        int initialValue);
```

```
    // Methods
+   public void addCommand(Command cmd);
    public int getMaxValue();
    public int getValue();
    public boolean isInteractive();
+   public void setDefaultCommand(Command cmd);
+   public void setItemCommandListener(ItemCommandListener l);
    public void setLabel(String label);
+   public void setLayout(int layout);
    public void setMaxValue(int maxValue);
+   public void setPreferredSize(int width, int height);
    public void setValue(int value);
  }
```

Class javax.microedition.lcdui.Graphics

```
    public class Graphics
        extends java.lang.Object {
    // Constants
    public static final int BASELINE;
    public static final int BOTTOM;
    public static final int DOTTED;
    public static final int HCENTER;
    public static final int LEFT;
    public static final int RIGHT;
    public static final int SOLID;
    public static final int TOP;
    public static final int VCENTER;


    // Methods
    public void clipRect(int x, int y, int width, int height);
+   public void copyArea(int x_src, int y_src, int width, int height,
        int x_dest, int y_dest, int anchor);
    public native void drawArc(int x, int y, int width, int height,
        int startAngle, int arcAngle);
    public native void drawChar(char character, int x, int y, int anchor);
    public native void drawChars(char[] data, int offset, int length,
        int x, int y, int anchor);
    public native void drawImage(Image img, int x, int y, int anchor);
    public native void drawLine(int x1, int y1, int x2, int y2);
+   public native void drawRGB(int[] rgbData, int offset, int scanlength,
        int x, int y, int width, int height, boolean processAlpha);
    public native void drawRect(int x, int y, int width, int height);
```

```
+   public native void drawRegion(Image src,
        int x_src, int y_src, int width, int height, int transform,
        int x_dest, int y_dest, int anchor);
    public native void drawRoundRect(int x, int y, int width, int height,
        int arcWidth, int arcHeight);
    public native void drawString(String str, int x, int y, int anchor);
    public native void drawSubstring(String str, int offset, int len,
        int x, int y, int anchor);
    public native void fillArc(int x, int y, int width, int height,
        int startAngle, int arcAngle);
    public native void fillRect(int x, int y, int width, int height);
    public native void fillRoundRect(int x, int y, int width, int height,
        int arcWidth, int arcHeight);
+   public native void fillTriangle(int x1, int y1, int x2, int y2,
        int x3, int y3);
    public int getBlueComponent();
    public int getClipHeight();
    public int getClipWidth();
    public int getClipX();
    public int getClipY();
    public int getColor();
+   public native int getDisplayColor(int color);
    public Font getFont();
    public int getGrayScale();
    public int getGreenComponent();
    public int getRedComponent();
    public int getStrokeStyle();
    public int getTranslateX();
    public int getTranslateY();
    public void setClip(int x, int y, int width, int height);
    public void setColor(int red, int green, int blue);
    public void setColor(int RGB);
    public void setFont(Font font);
    public void setGrayScale(int value);
    public void setStrokeStyle(int style);
    public void translate(int x, int y);
}
```

Class javax.microedition.lcdui.Image

```
public class Image
    extends java.lang.Object {
   // Static methods
   public static Image createImage(int width, int height);
   public static Image createImage(Image source);
   public static Image createImage(String name);
   public static Image createImage(byte[] imageData, int imageOffset,
       int imageLength);
+  public static Image createImage(Image image, int x, int y,
       int width, int height, int transform);
+  public static Image createImage(InputStream stream);
+  public static Image createRGBImage(int[] rgb,
       int width, int height, boolean processAlpha);

   // Methods
   public Graphics getGraphics();
   public int getHeight();
+  public native void getRGB(int[] rgbData, int offset, int scanlength,
       int x, int y, int width, int height);
   public int getWidth();
   public boolean isMutable();
 }
```

Class javax.microedition.lcdui.ImageItem

```
public class ImageItem
    extends javax.microedition.lcdui.Item {
   // Constants
   public static final int LAYOUT_CENTER;
   public static final int LAYOUT_DEFAULT;
   public static final int LAYOUT_LEFT;
   public static final int LAYOUT_NEWLINE_AFTER;
   public static final int LAYOUT_NEWLINE_BEFORE;
   public static final int LAYOUT_RIGHT;

   // Constructors
   public ImageItem(String label, Image img, int layout, String altText);
+  public ImageItem(String label, Image image, int layout, String altText,
       int appearanceMode);

   // Methods
   public String getAltText();
+  public int getAppearanceMode();
   public Image getImage();
   public int getLayout();
   public void setAltText(String text);
   public void setImage(Image img);
-  public void setLabel(String label);
   public void setLayout(int layout);
 }
```

Class *javax.microedition.lcdui.Item*

```
    public abstract class Item
        extends java.lang.Object {
      // Constants
+     public static final int BUTTON;
+     public static final int HYPERLINK;
+     public static final int LAYOUT_2;
+     public static final int LAYOUT_BOTTOM;
+     public static final int LAYOUT_CENTER;
+     public static final int LAYOUT_DEFAULT;
+     public static final int LAYOUT_EXPAND;
+     public static final int LAYOUT_LEFT;
+     public static final int LAYOUT_NEWLINE_AFTER;
+     public static final int LAYOUT_NEWLINE_BEFORE;
+     public static final int LAYOUT_RIGHT;
+     public static final int LAYOUT_SHRINK;
+     public static final int LAYOUT_TOP;
+     public static final int LAYOUT_VCENTER;
+     public static final int LAYOUT_VEXPAND;
+     public static final int LAYOUT_VSHRINK;
+     public static final int PLAIN;


      // Methods
+     public void addCommand(Command cmd);
      public String getLabel();
+     public int getLayout();
+     public int getMinimumHeight();
+     public int getMinimumWidth();
+     public int getPreferredHeight();
+     public int getPreferredWidth();
+     public void notifyStateChanged();
+     public void removeCommand(Command cmd);
+     public void setDefaultCommand(Command cmd);
+     public void setItemCommandListener(ItemCommandListener l);
      public void setLabel(String label);
+     public void setLayout(int layout);
+     public void setPreferredSize(int width, int height);
    }
```

Interface *javax.microedition.lcdui.ItemCommandListener*

```
+ public interface ItemCommandListener {
    // Methods
+   public void commandAction(Command c, Item item);
  }
```

Interface *javax.microedition.lcdui.ItemStateListener*

```
public interface ItemStateListener {
  // Methods
  public void itemStateChanged(Item item);
}
```

Class *javax.microedition.lcdui.List*

```
public class List
    extends javax.microedition.lcdui.Screen
    implements Choice {
  // Constants
  public static final Command SELECT_COMMAND;

  // Constructors
  public List(String title, int listType);
  public List(String title, int listType, String[] stringElements,
      Image[] imageElements);

  // Methods
  public int append(String stringPart, Image imagePart);
  public void delete(int elementNum);
+ public void deleteAll();
+ public int getFitPolicy();
+ public Font getFont(int elementNum);
  public Image getImage(int elementNum);
  public int getSelectedFlags(boolean[] selectedArray_return);
  public int getSelectedIndex();
  public String getString(int elementNum);
  public void insert(int elementNum, String stringPart, Image imagePart);
  public boolean isSelected(int elementNum);
+ public void removeCommand(Command cmd);
  public void set(int elementNum, String stringPart, Image imagePart);
+ public void setFitPolicy(int fitPolicy);
+ public void setFont(int elementNum, Font font);
+ public void setSelectCommand(Command command);
  public void setSelectedFlags(boolean[] selectedArray);
  public void setSelectedIndex(int elementNum, boolean selected);
+ public void setTicker(Ticker ticker);
+ public void setTitle(String s);
  public int size();
}
```

Class *javax.microedition.lcdui.Screen*

```
  public abstract class Screen
      extends javax.microedition.lcdui.Displayable {
    // Methods
-   public Ticker getTicker();
-   public String getTitle();
-   public void setTicker(Ticker ticker);
-   public void setTitle(String s);
  }
```

Class *javax.microedition.lcdui.Spacer*

```
+ public class Spacer
      extends javax.microedition.lcdui.Item {
    // Constructors
+   public Spacer(int minWidth, int minHeight);

    // Methods
+   public void addCommand(Command cmd);
+   public void setDefaultCommand(Command cmd);
+   public void setLabel(String label);
+   public void setMinimumSize(int minWidth, int minHeight);
  }
```

Class *javax.microedition.lcdui.StringItem*

```
  public class StringItem
      extends javax.microedition.lcdui.Item {
    // Constructors
    public StringItem(String label, String text);
+   public StringItem(String label, String text, int appearanceMode);

    // Methods
+   public int getAppearanceMode();
+   public Font getFont();
    public String getText();
-   public void setLabel(String label);
+   public void setFont(Font font);
+   public void setPreferredSize(int width, int height);
    public void setText(String text);
  }
```

Class javax.microedition.lcdui.TextBox

```
public class TextBox
    extends javax.microedition.lcdui.Screen {
// Constructors
public TextBox(String title, String text, int maxSize, int constraints);

// Methods
public void delete(int offset, int length);
public int getCaretPosition();
public int getChars(char[] data);
public int getConstraints();
public int getMaxSize();
public String getString();
public void insert(String src, int position);
public void insert(char[] data, int offset, int length, int position);
public void setChars(char[] data, int offset, int length);
public void setConstraints(int constraints);
public void setInitialInputMode(String characterSubset);
public int setMaxSize(int maxSize);
public void setString(String text);
public void setTicker(Ticker ticker);
public void setTitle(String s);
public int size();
}
```

Class javax.microedition.lcdui.TextField

```
public class TextField
    extends javax.microedition.lcdui.Item {
// Constants
public static final int ANY;
public static final int CONSTRAINT_MASK;
public static final int DECIMAL;
public static final int EMAILADDR;
public static final int INITIAL_CAPS_SENTENCE;
public static final int INITIAL_CAPS_WORD;
public static final int NON_PREDICTIVE;
public static final int NUMERIC;
public static final int PASSWORD;
public static final int PHONENUMBER;
```

```
+   public static final int SENSITIVE;
+   public static final int UNEDITABLE;
    public static final int URL;

    // Constructors
    public TextField(String label, String text, int maxSize, int constraints);

    // Methods
    public void delete(int offset, int length);
    public int getCaretPosition();
    public int getChars(char[] data);
    public int getConstraints();
    public int getMaxSize();
    public String getString();
    public void insert(String src, int position);
    public void insert(char[] data, int offset, int length, int position);
    public void setChars(char[] data, int offset, int length);
    public void setConstraints(int constraints);
-   public void setLabel(String label);
+   public void setInitialInputMode(String characterSubset);
    public int setMaxSize(int maxSize);
    public void setString(String text);
    public int size();
  }
```

Class javax.microedition.lcdui.Ticker

```
  public class Ticker
      extends java.lang.Object {
    // Constructors
    public Ticker(String str);

    // Methods
    public String getString();
    public void setString(String str);
  }
```

Package javax.microedition.lcdui.game

Class javax.microedition.lcdui.game.GameCanvas

```
+ public abstract class GameCanvas
       extends javax.microedition.lcdui.Canvas {
    // Constants
+    public static final int DOWN_PRESSED;
+    public static final int FIRE_PRESSED;
+    public static final int GAME_A_PRESSED;
+    public static final int GAME_B_PRESSED;
+    public static final int GAME_C_PRESSED;
+    public static final int GAME_D_PRESSED;
+    public static final int LEFT_PRESSED;
+    public static final int RIGHT_PRESSED;
+    public static final int UP_PRESSED;


    // Constructors
+    protected GameCanvas(boolean suppressKeyEvents);


    // Methods
+    public void flushGraphics(int x, int y, int width, int height);
+    public void flushGraphics();
+    protected Graphics getGraphics();
+    public int getKeyStates();
+    public void paint(Graphics g);
  }
```

Class javax.microedition.lcdui.game.Layer

```
+ public abstract class Layer
       extends java.lang.Object {
    // Methods
+    public final int getHeight();
+    public final int getWidth();
+    public final int getX();
+    public final int getY();
+    public final boolean isVisible();
+    public void move(int dx, int dy);
+    public abstract void paint(Graphics g);
+    public void setPosition(int x, int y);
+    public void setVisible(boolean visible);
  }
```

Class *javax.microedition.lcdui.game.LayerManager*

```
+ public class LayerManager
      extends java.lang.Object {
    // Constructors
+   public LayerManager();

    // Methods
+   public void append(Layer l);
+   public Layer getLayerAt(int index);
+   public int getSize();
+   public void insert(Layer l, int index);
+   public void paint(Graphics g, int x, int y);
+   public void remove(Layer l);
+   public void setViewWindow(int x, int y, int width, int height);
  }
```

Class *javax.microedition.lcdui.game.Sprite*

```
+ public class Sprite
      extends javax.microedition.lcdui.game.Layer {
    // Constants
+   public static final int TRANS_MIRROR;
+   public static final int TRANS_MIRROR_ROT180;
+   public static final int TRANS_MIRROR_ROT270;
+   public static final int TRANS_MIRROR_ROT90;
+   public static final int TRANS_NONE;
+   public static final int TRANS_ROT180;
+   public static final int TRANS_ROT270;
+   public static final int TRANS_ROT90;

    // Constructors
+   public Sprite(Image image);
+   public Sprite(Image image, int frameWidth, int frameHeight);
+   public Sprite(Sprite s);

    // Methods
+   public final boolean collidesWith(Sprite s, boolean pixelLevel);
+   public final boolean collidesWith(TiledLayer t, boolean pixelLevel);
+   public final boolean collidesWith(Image image, int x, int y,
        boolean pixelLevel);
+   public void defineCollisionRectangle(int x, int y, int width, int height);
```

```
+    public void defineReferencePixel(int x, int y);
+    public final int getFrame();
+    public int getFrameSequenceLength();
+    public int getRawFrameCount();
+    public int getRefPixelX();
+    public int getRefPixelY();
+    public void nextFrame();
+    public final void paint(Graphics g);
+    public void prevFrame();
+    public void setFrame(int sequenceIndex);
+    public void setFrameSequence(int[] sequence);
+    public void setImage(Image img, int frameWidth, int frameHeight);
+    public void setRefPixelPosition(int x, int y);
+    public void setTransform(int transform);
  }
```

Class javax.microedition.lcdui.game.TiledLayer

```
+ public class TiledLayer
      extends javax.microedition.lcdui.game.Layer {
    // Constructors
+    public TiledLayer(int columns, int rows, Image image,
         int tileWidth, int tileHeight);

    // Methods
+    public int createAnimatedTile(int staticTileIndex);
+    public void fillCells(int col, int row, int numCols, int numRows,
         int tileIndex);
+    public int getAnimatedTile(int animatedTileIndex);
+    public int getCell(int col, int row);
+    public final int getCellHeight();
+    public final int getCellWidth();
+    public final int getColumns();
+    public final int getRows();
+    public final void paint(Graphics g);
+    public void setAnimatedTile(int animatedTileIndex, int staticTileIndex);
+    public void setCell(int col, int row, int tileIndex);
+    public void setStaticTileSet(Image image, int tileWidth, int tileHeight);
  }
```

Package javax.microedition.media

Interface javax.microedition.media.Control

```
+ public interface Control {
  }
```

Interface javax.microedition.media.Controllable

```
+ public interface Controllable {
    // Methods
+    public Control getControl(String controlType);
+    public Control[] getControls();
  }
```

Class javax.microedition.media.Manager

```
+ public final class Manager
      extends java.lang.Object {
    // Constants
+    public static final String TONE_DEVICE_LOCATOR;

    // Static methods
+    public static Player createPlayer(String locator);
+    public static Player createPlayer(InputStream stream, String type);
+    public static String getSupportedContentTypes(String protocol);
+    public static String getSupportedProtocols(String content_type);
+    public static void playTone(int note, int duration, int volume);
  }
```

Interface javax.microedition.media.Player

```
+ public interface Player
      implements Controllable {
    // Constants
+    public static final int CLOSED;
+    public static final int PREFETCHED;
+    public static final int REALIZED;
+    public static final int STARTED;
```

```
+    public static final long TIME_UNKNOWN;
+    public static final int UNREALIZED;

     // Methods
+    public void addPlayerListener(PlayerListener playerListener);
+    public void close();
+    public void deallocate();
+    public String getContentType();
+    public long getDuration();
+    public long getMediaTime();
+    public int getState();
+    public void prefetch();
+    public void realize();
+    public void removePlayerListener(PlayerListener playerListener);
+    public void setLoopCount(int count);
+    public long setMediaTime(long now);
+    public void start();
+    public void stop();
   }
```

Interface javax.microedition.media.PlayerListener

```
+ public interface PlayerListener {
     // Constants
+    public static final String CLOSED;
+    public static final String DEVICE_AVAILABLE;
+    public static final String DEVICE_UNAVAILABLE;
+    public static final String DURATION_UPDATED;
+    public static final String END_OF_MEDIA;
+    public static final String ERROR;
+    public static final String STARTED;
+    public static final String STOPPED;
+    public static final String VOLUME_CHANGED;

     // Methods
+    public void playerUpdate(Player player, String event, Object eventData);
   }
```

Package javax.microedition.media.control

Interface javax.microedition.media.control.ToneControl

```
+ public interface ToneControl
      implements Control {
   // Constants
+    public static final byte BLOCK_END;
+    public static final byte BLOCK_START;
+    public static final byte C4;
+    public static final byte PLAY_BLOCK;
+    public static final byte REPEAT;
+    public static final byte RESOLUTION;
+    public static final byte SET_VOLUME;
+    public static final byte SILENCE;
+    public static final byte TEMPO;
+    public static final byte VERSION;


   // Methods
+    public void setSequence(byte[] sequence);
  }
```

Interface javax.microedition.media.control.VolumeControl

```
+ public interface VolumeControl
      implements Control {
   // Methods
+    public int getLevel();
+    public boolean isMuted();
+    public int setLevel(int level);
+    public void setMute(boolean mute);
  }
```

Package javax.microedition.midlet

Class javax.microedition.midlet.MIDlet

```
  public abstract class MIDlet
      extends java.lang.Object {
    // Constructors
    protected MIDlet();

    // Methods
+   public final int checkPermission(String permission);
    protected abstract void destroyApp(boolean unconditional);
    public final String getAppProperty(String key);
    public final void notifyDestroyed();
    public final void notifyPaused();
    protected abstract void pauseApp();
+   public final boolean platformRequest(String URL);
    public final void resumeRequest();
    protected abstract void startApp();
  }
```

Package javax.microedition.pki

```
+ public interface Certificate {
    // Methods
+   public String getIssuer();
+   public long getNotAfter();
+   public long getNotBefore();
+   public String getSerialNumber();
+   public String getSigAlgName();
+   public String getSubject();
+   public String getType();
+   public String getVersion();
  }
```

Package javax.microedition.rms

Interface javax.microedition.rms.RecordComparator

```
public interface RecordComparator {
  // Constants
  public static final int EQUIVALENT;
  public static final int FOLLOWS;
  public static final int PRECEDES;


  // Methods
  public int compare(byte[] rec1, byte[] rec2);
}
```

Package javax.microedition.midlet
Package javax.microedition.pki
Package javax.microedition.rms

Interface javax.microedition.rms.RecordEnumeration

```
public interface RecordEnumeration {
  // Methods
  public void destroy();
  public boolean hasNextElement();
  public boolean hasPreviousElement();
  public boolean isKeptUpdated();
  public void keepUpdated(boolean keepUpdated);
  public byte[] nextRecord();
  public int nextRecordId();
  public int numRecords();
  public byte[] previousRecord();
  public int previousRecordId();
  public void rebuild();
  public void reset();
}
```

Interface javax.microedition.rms.RecordFilter

```
public interface RecordFilter {
  // Methods
  public boolean matches(byte[] candidate);
}
```

Interface javax.microedition.rms.RecordListener

```
public interface RecordListener {
  // Methods
  public void recordAdded(RecordStore recordStore, int recordId);
  public void recordChanged(RecordStore recordStore, int recordId);
  public void recordDeleted(RecordStore recordStore, int recordId);
}
```

Class javax.microedition.rms.RecordStore

```
    public class RecordStore
        extends java.lang.Object {
      // Constants
+     public static final int AUTHMODE_ANY;
+     public static final int AUTHMODE_PRIVATE;

      // Static methods
      public static void deleteRecordStore(String recordStoreName);
      public static String listRecordStores();
      public static RecordStore openRecordStore(String recordStoreName,
          boolean createIfNecessary);
+     public static RecordStore openRecordStore(String recordStoreName,
          boolean createIfNecessary, int authmode, boolean writable);
+     public static RecordStore openRecordStore(String recordStoreName,
          String vendorName, String suiteName);
```

```
    // Methods
    public int addRecord(byte[] data, int offset, int numBytes);
    public void addRecordListener(RecordListener listener);
    public void closeRecordStore();
    public void deleteRecord(int recordId);
    public RecordEnumeration enumerateRecords(RecordFilter filter,
        RecordComparator comparator, boolean keepUpdated);
    public long getLastModified();
    public String getName();
    public int getNextRecordID();
    public int getNumRecords();
    public int getRecord(int recordId, byte[] buffer, int offset);
    public byte[] getRecord(int recordId);
    public int getRecordSize(int recordId);
    public int getSize();
    public int getSizeAvailable();
    public int getVersion();
    public void removeRecordListener(RecordListener listener);
+   public void setMode(int authmode, boolean writable);
    public void setRecord(int recordId, byte[] newData, int offset,
        int numBytes);
    }
```

Index

Symbols

+ (plus) operator, overloading, 245
+ (plus sign), meaning of, 50
_ (underline) in J2MEWTK emulator,
    meaning of, 88
| (pipe) separator, using with Preferences
    class, 129

A

ABB (Audio Building Block)
    content types supported by, 226–228
    explanation of, 219, 223
About command, using with alerts, 75–76
abstraction, explanation of, 61
Active state for MIDlets, meaning of,
    33–34
addCommand() method, using with
    alerts, 74
addRecord() method, using, 126
"Address" record store, opening, 122–123
alerts
    adding commands to, 74
    representing, 74
    using, 73–76
AlertType class, types provided by, 74
allowed permissions, explanation of, 43
alpha component, explanation of, 182
AMS (Application Management
    Software), role in MIDlets, 24
anchor points
    for images, 180
    role in drawing text, 172–173
animated tiles, using, 205
animation
    driving with GameCanvas class,
        195–198
    and multithreading, 188–192
Ant build tool, using, 29–31, 289
ANY constants
    using with TextBox screens, 70–71
    using with TextFields, 94
APIs (application programming
    interfaces)
    in CLDC, 8
    for MIDP applications, 7
    signaling dependence of MIDlet suites
        on, 39
    table of, 3

appearance mode in MIDP 2.0,
    explanation of, 92
append() method
    using with items on forms, 86
    using with List class, 81–82
application deployment, optimizing,
    249–250
application descriptors, using with
    MIDlets, 28, 35, 39
application manager, purpose of, 33
application speed, testing, 240
applications
    packaging, 27
    partitioning, 250
    testing with J2ME Wireless Toolkit
        emulators, 21–23
Apress Web site, 15
arraycopy() method, using with System
    class, 51
arrays
    freeing, 247
    versus objects, 246–247
attribute values, retrieving with
    getAppProperty() method, 40
attributes for MIDlet manifests
    explanations of, 37–38
    purpose of, 39
audio clips, jumping to points in, 230
audio data
    class relationships for, 226
    obtaining InputStream for, 223
    path of, 226
audio files, playing, 223–225
authentication
    explanation of, 264
    providing with TLS, 265
AUTHMODE_ANY, advisory about, 123
authorization mode for record stores,
    meaning of, 123

B

Back command, example of, 91–92
BACK command for Displayable class,
    meaning of, 65
baseline, locating for text, 178
benchmarking, overview of, 239–240
bits of color depth, parameters for, 61
blanket permissions, explanation of, 43
blitting, explanation of, 183

About Apress

A press, located in Berkeley, CA, is a fast-growing, innovative publishing company devoted to meeting the needs of existing and potential programming professionals. Simply put, the "A" in Apress stands for *The Author's Press™*. Apress' unique approach to publishing grew out of conversations between its founders, Gary Cornell and Dan Appleman, authors of numerous best-selling, highly regarded books for programming professionals. In 1998 they set out to create a publishing company that emphasized quality above all else. Gary and Dan's vision has resulted in the publication of over 70 titles by leading software professionals, all of which have *The Expert's Voice™*.

Do You Have What It Takes to Write for Apress?

A press is rapidly expanding its publishing program. If you can write and you refuse to compromise on the quality of your work, if you believe in doing more than rehashing existing documentation, and if you're looking for opportunities and rewards that go far beyond those offered by traditional publishing houses, we want to hear from you!

Consider these innovations that we offer all of our authors:

- **Top royalties with *no* hidden switch statements**
  Authors typically receive only half of their normal royalty rate on foreign sales. In contrast, Apress' royalty rate remains the same for both foreign and domestic sales.

- **Sharing the wealth**
  Most publishers keep authors on the same pay scale even after costs have been met. At Apress author royalties dramatically increase the more books are sold.

- **Serious treatment of the technical review process**
  Each Apress book is reviewed by a technical expert(s) whose remuneration depends in part on the success of the book since he or she too receives royalties.

Moreover, through a partnership with Springer-Verlag, New York, Inc., one of the world's major publishing houses, Apress has significant venture capital and distribution power behind it. Thus, we have the resources to produce the highest quality books *and* market them aggressively.

If you fit the model of the Apress author who can write a book that provides *What The Professional Needs To Know™*, then please contact us for more information:

editorial@apress.com